752

7.95
Harding, Wells
25 Aug 1995

McGILL AND ITS STORY

James McGill
1756-1813
Founder of McGill College

McGILL AND ITS STORY 1821-1921

By CYRUS MACMILLAN

Author of "Canadian Wonder Tales," Etc.

LONDON: JOHN LANE
NEW YORK: JOHN LANE COMPANY
TORONTO: CANADIAN BRANCH
THE OXFORD UNIVERSITY
PRESS

MCMXXI

TO

MY McGILL COMRADES

WHO FELL IN THE WAR 1914-1918

We who remain shall grow old,
We shall feel the snows of cheerless winter;
But you shall be forever young,
With you it shall be forever spring,
Where you wander through the willows
Of the valley in your West.

PREFACE

The following pages give in general outline the century story of McGill University. They have no pretension to the title of detailed History, for it has been possible to chronicle only the circumstances which shaped the University in its infancy and the important events of its succeeding years. The story is one of struggle and disappointment, of discouragement and controversy, and of ultimate success and triumph. The men who made McGill were men of far and clear vision, of unfaltering courage and unwavering faith. They never doubted the final breaking of the clouds; they were baffled only to fight better in their forward march on behalf of national enlightenment. They believed in the future greatness of Canada, and of the place of education in moulding their country's destiny. The students of to-day who enjoy the advantages of a great seat of learning are not always conscious of the toil and the anxiety, the weariness and the fret of their College's early years; they perhaps do not always appreciate their glorious heritage and the efforts and the sacrifices of those who scorned delights and lived laborious days in order to leave that heritage behind. The author's hope is that the story of struggle herein recorded may deepen our gratitude for our privileges, and our reverence for McGill and the men who made it.

It has been impossible here to enter into minute

details of organization or administration or personnel. The book is a story of epochs rather than of individuals,—but epochs in which the sign posts ever pointed onward. Biographical material has, therefore, been reduced to a minimum and no attempt has been made to give names or notices of Professors, many of whom, the writer is well aware, should otherwise receive appreciative reference as among the makers of McGill. With the exception of the portrait of the present Principal, too, the photographs include of necessity only those who are already numbered with the University's past.

The writer's deepest thanks are here expressed to those without whose assistance this story could not have been told. He is grateful to Professor Stephen Leacock for advice and encouragement; to the Principal, the Governors, and the Secretary of McGill, Mr. A. P. S. Glassco (Science, 1901), for permission to examine letters and minutes; to Dr. J. A. Nicholson, (Arts, 1887) for his valuable aid in locating and obtaining access to documents; to the staff of the Redpath Library, especially Miss D. A. Lomer, for their unfailing and patient help in the search for records; to Mr. J. W. Jeakins, Secretary of the Graduates' Society, and to Mr. E. Ardley of the Redpath Museum for kind assistance; to the attendants in Archives for many courtesies; to George B. Fraser, Esq., for permission to photograph prints; to the late Rev. Dr. Robert Campbell whose knowledge and memory of old Montreal was wide and vivid; and particularly to John Lane, Esq., of the Bodley Head for his personal interest and experienced advice in the preparation of this volume.

Since the information concerning the ancestry of

James McGill is at present meagre I should be glad
if any reader possessing information as to his ancestry and early career would communicate with me in
Canada, or with my publisher, Mr. John Lane, The
Bodley Head, Ltd., Vigo Street, London, England,
so that this section of the book may be amplified in
future editions.

C. M.

McGill University,
    July, 1921.

CONTENTS

xi

LIST OF ILLUSTRATIONS

The photographs from which the prints were made are the work of Norman and of the Rice Studios.

THE ROYAL INSTITUTION FOR THE
ADVANCEMENT OF LEARNING

CHAPTER I

The Royal Institution for the Advancement of Learning

THE Charter under which McGill University was established, was obtained on March 31st, 1821. The century mark in the University's history has now been passed. One hundred years is a long period in the life of a nation or a country; it is a longer period still in the life of an individual; but it is perhaps longest relatively in the life of an educational institution, particularly if that institution had its birth in struggling pioneer days. It is a period in university life which sees, as a rule, an undreamed of growth and development from small beginnings to unlimited influence, from scanty resources and great disappointments to a large if not always adequate endowment and equipment, from a merely local service to a national and even a world educational power. This is distinctly true of the century of McGill University's story. It began as a College, intended to minister to a very small community. It has grown in one hundred years to serve the world. It has graduated over twenty-five hundred Bachelors, over thirty-three hundred Doctors of Medicine, over nineteen hundred Engineers, over eight hundred Lawyers besides holders of higher or graduate degrees; it has given hundreds of graduates to high positions in the Church, the State, and

15

industrial and educational institutions.   It has drawn
its students from all lands, and it has sent its products in trained men and women into every country
on the globe.   Long ago it divested itself of the
merely local, and to-day the old term, *Studium Generale,* used in the middle ages to designate a University, may well be applied to McGill,—"a School
where students of all kinds and from all parts are
received."

The establishment of McGill University was but
part of a more comprehensive plan to improve educational conditions in Canada in the beginning of the
19th century.   After the peace treaty of 1763, which
ended the Seven Years' War and gave Canada to
the British, immigration to the colony was compara-
tively small, and little effort was made by the Home
Government to provide educational opportunities
for the children of those who sought happiness or
fortune in the new land beyond the ocean.   Indeed,
in that time the authorities were too busy trying to
solve difficult problems at home to devote much
energy to the internal problems of the colony.
They had no time and perhaps they had even less
care for their colonists.   The treaty of 1763 had
not brought peace.   The advocacy for political
change was causing deep anxiety and the new radi-
calism under the plea for the new democracy was
making a slow but steady advance which troubled
the statesmen of the age.   Then came in quick succession the American Revolution, the French Revolution and the Peninsular War, all of which absorbed the attention of the Home Government.   By
her steadfast attitude in 1776, Canada had proved
her right to expect and to receive sympathetic at-

tention and encouragement from the Home Government, but it is perhaps not to be wondered at that in the circumstances of the troubled period the educational advancement of Lower Canada was neglected or ignored, and that educational opportunities were practically non-existent.

In other parts of Canada education seems to have received more sympathetic interest. Particularly in the Maritime Provinces good schools had been established, largely, however, through the efforts of the colonists themselves. A new impetus was given to education by the arrival of many settlers from the United States during and after the Revolution. These settlers had enjoyed in New England excellent educational advantages; they had lived close to great universities with their beneficent influence, the Universities of Harvard and Yale, of Williams and Dartmouth and Brown, and they determined to establish in their new home the educational facilities which they had already enjoyed in another land. It was felt in Lower Canada that similar opportunities should be speedily provided for the English-speaking children of the country. The majority of settlers in Lower Canada were of Scottish origin. They were largely soldiers or the descendants of soldiers who had fought in the Highland Regiments during the campaign of 1759, and who after the Treaty of Paris in 1763 had taken up the land assigned to them by the Crown. Many of these soldiers, too, later became fur-traders and entered the service of the North-West Company. These settlers were all eager that their children should have at least an elementary education. It was felt, too, that in the unrest and the uncertainty of the period immediately following the American Revolution it was not advisable to send students in search of higher professional training to the universities of the United States, which in the days of their British allegiance had attracted Canadian students in large numbers. But above all, the settlers realised the necessity for the establishment of schools in which the children of the French-Canadians should be taught English. It was declared that from the national point of view such training would have a far-reaching influence on the future of Canada as an integral part of the British Empire, and that without such instruction, which would result in a bond of language, Canada could never be a united land.

Efforts were accordingly made to establish a system of free schools, with the hope that later a university might be founded. As early as 1787 the matter received the serious consideration of the Legislative Council, and a scheme of education in the Province was actually prepared. But the scheme met with vigorous and determined opposition from one section of the community and it was in the end abandoned by the authorities after a somewhat bitter controversy. Some years passed without further action. In 1797 General Simcoe, the first Governor of Upper Canada, and his Executive Council decided to establish a Seminary for higher learning in that Province. They invited Mr. Strachan, a graduate of St. Andrews' University, Scotland, to organise the College but before he arrived in Canada General Simcoe was removed from office and the establishment of the proposed university was long delayed. The plans of Upper

Canada in 1797 to establish a university, although their fulfilment was long postponed, inspired the people of Lower Canada to greater efforts on behalf of education. They continued their agitation, but their efforts had little immediate success. The conditions in Lower Canada were earnestly and anxiously set forth in the following appeal made to the Governor-General, Sir R. S. Milnes, by the Rev. Dr. Jacob Mountain, Lord Bishop of Quebec, on October 19th, 1799:

"There is so intimate and obvious a connection between the education of youth and the general state of public morals, that I trust I shall not be thought to deviate from the duties that are more particularly assigned to me, if I presume to solicit your Excellency's attention to the disadvantages under which the Province has long laboured from the want of proper schools for the instruction of the children both of the higher and of the lower orders of the community.

"In doing this, it is by no means my intention to enter into the examination of these disadvantages so far as they are common to us with every other society which is without proper institutions for the education of youth; I shall take the liberty of mentioning such only as appear to be in a great measure peculiar to ourselves.

"Let me be permitted, then, to suggest the danger which may result to the political principles and to the future character as subjects of such of our young men among the higher ranks as the exigency of the case obliges their parents to send for a classical education to the colleges of the United States.

"In these Seminaries, most assuredly, they are not likely to imbibe that attachment to our constitution in Church and State, that veneration for the Government of their country, and that loyalty to their King, to which it is so peculiarly necessary in the present times to give all the advantage of early predilection in order to fix them deeply both in the understanding and the heart.

"To obviate this danger, it would seem expedient to found at least one good Grammar School in this Province and to invite able Masters from England by the liberality of the endowment.

"It may not be improper to state here that there is already at Quebec a respectable school, which offers the means of instruction to those who are designed for the more accurate professions, or for the pursuits of Trade and Commerce in which, together with the lower branches of education, are taught the Latin language, Mathematics, and Navigation, by a master well qualified for the task he has undertaken. I would wish to suggest the expediency of insuring the continuance of this advantage (which has not hitherto been duly appreciated) by some mark of the protection of the Government.

"But it is not only good Grammar Schools for the education of such young men as are designed for the learned Professions or who from their rank in society may hereafter fill situations of great political importance in the Province that are wanted; a more humble but a not less important branch of the community seems to call also for your Excellency's benevolent attention.

"It is well known that the lower orders of the people in this Province are for the most part de-

plorably ignorant; that the very slender portion of
instruction which their children obtain is almost entirely confined amongst those, who do not live in
the Towns, to the girls alone; and more especially,
it is notorious that they have hitherto made no
progress towards the attainment of the language of
the country under which government they have the
happiness to live.

"This total ignorance of the English language
on the part of the Canadians draws a distinct line of
demarcation between them and His Majesty's British subjects in this Province, injurious to the welfare
and happiness of both; and continues to divide into
two separate peoples those, who by their situation,
their common interests and their equal participation
of the same laws and the same form of Government,
should naturally form but one.

"If the evils are confessedly great which arise
from this want of a community of language, it
should seem expedient to endeavour to provide an
immediate remedy for the defect, and it should also
seem that this can only be done by facilitating as
much as possible the means of acquiring the English language to the children of the Canadians.

"The plan which I would beg leave to submit for
this purpose is simple and I trust practicable. Its
aim may appear to be humble, but its effects, I am
persuaded, would be in a high degree beneficial and
important.

"It is briefly this :—that a certain number of English School Masters, to be hereafter determined,
should be employed and paid by the Government;
that one of these should be placed in each of the
cities and towns, and in the most considerable vil-

lages for the purposes and under the express obligation of teaching the English language *gratis* to a
certain number of the Canadian children, and writing and arithmetic when required, at an easy rate;
that Trustees or Commissioners should be appointed
to manage the fund which the Government in its
bounty may see fit to appropriate to the end, to determine the number of Masters that may be required, their respective salaries, and the number of
children they shall respectively teach *gratis,* to fix
the rate at which Writing and Arithmetic shall be
taught on, and to have the power of removing the
Masters for incapacity or neglect of duty, and of
promoting them successively to the more lucrative
situations for able and meritorious conduct.

"I would barely hint, by way of a leading idea
upon this subject, that the salaries might perhaps
extend from £20 to £60 per annum according to
the number of inhabitants in the Village, Town, or
City in which the Teacher should be placed, and
that it might perhaps not improperly be a condition that he who received a payment of £20, should
be obliged to teach English *gratis* to *ten* Canadian
children, he who received £30 to fifteen children,
and so on in proportion.

"The importance and extent of this subject demand, I am well aware, more local information and
better judgment than I have been able to apply to
it;—I presume only to suggest it as an object not
unworthy of immediate consideration to your Excellency's superior wisdom."

This appeal was submitted by the Governor-
General to the Executive Council of Lower Canada
and was approved by that body. It was then for-

warded to the Colonial Office for further consideration. As a result, on July 12th, 1800, the Duke of Portland, sent to the Lieutenant-Governor a long despatch from which the following extracts indicate that the Home Government sympathised with the Lord Bishop's suggestion:—

"With respect to making a suitable provision for the education of youth in Lower Canada, and more particularly for laying a foundation for teaching the English tongue generally throughout the Province, I not only fully coincide with the sentiments expressed by the Bishop of Quebec and concurred in by the Executive Council on this point, but I am of opinion that the proposed Free Schools for this purpose should be established under the express condition of teaching the English language *gratis* to the children of His Majesty's subjects resident within the district for which such schools are established, without any limitation as to the number of such children.

"The Master should certainly be authorised to make a reasonable demand for teaching Writing and Arithmetic or, what would be still better, the terms may be settled from time to time by the Trustees or Governors of such Free Schools in the appointing of which it is His Majesty's pleasure that the Governor, Lieutenant-Governor, or person administrating the Government for the time being, the Bishop of Quebec, the Chief Justice of the Province, and the Speaker of the Assembly should always be of the number.

"In addition to the Free Schools for teaching the English language, (which I consider to be of the first necessity, and for the establishment of which you will consider yourself hereby authorised to appropriate from the Provincial revenues such sums as may be necessary to pay the salaries of the Masters who shall from time to time be appointed by you), it will be necessary in one or perhaps two instances to have recourse to others of the higher order and of the nature of our Public Schools here, in order that neither the means nor the necessary encouragement may be wanting to cultivate the study of the learned languages. It appears to me that this establishment will be sufficient for the present, although in due progress of time Foundations of a more enlarged and comprehensive nature will be requisite for the promotion of Religious and Moral Learning and the study of the Arts and Sciences. With this view His Majesty, ever ready to manifest his paternal consideration and regard for his subjects, and desirous to afford all possible assistance and encouragement to his Province in carrying into execution an object of such importance as the instruction and education of youth, has signified to me his Royal pleasure that you should upon consulting the members of His Majesty's Executive Council report to me in what manner and to what extent it would be proper to appropriate a portion of the Crown Land or revenues arising therefrom for this purpose."

As a result of the agitation for the providing of educational opportunities in Lower Canada, the Royal Institution for the Advancement of Learning was established by Act of the Legislature in 1801. Under this Act, the King gave directions for the establishment "of a competent number of Free Schools for the instruction of children in the first rudiments of useful learning; and also as occasion should require for foundations of a more comprehensive nature." It was declared that "His Majesty had further signified his intention that a suitable portion of the Lands of the Crown should be set apart, and the revenue thereof appropriated to these purposes." The Act provided that all property which should thereafter be given, bequeathed or purchased for educational purposes was to be vested in the trustees of the Royal Institution, with the necessary powers of management. Provision was made for the establishment of Free Schools at specified places throughout the Province by the authority of the Government, and for the building and repairing of schoolhouses, but not for the salaries of the masters. Accordingly, elementary free schools were soon erected in different parts of the Province, and several teachers were appointed by the authorities.

Notwithstanding the passing of the above Act, educational advancement in the Province for many years made but slow progress. There was no adequate system of management. In 1803, Lord Hobart issued instructions to the effect that a portion of the Crown Lands was to be set apart for the promotion of education. These instructions were not carried out; at best such a scheme would have been insufficient for the purpose; subsequent experience in the case of the Clergy Reserves proved the inefficacy of such an appropriation. There was a long delay in establishing the Corporation which the Act of 1801 had in view. In 1815, the Home Government directed the Provincial Government to proceed with the election of trustees under the Act, but it was not until 1818 that trustees were finally appointed. The trustees included the Lord Bishop of Quebec as Principal; the Lord Bishop of Montreal; the Chief Justice of Lower Canada; the Speaker of the Legislative Council; and the Speaker of the Legislative Assembly.

It is unnecessary to enter here into the details of the early history of the Royal Institution. Its first years were years of struggle. The schools erected under its authority were one-room buildings of cedar logs. Indeed, they were mere log-huts, but they provided the first free English Education in Lower Canada, and laid the foundation for a Canadian nationality. The records of the Royal Institution indicate the determination with which teachers and officials battled sturdily with poverty, and with discouraging conditions. The Secretary's salary was always many months in arrears, and he frequently complained, with unfortunately but little satisfaction, that not only had he given his time for some years without remuneration, but that he had expended even his own fuel and candles. In 1819, thirty-seven schools were in existence in the Province; these were occupied by fifty-three Teachers; the total expenditure for education was £883.10; the highest salary paid was £100,—at Quebec and at Montreal; the lowest salary was £11.5; the average salary was £18. It was pointed out by the authorities that these salaries were not intended to be the sole support of the teachers, but that they were meant "to operate as an aid and encouragement for the exertions and contributions of the inhabitants themselves."

Although the salaries were small and the school-buildings and equipment very poor and uncomfortable, the discipline of the Royal Institution seems to have been surprisingly strict and exacting. Criticism of teachers, their methods and the books they used, was plentiful and continuous. It was not unusual for teachers to be censured "for not keeping school at all," or for giving too many holidays, or for tardiness in opening school in the morning and eagerness in closing it in the afternoon. At least one teacher was warned that his arrears in salary would not be paid, and that he would be instantly dismissed "if he did not treat his wife with greater kindness." The teachers were billetted among the inhabitants in their respective districts; after a few days' sojourn in one house they moved on to another, thus making all the settlers bear in turn the burden of providing their food and lodging. In this way they managed to exist on their scanty salaries, which were frequently unpaid for many months. The school-buildings were used at times by travelling missionaries for religious services. This seems to have been a source of much annoyance to the authorities; the teachers rather than the inhabitants of the district were always held responsible, and were frequently severely reprimanded for permitting such use of the schoolhouses. It was not unusual for teachers to be told plainly by letter from the Secretary that they would be dismissed or "that no part of the salary hitherto granted by the Government would be allowed, unless the Methodists were wholly and immediately excluded from using the school-room as a place of worship."

The Royal Institution had many difficulties to contend with. Although its methods were not always

efficient and its management was not always adequate, it is deserving of gratitude for laying the
foundation of English education in what was to be
later the Province of Quebec. It not only guided for
many years elementary and grammar school education, but it planned for the establishment of a State
or Government College where higher education could
be obtained.   But before the proposed plan was
carried into effect, provision was made by a citizen
of Montreal for the endowment of a College to bear
his name. As a result, the Royal Institution for the
Advancement of Learning supervised the establishment of McGill College and directed it in its infancy,
for under the Act of 1801 all property and money
given for educational purposes in the Province of
Lower Canada was placed under its control.

CHAPTER II

The Dawn of McGill

DURING the discussion in the Legislature of educational conditions in Lower Canada which resulted in the establishment of the Royal Institution for the Advancement of Learning under the Act of 1801, one of the most prominent members of the Provincial Parliament was James McGill, a merchant and fur-trader who represented the West Ward of Montreal in the Legislative Assembly. Only meagre facts about the life of James McGill are available and the documentary evidence bearing on his career is scanty. He was born in Glasgow, Scotland, on the 6th of October, 1744. His parents were natives of Banffshire. After an elementary school education in his native town he entered Glasgow University at the age of twelve, in accordance with the custom of those days which permitted attendance at a University at a very early age. The Matriculation Album of Glasgow University contains the following entry:

1756, Jacobus McGill, filius natu maximus Jacobi mercatoris Glasguensis.

Nine years later, his younger brother Andrew entered the University, as indicated by the following record in the Matriculation Album:

1765, Andreas McGill, filius natu quintus Jacobi mercatoris Glasguensis.

Like so many other adventurous Scotchmen of that period, after completing his education James McGill determined to seek his fortune in the new land beyond the horizon, from which wondrous stories of the wealth and romance of the fur-trade were drifting to the old world. He emigrated to the American Colonies, where he remained for some years, and where he was later joined by his younger brother, Andrew. But before the American Revolution the brothers moved to Canada and in 1775 they were firmly and prosperously established in business in Montreal, where the older brother became connected with the famous fur-trading North-West Company. That he was at that time regarded as one of the leading citizens is evident from the fact that he was selected for many important and responsible civic duties. During the American Revolution when Canada was invaded and General Guy Carleton withdrew all the troops to Quebec and left Montreal to its fate, James McGill was one of those who saw the folly and uselessness of resistance. He preferred to save the city from unnecessary destruction and he was one of the twelve citizens,—six French and six English,—who were selected to sign the capitulation of the city to General Richard Montgomery on November 12th, 1775. His five associates were John Porteous, Richard Huntley, John Blake, Edward Gray and James Finlay. On December 2nd, 1776, he married Mrs. Marie Charlotte Guillemin, a French Roman Catholic lady, the widow of a French Canadian gentleman, Joseph A. T. Desrivières. The ceremony was performed by the Rev. David Charbrand Delisle, Rector of the Protestant Parish of Montreal and Chaplain of the Garrison.

The Church record reads:—"1776, James McGill, Esq., and Mrs. Charlotte Guillemin, widow, were married by Licence the 2nd December, 1776." Mrs. James McGill was born in Montreal in 1747, the daughter of William Guillemin and Claire Gene-vieve Foucault. She married Joseph A. T. Desri-vières in Montreal on the 19th of September, 1763, at the age of sixteen.

Soon after his arrival in Montreal James McGill acquired the Burnside estate of forty-six acres, with the Burnside Manor, in which he resided during the remainder of his life. He took into partnership, under the name of "McGill and Todd," his friend, Isaac Todd, a man of keen business ability and of civic prominence.

James McGill is described by his contemporaries as of "a frank and social temperament," in figure "tall and commanding, handsome in youth and be-coming somewhat corpulent in his old age," and in his leisure time "much given to reading." He was a prominent member of the Beaver Club, the members of which were all fur-traders who had amassed con-siderable wealth in their calling. A contemporary had a memory of him in jovial mood at one of the festal meetings of this Club, "singing a voyageur's folk-song with sonorous voice, and imitating, paddle in hand, in time with the music, the action of the bowman of a canoe ascending a rapid."

Because of his pleasing personality, his prosperity and business strength, and his marriage connections with another race and religion, he was held in respect and popularity by all classes, irrespective of nation-ality or creed. It was therefore but natural that he should enter political life after the granting of the

Constitutional Act by the Home Government in
1791. He was selected, with J. B. Durocher as
his colleague, to represent the West Ward of Montreal in the first parliament of Lower Canada which
met on the 17th of December, 1792. Later he became a member of the Legislative Council, and in
1812 he was appointed one of the commissioners
for removing from the city the old walls which had
been built in 1724. He took a prominent part in
the Militia organisation; during the war of 1812 he
was honorary Colonel of the Montreal Infantry
Volunteer Regiment; later and before hostilities
ended, although he was too old for active service,
he was promoted to be Brigadier General, and he
seems to have had a large part in directing the administration of the various Militia units. After a
busy, active and strenuous life of unselfish service
for his community and of devoted efforts for the promotion of tolerance and harmony between races and
creeds as the one sure foundation for a united Canadian nationality, he died in Montreal on December
19th, 1813, at the age of sixty-nine, and was buried
on December 21st. The official record of his death
reads: "On the nineteenth day of December, one
thousand eight hundred and thirteen, the Honourable James McGill, Colonel, Commandant of the
Montreal Militia, died, and was buried on the
twenty-first following." The certificate of death
was signed by his partner, Isaac Todd, and by
Thomas Blackwood, a native of Lanarkshire, Scotland, who was at one time employed in the firm of
McGill and Todd, and who later formed a business
partnership with Francis Desrivières.

Mrs. James McGill survived her husband less

Thomas Pattendel

P. Canot Sculpsit

Montreal as James McGill knew it

than five years. She died in Montreal on the 16th of April, 1818, aged seventy years and nine months, and was buried on the 18th following. There were no children from the marriage.

James McGill was born of Scotch Presbyterian parents and he grew up in the church and religion of his fathers. When he settled in Montreal there was no Church of Scotland in the city. The first Presbyterian congregation in Montreal consisted of a small group of Scottish settlers. It was organised without a church building in 1786 by the Rev. John Bethune, who ministered to its members from March 12th in that year until he moved to Upper Canada in May, 1787. But it was but a temporary organisation and had no continuous status. From 1787 to 1790 there is no record of the holding of a strictly Presbyterian service in the city. The only Protestant body holding service regularly was known as "the Protestant Congregation of Montreal," the pastor of which was the Rev. David Charbrand Delisle, one of the three clergymen who had been employed by the Church of England to labour among the French-Canadians. He was Rector of the Parish of Montreal and Chaplain of the Garrison. This congregation worshipped until 1789 in the Church of the Recollet Fathers, which with great tolerance and courtesy was for twenty years at their disposal; in 1789 they were given the Chapel belonging to the Jesuits' College, then Government property; they opened it for public worship in December under the name of Christ Church.

Like all the young Protestant Scotchmen living in Montreal at that time, James McGill became by necessity a member of the Protestant Episcopal

Congregation. The adherents to the two Protestant
creeds were tolerant and harmonious in their relations one with the other and they were content to
worship together. In 1789 when the Bishop of
Nova Scotia visited Montreal an address was presented to him by the Church Wardens, and by "a
committee of the Protestant inhabitants of Montreal," irrespective of their former creed. The majority of the latter were Scotch Presbyterians. The
Bishop was met at Pointe aux Trembles by the reception committee. One of the "Protestant inhabitants" who signed and presented the address was
James McGill. There is no doubt that the larger
number of this "committee of Protestant inhabitants," at that time identified with the Protestant
Episcopal Congregation of Montreal, returned to
the Church of their fathers as soon as a Church was
built, several of them becoming office-bearers. The
precise action taken by James McGill is uncertain.
He seems to have divided his allegiance between the
two communions; while not severing his connection
entirely with the Church of England he gave his
support to the establishment of a Church of Scotland and later became identified with it. When the
St. Gabriel Street Church, the first Presbyterian
Church in Montreal, was built in 1792, he subscribed
ten guineas towards the construction of the building.
He signed the call to the first pastor of the Church,
the Rev. James Somerville; he thereafter contributed
three pounds a year to his stipend and occupied pew
No. 16 in the Church. His brother Andrew later
contributed five pounds towards removing the remaining debt from the building. The Rev. Mr.
Somerville, the pastor of the Church, officiated at

Andrew's funeral. There is little doubt from the records that James McGill regarded himself as of the Church of Scotland although he was for a time, in those days of somewhat surprising religious harmony and tolerance, a member of the Protestant Episcopal Church of Montreal.

One of James McGill's most intimate friends and confidants in Canada was the Rev. John Strachan, afterwards the Right Reverend Bishop of Toronto, who was thirty-four years his junior. He was a native of Aberdeen, Scotland. He received his M. A. from King's College, Aberdeen, in 1797, and then attended for some months Divinity Classes at St. Andrew's University, near which he had a post as a Parish schoolmaster. Towards the end of 1797, he came to Canada by invitation to organise a seminary of learning in Upper Canada, but the plan was abandoned and he became tutor in a private family in Kingston, Ontario. He offered himself as a candidate for the pastorship of the St. Gabriel Street Presbyterian Church on September 21, 1802, but before his letter was received another applicant, the Rev. James Somerville, had been accepted. Later he took orders in the Anglican Church and was appointed to the Church at Cornwall. He opened there a school and his fame as a teacher was soon widespread. Among his pupils were the three sons of the Rev. John Bethune who had established the first Presbyterian Congregation in Montreal, one of whom afterwards became Rector of Christ Church and acting-Principal of McGill University. In 1807, he married the widow of James McGill's younger brother, Andrew, formerly Miss Wood of Cornwall, and he was thus brought into closer relation-

ship with the McGill family.   His enthusiasm for
education and for its advancement in Canada was
unbounded and it is evident that he impressed his
ideas as to ways and means and methods on the mind
of his wealthy merchant friend.   James McGill was
a believer in the value of education; he knew what
it had done for his own home-land, and what Scotland, educationally, was doing for the world.   He
determined that the torch which for him had been
lighted in Glasgow University should burn likewise
for those who would succeed him in the land of his
adoption.   He had indicated that determination
during the consideration of the subject in the Legislature.   But on the question of method he sought
advice from his young teacher friend, Strachan,
whom he frequently visited in the latter's home in
Cornwall.   During these Glengarry visits there was
many a happy and roseate night of mingled sociabil-
ity and high seriousness, after the custom of their
race and time, when the two friends, the young educationalist and the older man of wealth, with similar
vision, sat late in discussion of the Canadian educational problem and of plans for its solution.

In a letter to the other surviving executors of
James McGill's will, written from York [Toronto]
on May 31, 1820, seven years after James McGill's
death, the Rev. Dr. Strachan gave interesting information on these discussions and their bearing on
the circumstances leading up to the practical working
out of James McGill's dreams on education as evidenced later in his will.   He wrote: "It was, I
believe, at Cornwall during one of the visits which
Mr. McGill made to Mrs. Strachan and me that his
final resolution respecting the erection of a College

after his name, endowing it, etc., was taken. We had been speaking of several persons who had died in Lower Canada and had left no memorial of themselves to benefit the country in which they had realised great fortunes. And particularly I mentioned a University, as the English had no Seminary where an Academical Education could be obtained. We had repeated conversations upon the subject, and he departed determined to do something and with some inclination to leave twenty instead of ten thousand pounds, together with Burnside, and even to make some preparations before his death, expressing at the same time a wish that if he did anything I should take an active part in the proposed College."

It was soon after the visit referred to that James McGill made his will,—on March 8, 1811. He bequeathed to the Royal Institution for the Advancement of Learning, in trust, the sum of £10,000 and his Burnside Estate of forty-six acres, together with the dwelling house and other buildings, for the erection on the estate, and the endowment, of a University or College on the express conditions,—and these were the only conditions imposed,—that the University be erected and established within ten years of his death and that one of the Colleges to be comprised in the University should be called "McGill College." If the College was not erected in the time specified the conveyance to the Royal Institution was to be null and void; and the estate and endowment were to revert to his widow, and after her death to her first husband's nephew, Francis Desrivières and to his legal heirs. He named as executors of the will John Richardson, James Reid, John Strachan, and James Dunlop.

These executors were all close personal friends of
the testator.   The career of John Strachan has
already been outlined.   Although it was not specified
in the will that he should be connected with the
proposed College, it may be assumed that because
of his close friendship, his marriage connection, and
his established reputation as a brilliant and successful educationalist with definite ideas on Canadian
nationality, James McGill desired that he should have
a prominent part in the organization of the College
and that possibly he should be its first Principal.
That this desire was stated to the trustees seems certain.   In a letter written from Toronto some years
after James McGill's death, while the trustees who
knew the circumstances were still living, Bishop
Strachan said:

"If it had been my desire, it was certainly in my
power to have been at the head of it [McGill Col-
lege] for it so happened that I had some difficulty in
prevailing with my friend, Mr. McGill, to forbear
annexing it as a condition to his bequest that I should
fill that situation;" and he added that "a Professorship in McGill College was never desired or
thought of by me, nor could any situation in that
institution have formed an inducement to me to
leave this Province to which I have been for so many
years devoted."

The three trustees associated with the Rev. Dr.
Strachan as administrators of the will were all prominent in civic and provincial affairs.   They were all
Scotchmen and were connected with St. Gabriel
Street Presbyterian Church.   John Richardson, partner in the mercantile house of Forsyth, Richardson
and Co., was a native of Banffshire, Scotland.   He

represented the East Ward of Montreal in the first Parliament of Lower Canada, which met in 1792, and he took his seat at the same time as James Mc-Gill, his colleague from the West Ward. With the latter, he was one of the commissioners appointed for the removing of the old city walls in 1802 and it was through his influence that the bill providing for the construction of a canal to Lachine was passed. The firm of which he was a member contributed £20 towards the building of St. Gabriel Street Presbyterian Church and he personally subscribed £3 a year towards the minister's stipend; he occupied pews No. 6 and No. 47. He was one of a committee of three formed to purchase the land on which the General Hospital now stands; he was chairman of the committee which superintended the construction of the Hospital and was later chosen as its first president. He died in 1831, aged seventy-six.

The Honourable James Reid, the second trustee named, was admitted to the Bar of the Province in 1794; he was raised to the Bench as a puisne Judge in 1807, and later in 1823 he was made Chief Justice of Montreal. He subscribed one guinea a year to the stipend of the first pastor of St. Gabriel Street Presbyterian Church and occupied pew No. 14. He died in 1848 at the age of seventy-nine. After his death, his widow erected to the memory of her husband the southwest wing of the Montreal General Hospital.

James Dunlop, the fourth trustee named, settled in Montreal in 1777 and established a general store in St. Paul Street. He took an active part in the military organisation during the War of 1812, and served as Major under Brigadier General James

McGill. He subscribed ten guineas towards the
building of St. Gabriel Street Presbyterian Church
and his name appears for ten pounds on a special
subscription list for liquidating the debt on the original building; he signed the manifesto in favour of the
first pastor of the Church, the Rev. James Somerville; he contributed five pounds annually towards his
salary and occupied pews No. 19 and No. 99. He
died in 1815 at the age of sixty.

James McGill's estate sloped from the base of
Mount Royal towards the St. Lawrence River. It
consisted of forty-six acres of fertile land extending
south to what is now Dorchester Street and reaching
from the present University Street on the east to
what are now McTavish and Metcalfe Streets on
the west. St. Catherine Street and Dorchester
Street were not then in existence and Sherbrooke
Street was but a narrow road running through the
farm. East, west and south of the estate were open
fields and a few scattered houses, and the city proper
lay a long distance away, beside the water-front. A
small stream of water passed through the farm. It
entered from the east near the present Milton Street
entrance on University Street; it then turned south
and was increased in volume by the water from a
spring near the site of the Macdonald Engineering
Building. It passed on through the present tennis
courts in "the hollow" by the Physics Building,
crossed Sherbrooke Street where it was joined by
another small stream from the southwest, and then
flowed close to Burnside House and on towards
the city. It is recorded that the name Burnside
was given to the estate because of this stream or
"burn" as the Scotch called it. James McGill's home,

Burnside House, a large stone building, was situated on the present McGill College Avenue, about midway between the present Sherbrooke and Burnside Streets on the left-hand side looking south; it was demolished in 1860 to make room for the buildings now in that locality. A narrow road led from near the front of the house to what is now St. Antoine Street. The estate was divided into small sections which were later rented for purposes of cultivation or pasture. It contained numerous trees and shrubs, and was at that time regarded as one of the most valuable and desirable parts of the district of Montreal.

In the days of James McGill, Montreal was a small town of from twelve to fifteen thousand inhabitants, and of these the large majority were French. Indeed, the whole province had but a scanty population. One-third of the houses were wooden huts. The town stretched out along the water-front in a series of narrow blocks and straggling streets. The trade with foreign countries was exceedingly small. The entire carrying capacity of ships annually arriving at Quebec did not exceed 12,-000 tons, and only a few of these ships went on to Montreal. In 1813, the year of James McGill's death, only nine vessels entered Montreal from the sea, and their total capacity was but 1,589 tons. At the end of the 18th century, the exports of furs and other products from the entire province was little more than half a million pounds sterling. Strange and primitive customs were still in vogue in the city. The price of bread was regulated by "His Majesty's Justices of the Peace," and bakers were required to mark their bread with the initials of their name.

Slavery was not unknown, and a sale advertisement towards the end of the century included in the articles to be sold "a stout, healthy negro man about 28 years of age,—an excellent cook, and very fit for working on a farm." A mail for England was dispatched about once a month. It went by way of New York and took from three to four weeks to reach that city; it was then forwarded by packet-ship to England, and usually at least four months passed before an answer could be received. The incoming mail was put off the New York packet at Halifax; it came overland from Halifax to Montreal, this part of the journey alone taking nearly four weeks.

Such was the somewhat primitive city in which James McGill lived and laboured and amassed his wealth. Such was the community to the service of which he contributed unstintingly of his material substance, his energy and his talent. Such, too, were the conditions in which this hard-headed, practical business man dreamed a dream,—a dream of a greater Canada with a distinctly Canadian nationality trained to solve its own problems in its own way, and of the necessity for providing for the youth of the great land mirrored in his mind the privileges of an adequate education similar to that which he had enjoyed in his own native country. For James McGill seems to have been a combination of the practical Scottish business man and the dreaming Scottish mystic. Like the other early Canadian pioneers of his race he was a hard-fisted man battling by necessity in a hard-fisted new world, but he kept in that new world the spiritual vision born of Scottish glens and mists and hills. He worked like his ancestors for the building of churches and schools and court

Photo Rice Studios

The Burnside Estate

houses, symbolic of religion, education and law, as milestones of civilisation in a new land and without which no country could make progress. He knew that without the torch of a free and liberal education the land of promise to which he had come and from which he had received much, could not advance to what he believed to be its destined place of power and service in the world. And so he dreamed of a great University which would not only be local in its usefulness, serving a small city which his faith told him would one day grow to giant size, but also national in its influence, and ministering to the enlightenment of that larger Canada which his vision saw in the far and dim distance. The making of his bequest two years before his death for the establishment and the endowment of McGill College was the first step towards the fulfilment of his hopes. But between the dream and its ultimate realisation lay long and troubled years of baffling difficulty and bitter discouragement, and at times, despair.

CHAPTER III

Delay and Difficulty

LESS than three years after he had made his bequest, James McGill died, in December, 1813. Soon after his death the executors of his will sought to fulfil his desire with reference to the establishment of a College, and to ensure that the conditions imposed with regard to time would be complied with as speedily as possible. But they were confronted by obstacles over which they had no control. The will bequeathed the Burnside Estate and the Endowment Fund to the executors in trust, on the understanding that they should as soon as convenient after the testator's death convey it to the Royal Institution for the Advancement of Learning, to be used by them as provided under the Act of 1801. But, as we have seen, the organization of the Royal Institution was bitterly opposed by one section of the community. Every effort to have trustees appointed and to have the Institution put in actual operation was frustrated. The authorities feared to cause friction or discord, and they preferred postponement. There was therefore no Royal Institution, other than in name only, to which the McGill bequest could be conveyed. There were no trustees. It was necessary first for the executors and those interested in the establishment of the College to effect the actual organization of the Royal

44

Institution by securing the appointment of trustees as called for by the Act. They continued, with vigour, to impress this necessity upon the authorities in order that the McGill bequest should not lapse, and they were promised prompt action. But in that troubled period of warfare the Home Government was involved in too many difficulties to devote time to the problem. Action was for these various reasons consequently long delayed and it was not until 1818 that the promise was fulfilled and that the authorities at last appointed Trustees and established in fact the Royal Institution. Were it not for the fear of losing the legacy,—a misfortune which after all was narrowly averted,—and the persistent efforts of the executors, the appointment would have been doubtless longer delayed. The Provincial Legislature could not appoint trustees without orders and they were unwilling to make any grant of money without authority from the Colonial Office.

But as a result of the hopeful promise made to the executors by the authorities towards the close of 1814, the former began to discuss and to put forward plans for the carrying out of the desire of the founder of the College. The Rev. Dr. Strachan was their spokesman. On February 14, 1815, he wrote to three personal friends who were then members of the Legislature of Lower Canada asking their co-operation and assistance, advising haste, and setting forth his own ideas on the establishment of McGill College,—ideas based on his knowledge of educational conditions in Canada and on his own experience of nearly twenty years in educational work. He urged the Provincial Legislature to act independently of the Home Government and to grant the funds necessary to put the College at once in operation, and he suggested making use of the Jesuits' Estates or the Crown Lands for this purpose. From this letter the following extracts are of interest:

"As we [the Executors] have sent the necessary documents to the Commander of the Forces to point out the necessity of his acting promptly in establish, ing a College according to the conditions of Mr. McGill's Will, and as it is probable he may apply to the House of Assembly upon the subject, I furnish you with my ideas.

"The scheme enclosed for the two Schools and College is as economical as it can well be to render it respectable and useful. The number of students will not be great for some years, nor will it ever be such as to make the Professorships lucrative. Even the Principal will hardly ever be able to reach one thousand pounds per annum, a remuneration suffi- ciently moderate for the accumulated duties which he will have to perform and to maintain in such an expensive place as Montreal the dignity of his station. If the Provincial Parliament waits for something to be done by the King all will be lost,—for the Gov- ernment have too many things to call their attention. But when the matter is once set on foot, an address from the Legislature can at any time procure assist- ance from His Majesty's Ministry. Yet six thousand pounds per annum appears to me a trifle, considering the increased opulence of the country. It is not prob- able that the Roman Catholics will object to such an arrangement,—they have already three Seminaries said to be well endowed,—but if any of them be poor the Legislature ought to grant them pecuniary relief.

"I say nothing respecting religion, but in the Chapel of the University Lectures on Theology may be given to Protestant students, which Roman Catholics shall not be required to attend. There are many particular regulations which I do not mention, I just furnish a crude outline.

"You are to recollect that if nothing be done, you will soon lose Mr. McGill's donation. The time will never again be so propitious. I say nothing about the nomination of Professors; men of some talent must be selected and of great zeal for the promotion of the Sciences. The first Principal will have many difficulties to encounter and may not live to see the Seminary in a very flourishing condition, but it will ultimately exceed the most sanguine expectations.

"I prefer the form of the Scotch and German Universities to the English, or rather a mixture of both plans, because much more may be done at one-fourth of the expense. In the English Universities the public Professors seldom lecture more than once a week, —many of them not at all; the whole system of teaching is conducted by Tutors and emulation and a love of study is kept up among the students by fellowships, etc. The great opulence of Cambridge and Oxford is far beyond our reach, and although I should be sorry ever to see them lose a shilling, for I think them wisely adapted to so rich and populous and learned a country as England, I consider them unfit for this country. Our professors must each during the session, give two, three, or even four courses of lectures, till the funds afford the means of increasing their number.

"I must further add on the subject of finding Professors, that gentlemen newly from England, and accustomed to the wealthy Universities of that country, may not always possess the qualities necessary to make them useful in this projected Seminary. Learning they may have in abundance, but the industry, labour (I may say drudgery) and accommodation to circumstances cannot be expected from them. There are several gentlemen in this country qualified for the first race of Professors, and after the Seminary is once set agoing there will be no risk in electing Englishmen to fill vacant chairs, because the rules and regulations being established, all must submit.

"I have only mentioned one restriction, the Principal to be of the Church of England. This, I think necessary on many accounts. The Seminary must and ought to have a distinct religious character, and this simple regulation will confer it without circumscribing its liberality and openness to all persuasions. I think also the Principal's department should be Moral Philosophy or Theology."

In the same letter Bishop Strachan outlined his suggested scheme for the organisation of McGill College. He pointed out "that the necessity of sending young men out of the Province to finish their education has been found both dangerous and inconvenient; that reason and policy equally demand that our youth be educated in the Province, or in England, if we wish them to become friendly to our different establishments and to the Parent State; that few can defray the expense of sending their children to England, and, if they could, the distance from parental authority is dangerous to their morals; and that there is at present no Seminary in which the English youth of Canada can obtain a liberal education."

To remedy these alleged evils, he therefore proposed that there should be established "two Grammar Schools, one at Quebec, and one at Montreal, each under a Rector or Head Master and three Assistants, at which the following branches of education shall be taught: the Greek, Latin, French and English languages, Writing, Arithmetic, Geography, and Practical Mathematics.   These schools, to be appendages and nurseries for a University to be established on the model of the Scotch and German Universities in the neighbourhood of Montreal, on the property bequeathed for that purpose by the late Honourable James McGill, and to be named as he desired, McGill College or University; that the following branches of academical education be taught in the said University, (1) Greek and Latin; (2) Natural History and Botany; (3) Mathematics and Astronomy; (4) Natural Philosophy and Chemistry; (5) Moral Philosophy, Logic and Rhetoric; (6) Surgery and Anatomy; (7) Civil and Public Law; that the Professors of Surgery and of Civil and Public Law shall not be required to reside within the College; that a house be provided within the College for a Principal and four Professors; that the members of the University be constituted a Corporation capable of sueing and being sued, and of receiving donations of money and lands, etc., for the benefits of the Institution; that the Principal be always a clergyman of the Church of England; that young men of all denominations, as Christians, be freely admitted to the different lectures; that new Professorships be established as soon as the funds will admit; that the University be represented in the House of Assembly by two Members; that no degree be conferred upon a student who has not resided three years; that an attendance of three years at the University shall entitle a student to be called to the Bar one year earlier than any other, provided he be of age; that a report of the state of the University be annually laid before Parliament; that there be frequent Visitations by the Bishop, the Chief Justice, the Speaker of the House of Assembly, etc., appointed a committee for that purpose; and that there be two public examinations every year."

Dr. Strachan estimated the expense of the necessary buildings to be £18,000, "made up of £4,000 for each of the two Grammar Schools including residence for the Head Masters, and £10,000 in addition to James McGill's bequest of £10,000, an excellent site and house extremely commodious for the Principal or one of the Professors." The annual expense of the Grammar Schools was estimated at £2,000, "made up of £300 a year to each of the Head Masters, £200 a year to each of two second Head Masters, £100 a year to each of four Under Masters, and £300 to each school for servants, repairs, library, premiums, etc." It was added that "this will render them desirable, and together with a moderate fee, payable by each scholar to his respective Teacher, will make them an object to men of talent!"

The total annual expense of the University was estimated at £4,000, made up as follows: "The Principal to be also a Professor, £750; the Senior Professor, £500; three Professors, £400 each; the Professor of Surgery and Anatomy, and the Professor of Civil and Public Law, £200 each; in addition each Professor is to enjoy a moderate fee from the students attending his lectures; for the purchase of books for the Library, £300; for the purchase of Philosophical and Chemical apparatus, £250; for the purchase of Plants for the Botanic Garden, £100; Librarian's salary, £100; Gardener's salary, £100; Servants and Contingencies, £300." It was explained that smaller salaries were given to the Professors of Surgery and Law because "they will be Professional men not expected to reside in the College or to be exclusively confined to its duties, but attending at the same time to their private practice."

Three reasons were given by Dr. Strachan for preferring Montreal to Quebec as the place for the establishment of the University: "its more central position; its greater suitability for a Botanic Garden; and the large sum of money and a most beautiful estate already given for the express purpose." In conclusion, Dr. Strachan wrote: "Thus it appears that for an appropriation of £18,000, and six thousand pounds per annum, an establishment may be formed of incalculable importance to the Province, in a religious, moral and political light. The Legislature might in a few years be relieved from the burden by procuring from the Crown the Jesuits' Estates to be given for the support of the Institution, and by grants of lands capable of becoming productive. The allowance for Philosophical and Chemical apparatus will in a few years become too great; the surplus may then assist the library."

The three members of the Legislature to whom this letter was sent by Dr. Strachan at once brought it to the attention of their colleagues, and the question was again referred to the Home Government. It seems to have been pressed with earnestness and persistence but it was apparently not regarded as very urgent by the Colonial Office. The authorities were evidently too busy with the Napoleonic Wars in Europe and America, and with their own internal problems to give much attention to Colonial education, and the year passed without further action. Finally, on the 30th of December, 1815, Lord Bathurst wrote from Downing Street to Sir Gordon Drummond, then administering the Government of Lower Canada, the following letter asking for information about the Jesuits' Estates, and intimating the intention of the Government to proceed with the establishment of a College or Colleges in the Province, for the erecting of which the revenues of these estates might be used:

"His Royal Highness, the Prince Regent, being desirous of marking by some permanent establishment the high sense which he entertains of the exertions made by the Provinces of Canada during the late war with the United States, has been pleased to signify his intention of founding and endowing in the Province one or more Colleges for the education of youth. An establishment so necessary cannot be too early accomplished, and although the details of such a measure are not completely arranged, yet Montreal has been from its central situation selected as the town best fitted for such a purpose. There does not appear any reason why the commencement of the work should not take place immediately. You will, therefore, lose no time in selecting such a spot in the immediate vicinity of Montreal, taking care that the ground selected be sufficiently extensive to leave an adequate space for the formation of walks and gardens, and you will proceed without delay to enclose it for that purpose. You will further take the necessary measures for acquainting the trustees in whose hands the late Mr. McGill deposited by will a sum of £10,000 in aid of this object, that it is the intention of His Majesty's Government to commence such an undertaking and to call upon them as soon as the plan shall have been definitely settled for the application of the funds entrusted to them for the purpose of erecting the building. I forbear in this first stage of the undertaking to mention either the assistance which His Majesty's Government is prepared or may be enabled to give or that which the Province may be disposed to contribute. The benefits of such an establishment are such as must be felt both in the Colonies and in the Mother Country, and when felt cannot but ensure on the part of both a hearty co-operation and liberal support.

"With a view to the endowment of a College, the estates lately belonging to the Jesuits and now in possession of the Crown, afford a resource of which His Majesty's Government are to a certain extent determined to avail themselves. But previous to deciding upon the extent of the establishment it is necessary that I should be informed of the present value of these Estates, of their capability of improvement and of the mode in which their revenues have hitherto been disposed of.

"I have therefore to desire that you will as early as possible furnish me with adequate information upon these several points. Upon the receipt of which His Majesty's Government will lose no time in entering upon the final arrangement of an establishment calculated to afford to all classes of His Majesty's subjects in the Province that degree of education and those means of improvement which they have hitherto been compelled to seek at a distance from home."

It is evident from the above letter that the writer had no knowledge of the conditions of James McGill's will nor was he aware that before Colleges could be established it was first necessary to appoint Trustees for the Royal Institution and thereby to enable that body to assume control of educational institutions established in the Province, as already provided for by the Act of 1801. However, the Executors of the McGill will were informed, as requested, of the Home Government's intention, and the information asked for with reference to the Jesuits' Estates was forwarded to the Colonial Office. Lord Bathurst was apparently meanwhile made acquainted with the conditions of the will and with the Act of 1801. A few weeks later, on March 14th, 1816, he again wrote to Sir Gordon Drummond, as follows:

"My despatch of the 30th December will have informed you of the determination of His Royal Highness the Prince Regent to avail himself of the return of peace to forward the important objects of education and instruction in His Majesty's Dominions, and especially in the Provinces of Canada. When I then addressed you I had not had an opportunity of perusing the will of Mr. McGill which afforded by the liberality of his bequest such important assistance in carrying such an object into effect. I have since been furnished with a copy of the will of which an extract is enclosed for your consideration. You will no doubt observe that the mode in which the bequest is directed to be made, no less than the nature of it, superseded the necessity

of carrying into effect the instructions conveyed to
you on the 30th December under an erroneous impression of its contents. You will therefore consider
that instruction to be recalled and in lieu of adopting
any measures for enclosing a spot well fitted for the
erection of the University, you will suspend all
measures of such a nature till the necessary preliminary arrangements have been made in conformity
with the Act of Parliament of the Province of Lower
Canada passed in the 41st year of His Present
Majesty, entitled 'An Act for the Establishment of
Free Schools and the Advancement of Learning in
this Province.' Those arrangements you will immediately carry into effect, by appointing under the
Great Seal of the Province the following persons to
be Trustees of the Schools of Royal Foundation in
the Province in the manner and for the purposes
specified in the Act and constituting them a Body
Corporate by the name of the Royal Institution for
the Advancement of Learning. The persons to be
nominated in the first instance are the Governor,
Lieutenant-Governor, or person administering the
Government for the time being; the Right Reverend
Jacob Mountain, Bishop of Quebec; Jonathan Sewell,
Esq., the Chief Justice of the district of Quebec;
James Monk, Esq., the Chief Justice of the district
of Montreal; the Reverend J. O. DuPlessis, Super-
intendent of the Romish Church.

"As soon as this preliminary arrangement shall
have taken place you will call upon the persons named
in Mr. McGill's will for the execution of the trust
reposed in them, and you will by an early opportunity
receive detailed instructions for your future proceedings."

Three weeks later, on the 9th April, 1816, Lord Bathurst forwarded to Sir Gordon Drummond the following despatch containing the names of additional Trustees and cancelling for obvious religious, political and racial reasons which would prevent criticism the former appointment of the Governor:

"In my despatch of the 14th ult., I conveyed to you the instruction of His Royal Highness, the Prince Regent, to nominate and appoint under the Provincial Act of 1801 a Body Corporate for the Advancement of Learning, and I communicated to you the names of several persons who appeared best qualified for such a duty. It has since appeared more advisable to increase the number of Trustees to eight in order to obviate the inconveniences which if the number were less might arise from the non-attendance of individual members. It has been deemed proper also in order to obviate all objections which might be grounded on the circumstances of the peculiar situation in which with regard to this commission the Governor is placed, to withdraw from that commission the name of the Governor or Officer administering the Government. You will therefore take the necessary measures for inserting in the Patent the following names in lieu of those which I have previously specified, viz.—Jonathan Sewell, Esq., Chief Justice of the district of Quebec; James Monk, Esq., Chief Justice of the district of Montreal; the Right Rev. Jacob Mountain, Bishop of Quebec; Rev. J. O. DuPlessis, Superintendent of the Romish Church; the Rev. Dr. Alexander Sparke of the Church of Scotland; John Richardson, Esq., of Montreal, a member of the Executive and Legislative Councils; William Bachelor Coltman, Esq., of Quebec, a member of the Executive Council; and John Reid, Esq., of Montreal, one of the Judges of the Court of King's Bench."

Notwithstanding the above instructions the Provincial Government was slow to act, for reasons already specified. Opposition to the establishment of the Royal Institution continued to be powerful and somewhat bitter, and two years passed before trustees were finally appointed. The Rev. J. O. DuPlessis, the Superintendent of the Romish Church, objected to becoming a member of the Board, and later declined. Meanwhile vigorous efforts were made to have the grants for schools and the McGill bequest augmented by the Crown, through the use of Crown Lands or the revenues of the Jesuits' Estates as partly promised in Lord Bathurst's letter of December 30, 1815.

As a result of these persistent efforts by some members of the Legislature and by church authorities interested in education, the Home Government realised that the funds devoted to educational institutions were lamentably insufficient and that additional means should at once be provided for the better equipment of schools and for the engagement of a greater number of teachers. They seem to have realised, too, that the bequest of James McGill was not in itself sufficient to provide for the erection of College buildings and for a subsequent endowment. They therefore decided after much consideration to make use of the estates of the Jesuits which had reverted to the Crown on the extinction of the order. For several years the assigning of the revenues of these estates to educational and religious purposes under Protestant control had been advo-

cated and by the strange irony of history this was
in time brought about.   Indeed, as early as February
10th, 1810, Sir Gordon Drummond, then administering the Government of Lower Canada, wrote from
Quebec to the Colonial Office stating that the Anglican Cathedral in Quebec "was badly in need of
repair and that for the purpose of repair there was
little hope of obtaining from the inhabitants of
Quebec any contribution worthy of consideration."
He therefore asked that the Home Government
should authorise him to devote to the purpose part
of the revenue arising from the Jesuits' Estates, the
whole of which "to the amount of more than £4,500
annually has hitherto been transferred to the Military chest."   And he added, "I beg leave to suggest
my opinion that this is the most proper source from
which the means of repairing the cathedral can be
drawn, and indeed, that this fund might with propriety in the future be applied to the general support
of the places of worship of the Established Church
throughout the Province."

In answer to this request, however, no immediate action was taken, for although the Home Government had a legal right to dispose of the Estates
as they saw fit, they naturally wished to proceed
slowly and tactfully in order to avoid religious friction or bitterness within the Province.   In 1815,
when, as already pointed out, it was intimated by
the Colonial Office that the Jesuit Estates might
possibly be appropriated in aid of the McGill bequest,
there seems to have been no intention to limit the
assistance which should be provided by this increased
revenue to McGill College alone.   On the contrary,
the object appears to have been to use the additional

funds in order that, irrespective of race or creed, the benefits of education might be diffused as widely as possible throughout the country. But delay again followed, and it was not until the next year that definite instructions were issued by Lord Bathurst for the transfer of the Jesuits' Estates to the Royal Institution for the Advancement of Learning. These instructions were contained in the following historic letter, destined to have so large a part in the establishment of McGill College and in Canadian education, and forwarded to the Officer Administering the Government of Lower Canada by Lord Bathurst from Downing Street on May 10th, 1816:

"I have already expressed to you the gracious intention of His Royal Highness, the Prince Regent, to forward the extension of education in the Provinces of Canada and I have pointed out the preliminary measures necessary on your part to give effect to that intention. In furtherance of this object, I have received the commands of His Royal Highness to instruct you to transfer to the Trustees of the Royal Institution for the Advancement of Learning all those estates which formerly belonged to the Society of Jesuits, which, since the abolition of that order, have been vested in the Crown, in order that the Royal Institution for the Advancement of Learning may possess present means for establishing and maintaining the Seminaries which it may be necessary to found and may possess the revenue which cannot fail progressively to increase in proportion to the improvement of the Provinces and the consequent demand for additional means of instruction.

"In transferring, however, those estates to the management of the Royal Institution for the Ad-

vancement of Learning, you will retain for the future
disposal of His Royal Highness the accumulation
of the rents and profits of preceding years which
may be either in the hands of the Receiver of those
estates, or which may have been by him paid to the
Colonial Government, and you will with as little
delay as possible transmit to me a detailed account
of the amount of the Fund which has been so
created."

Meanwhile the executors of the will of James
McGill had been again informed of the definite intention of the authorities to proceed with the erection and endowment of a College at Montreal, and
on May 13th, 1816, John Richardson, one of the
surviving executors, acknowledged on behalf of
himself and his colleagues receipt of the information
in the following letter, in which, remembering perhaps Lord Bathurst's letter of December 30, 1816,
they emphasised the conditions imposed in the will:

"We have the honour of receiving your letter of
the 9th inst., written by command of His Excellency,
the Administrator in Chief, to acquaint us that His
Majesty's Government have it in contemplation to
erect and endow a College at Montreal and that it
is their intention as soon as the plan of this establishment shall be definitely settled, to call upon us as
Trustees of the Will of the late Mr. McGill for
the application of the lands entrusted to us for that
purpose.

"And further desiring to be acquainted for His
Excellency's information, what are the extent and
advantages considered with reference to the object
proposed of the House and property of the late
Mr. McGill in the vicinity of Montreal and whether

the grounds are sufficiently extensive to have an adequate space for the formation of walks and gardens, —in compliance with His Excellency's desire, we have to acquaint you that the grounds above mentioned contain about forty-six superficial arpents in a very healthy, moderately elevated, and pleasant situation, well watered, at a convenient distance from the city towards the mountain, and consequently appear to be sufficiently extensive and well calculated for every purpose of the contemplated establishment. There are already upon the premises a good stone house of two and a half stories, a barn, office, and a large garden, which may be applied to the residence of the President or some of the Professors or to other useful purpose connected with the object in view.

"We have further to acquaint you for His Excellency's information that the devise by the late Mr. McGill is upon several conditions, one whereof is that 'one of the Colleges be named McGill College, or if only one College should be selected, then that the said one shall be called McGill College!' Another of the conditions is 'that it be erected upon the tract so devised.'

"We therefore take the liberty of suggesting that it will be needful in forming the plan of the establishment to attend to these conditions so as to enable the Trustees to act in conformity to the trust reposed in them by the will of the deceased."

Two years of inaction followed, and even after the trustees of the Royal Institution were appointed, delay characterised the efforts of the authorities. There seems to have been considerable disagreement between the Home Government and the Provincial Government with regard to the exact objects for

which the revenue of the Jesuits' Estates was intended, and on the method of distribution.   The
Home authorities would not agree to assign any
of the revenue to aid in the establishment of McGill
College.   Finally, in 1819, Lord Bathurst directed
the Duke of Richmond, the Governor-General, immediately to commence the building of McGill College, and he authorised him to defray the expense
which it might in the first instance be necessary to
incur "from any funds which might be in the hands
of the Receiver of the Jesuits' Estates."   But this
instruction was not carried out.   Its object seems to
have been merely to prevent the lapse of the McGill
bequest in conformity with the expressed condition
of the will that the College should be erected within
a definite time.   Further, the proposed assistance
from the Jesuits' Estates seems to have been an
advance and not a gift.   It is unnecessary here to
follow in detail the disagreement and the struggle
arising from the distribution of the revenue of these
estates.   For several years the subject was one of
controversy, and meanwhile the cause of education
suffered.   In 1823 Lord Bathurst recommended to
the Lords Commissioners of the Treasury that a loan
of £50,000 at 4% interest should be granted to the
Royal Institution, but this recommendation was not
complied with.   In 1825 a system was proposed by
Lord Dalhousie, and subsequently followed, by which
the management of the estates was taken over by the
Inspector of the King's Domain under the control of
the Governor in Council.   He was allowed an agent
in each district to collect the rents which were then
turned in at stated periods to the Receiver General.
For several years, however, particularly in 1830 and

1831, the question of assigning the revenues from the estates for the purpose of education was repeatedly under discussion, but no pledge for such financial assistance was given by the Home Government. At last, in 1831, the Home Government surrendered the Jesuits' Estates to the Provincial Legislature, and against much opposition the schools were placed under the control of the House of Assembly. The salaries of teachers were greatly reduced; they were granted on an annual vote on condition that instruction be given by each teacher to at least twenty pauper scholars. As a result, it was stated by those opposed to this new plan that "the schools were nothing more than places of cheap education for the children of people in the lower walks of life." But notwithstanding this criticism the schools of the Province seem to have flourished to some extent at least under the new system. But it should not be forgotten that the Jesuits' Estates which had so long been the subject of discussion and controversy had in the end a very prominent part in the early history of McGill College. It was because of the funds derived from them when all other sources of revenue were exhausted that the trustees of the Royal Institution, and the executors of the will of James McGill, were permitted to prove in the courts the legality of the McGill bequest and to prosecute successfully their claims to his Burnside estate.

In accordance with Lord Bathurst's instructions to the Duke of Richmond in 1819, the Royal Institution for the Advancement of Learning proceeded to have the McGill property transferred from the executors of the will to their own control. They gave a power of attorney to S. Sewell, who subse-

quently continued for several years to act on their
behalf. But delay again characterised the efforts of
the Royal Institution, and it was not until January
18th, 1820, that final application for the transfer of
the McGill estate was made to the three surviving
executors, Hon. John Richardson, Hon. James Reid,
and the Rev. Dr. Strachan. The estate was then in
possession of Francis Desrivières, the nephew of the
first husband of Mrs. James McGill. He was occupying Burnside House, James McGill's former
home, and he was in control of the lands, products
and rents of the estate. On receipt of the request
from the Royal Institution, the executors wrote to
Mr. Desrivières on January 20th, 1820, informing
him that a University or College was about to be
erected and established "for the purpose of education
as designated in the will and in conformity to the
conditions therein presented," and asking "when the
tract of land and premises now in your possession
can be delivered over without subjecting you to
unnecessary inconvenience."

This inquiry was the beginning of a long and
wearying controversy which resulted in protracted
litigation and ended finally in an appeal to the Privy
Council. The reply to the above request indicates
that the Desrivières family was not inclined to give
up the property without a struggle. Francis Desrivières wrote, "I beg leave to mention that when the
demand for the property in question is made by the
Corporation referred to [The Royal Institution], I
will determine how far a compliance with that demand ought to take place on my part." The executors forwarded this reply to the Attorney for the
Royal Institution with the comment "you will per-

ceive that it is evasive." They further stated their
intention to proceed nevertheless with the conveyance,
"which, when completed, will be handed over to you;
it will then rest with your Corporation to pursue
such measures as may be considered proper on the
occasion."

The necessary papers for the transfer of the estate,
but not the endowment fund,—from the executors
of the will to the Royal Institution were finally completed in May, 1820; on June 7th following, the
conveyance was effected and the Deed was recorded
on August 3rd. It was evident, however, to the
executors that difficulties were in the way of securing
possession of the property. In a letter to the Rev.
Dr. Strachan, written on the 24th of May, 1820,
the two remaining living executors, John Richardson
and James Reid, said: "We are sorry to say that a
general belief prevails, and we fear is too well
founded, that Mr. Desrivières, the residuary legatee,
means to contest this bequest of his venerable benefactor. If that shall be really his intention, it will
speedily be known by a refusal after a formal demand
is made by the Corporation for the delivery of possession of the aforesaid grounds and premises,—
whereupon a suit will be instituted against him in the
October term." To this letter Dr. Strachan replied,
"I should hope that Mr. Desrivières will have a
greater respect for the memory of his greatest benefactor than to contest a Legacy which goes to establish an institution which he had so much at heart."

That the "general belief" and the fears above
referred to were not groundless was soon apparent.
Formal application for the vacating and the giving
up of the estate was made by the trustees of the

Royal Institution.   The application was curtly refused.   Francis Desrivières was in possession of the
estate and he determined to remain in such possession
until the Courts should decide otherwise.   His solicitors based their claim, on his behalf, on the plea that
a college had not yet been erected, that no steps had
been taken towards its erection, that there was no
intention to proceed with its establishment, and that
it was now too late to comply with the conditions of
the will with reference to time.   With respect to the
endowment fund, they claimed that they were not
obliged to pay it until a college had been actually
erected as provided in the will.   As a result of these
claims, a suit was at once instituted in the Courts by
the Royal Institution for the purpose of obtaining
possession of the estate, and on October 3rd, 1820,
the Board passed a resolution authorising their attorney, Mr. Sewell, to secure the aid of Mr. Stuart
as counsel in the case.   Mr. Sewell subsequently had
the assistance of Mr. Ogden, Mr. Vallières de St.
Real, Mr. Griffin, and Mr. Cochrane.

The Board soon realised that if their suit was to
be carried to a successful conclusion they must have
funds to meet necessary expenses.   They applied to
the Governor-General for financial assistance, and as
a result a sum of £200 was advanced to them as a
loan, from the proceeds of the Jesuits' Estates.
They realised, too, that it was necessary at once to
give the College some semblance of organisation.
Their solicitors advised the securing of a Charter
without delay, and on February 7th, 1821, the Secretary of the Board wrote to Mr. Sewell, stating that
"application for a Charter will be made to His
Majesty's Government without loss of time, but it

is the unanimous opinion of the Board that the case
should proceed." The Charter [here included as
appendix B] received the sanction of the Crown on
March 31st, 1821, and formed the basis of the court
plea of the Royal Institution. Two years later the
Board decided to secure a teaching staff, and by 1824
they had appointed a Principal, who was to be also
Honorary Professor of Divinity, and four Professors. The latter held merely *pro forma* appointments, and were intended to fulfil a technical legal
requirement; none of them ever lectured in the University, and when the College was actually opened
five years later those who still remained willingly
resigned to leave the Governors free to fill all Professorships as they desired. But the fact of their
appointment doubtless helped the Board in the suit
then pending.

It is needless here to outline in detail the litigation
that followed. In answer to the Desrivières claim,
the Board contended that, as required by the testator,
McGill College had now been, to all intents and purposes, erected and established by Letters Patent under
the Great Seal, and by the appointment of Professors.
All the conditions of the will had therefore, they
said, been fulfilled. Accordingly on November 8th,
1821, they made a formal demand upon the executors, the Hon. John Richardson and the Hon. Justice
Reid, for the transfer of the legacy of £10,000 with
interest due since the death of the testator. Francis
Desrivières was in possession of this money, and on
December 4th, 1821, the executors called on him
for its payment. He replied that it would not be
paid until the college had been built and established,
as the case connected with property only had not yet

been decided, and he did not regard the mere obtaining of a Charter as fulfilling the conditions of the will. As a result the executors and the Board issued instructions on December 26th, 1821, for the instituting of a second suit to obtain possession of the endowment fund, and the two suits proceeded.

The settlement of the first case was long delayed, and was attended with numerous discouragements. It involved, too, great expense, which the Board was not always able to meet. The judgment of the Court of King's Bench in Montreal was in favour of the Royal Institution. Mr. Desrivières then appealed from this judgment to the Privy Council, and again an irritating delay ensued before the appeal was heard. In July, 1823, the Board asked the Governor-General for a further loan of £300 from the revenues of the Jesuits' Estates as they were again in financial straits. The advance was made, but it was soon expended, and when forwarding a payment on account to Mr. Sewell on April 15th, 1824, the Secretary of the Board wrote, "this payment exhausts within a few pounds all the money of the Royal Institution. We are therefore in no very enviable situation as to funds." Four more years passed before the first suit was finally settled; they were years during which in the face of obstacles that threatened the very existence of the College, the Board frequently despaired of success. On August 17th, 1824, the Secretary wrote to the Lieutenant-Governor of the Province, Sir F. N. Burton, pleading for his assistance and co-operation in bringing the case to a speedy conclusion, and asking for further financial assistance. The following extract from his letter indicates that the outlook was not entirely hopeful:

"The judgment of the Court of King's Bench at Montreal in favour of the Institution in suit against Mr. Desrivières has been confirmed by the Court of Appeals; but a further appeal has been made to the Privy Council; the sum of £300, advanced by way of Loan, by order of His Excellency, the Governor in Chief, in consequence of the address above referred to (in addition to £200 before received), from the proceeds of the Estates heretofore belonging to the late Order of Jesuits' has been subsequently expended. Your Excellency is likewise aware that not only is a question arising out of these complicated legal proceedings now pending in the Court of Appeals, but also that the action for the £10,000 which promises to be at least as expensive to the Institution as that for the Estate of Burnside, is as yet undecided in the Court of King's Bench at Montreal. Of the final result of these proceedings no doubt can reasonably be entertained; but the Institution have before them in the meantime the prospect of protracted Litigation without any means whatever of meeting the heavy expense attendant upon it,—or even of defraying their ordinary contingent expenses, however trifling their amount. In these circumstances of unexampled difficulty, the Institution once more humbly pray that your Excellency in transmitting their Memorial to His Majesty's Government, will be pleased to accompany it with such representations as to your Excellency may seem best calculated to relieve them from the extreme embarrassment of their situation; from which, if it is not speedily extricated, not only must all hope be relinquished of the actual establishment of McGill College, already erected by the Royal Charter, but their operations must be suspended altogether and their very existence as a Corporation virtually cease."

The reply to this letter was unfavourable, or at least indifferent, and on November 14, 1824, an appeal was made for a grant or a loan of £50 from the revenues of the Jesuits' Estates. Finally, towards the close of 1828, the judgment previously given in favour of the Royal Institution was confirmed by decree of the Privy Council in Appeal, and early in 1829 the Burnside Estate was given into the Board's possession. The suit in connection with the endowment fund was still pending. Because of the judgment given in the first suit, there was no doubt, however, about its ultimate result, but it was not finally settled by the Privy Council in favour of the Royal Institution until 1837.

When the Board took possession of the Burnside Estate they decided to lease to a farmer named O'Connor, the farm and garden for one year, "on the halves," on condition that the lease could be cancelled by the Board on three months' notice. The leasing of the property was frequently the cause of controversy and annoyance. O'Connor contracted a bill for garden seeds amounting to over £3. He was unable to pay it and the seed merchant held the Estate liable, as the products of the seeds had improved the property. There was a long and technical discussion, until at last the bill was paid from the proceeds of the sale of wood from apple trees O'Connor had cut down, apparently to end the trouble. On the whole, the leasing was for a time profitable to the Board, but it was not always attended with harmony. Later, the land was leased to another farmer named Kelly for seven years, on condition that the lease could be surrendered on four months' notice, "and that Kelly should cut down the poplar trees." Subsequently, the estate was leased in smaller sections.

In order to strengthen the claims then before the courts for the possession of the endowment fund, it was desirable actually to open the College in Burnside House as speedily as possible. It was decided that the opening should take place on Wednesday, the 24th of June, 1829, and notification of this intention was published in the press. In April a committee of the Board was appointed to draw up a Code of Statutes for the government of the College. The Rev. Archdeacon Mountain, son of the Principal of the Royal Institution for the Advancement of Learning, had been appointed Principal of the proposed University five years before. But no arrangements had been made for the future. There was apparently but little promise of a grant from the Government, and until the second suit should be settled in the courts and money thereby made available, it was obvious that all plans must be indefinite. The future would, it was hoped, take care of itself; the main object to be considered for the present at least was the opening of the College. With that accomplished, and the endowment fund paid, all difficulties, it was thought, would vanish, and the College would go forward to its intended place. But before it lay troubled years of uncertainty and anxiety. It was only the firm determination and the undefeated optimism of those who believed in its destiny that kept it from being merely the hope or the dream of a

Scottish pioneer rather than a place of everlasting influence in our national life. The struggle of those years was not always without great disappointment, and even bitterness. But the product that emerged from the turmoil was perhaps greater and stronger for that fact.

CHAPTER IV

THE COLLEGE OPENED

THE Principal who guided McGill College in its infancy and for six years after its opening, was the Rev. George Jehosophat Mountain. He was appointed to the Principalship in 1824, while the University was a name only. The family from which he was descended had won distinction in education and in the church, and it was fortunate that the young College should be cradled under the care of a guardian of his learning, his traditions and his breadth of vision. His father, the Rev. Jacob Mountain, was given livings by the younger Pitt in Lincolnshire and Huntingdonshire in England, and later a prebend's stall in Lincoln Cathedral. When a diocese was created in Canada his name was at once suggested, because of his success at home, and in 1793 he came to Canada to become the first Anglican Bishop of Quebec. He subsequently acted as Principal of the Royal Institution for the Advancement of Learning and as such he had an active part in the educational affairs of the Province. His son, George, was born in England in 1789 and when he arrived in Canada with his parents he was but four years old. He therefore justly regarded himself as a Canadian. He received his early education in Quebec and continued his studies in England, where he took his B.A. degree at Trinity College, Cambridge. He then

73

returned to Canada and assisted his father as Secretary until he was ordained in 1816, at a time when the establishment of McGill College and the methods of fulfilling James McGill's desire were under discussion. In 1817 he became Rector of Quebec, and in 1821 Archdeacon of Lower Canada. When in 1824 the Board of the Royal Institution found that it was necessary, in order to secure the McGill bequest, to appoint Professors to the proposed College they selected Archdeacon Mountain as Honorary Professor of Divinity and Principal of McGill College. But he gave no lectures and received little or no remuneration for his work. His duty seems to have been mainly to preserve the forms which the terms of the will required. He laid the foundation for the creation of the Faculty of Arts, and while he believed that instruction should be given in a manner consistent with the English National Establishment, he desired that the University should be open to students of all creeds with equal privileges and that Professorships should be tenable by graduates of the Scotch Universities. He retained the Principalship until 1835, when he retired, to return for a time to England. It is unnecessary here to follow in detail his subsequent career. In 1836 he was made coadjutor of Dr. James Stewart, Bishop of Quebec and became thereby Bishop of Montreal, the consecration ceremony being performed at Lambeth. After his retirement from the Principalship he continued, as we shall see, to devote much time and attention to the affairs of the growing University as a Governor, and he lived to see the College of which he was the first guardian advance to growth and usefulness even far beyond his dreams. Dur-

Rev. George Jehoshaphat Mountain
1789-1863
First Principal of McGill University 1829-1835

ing his last years he occupied the Anglican See of Quebec, where he died in 1863.

The ceremony which marked the official opening of McGill University was held on Wednesday afternoon, June 24th, 1829. It had been advertised in the press for some time, and in addition special invitations were sent out to many citizens interested in educational advancement. It was therefore attended by what the contemporary press called a gathering of "numerous and respectable individuals." Because of the historical importance of this meeting, the report of it, which appeared in the *Montreal Gazette* in the issue of Monday, June 29, and which is similar in its details to the Governors' minutes of the meeting, is here given in full:

"In consequence of a notification having been published—that this College would be opened, and that formal possession of the estate of Burnside, upon which it was established, would take place on Wednesday, a very numerous assemblage of the inhabitants of this City were present at what we consider to be one of the most important and interesting ceremonies lately witnessed in this part of the Province. Though there was none of the gaudy appearance and display characteristic of religious or Masonic Processions, yet to the mind of the philosopher and friend of education, the simple and appropriate ceremony, an account of which we are about to lay before our readers, presented more charms than if decked out with all the pageantry of chivalry and romance.

"A large room in the house which has been for some time existing on the estate having been fitted up, it was soon after one o'clock filled by the numerous and respectable individuals who had assembled to witness the ceremony. Among the company we noticed several officers of the government, the principal members of the Bar, the lecturers at the Montreal Medical Institution and several gentlemen, more or less connected with the proposed College.

"The Right Reverend the Lord Bishop of the Diocese, attended by the Rev. G. J. Mountain, D.D.; the Rev. J. L. Mills, D.D.; the Rev. B. B. Stevens, A.M.; the Rev. A. Norman; and the Rev. A. F. Atkinson of Montreal; the Rev. James Reid of St. Armand; the Rev. W. Abbott of St. Andrews; the Rev. J. Abbott of Yamaska; the Rev. I. Braithwaite, A.B., of Chambly, and the Rev. H. Esson, and E. Black of the Kirk of Scotland in Montreal having entered the Hall, the business of the day was soon after proceeded upon.

"The Royal Charter incorporating the Governors and Professors of the University being placed on the table, His Lordship the Bishop of Quebec rose and addressed the assembled body. He stated that in consequence of the absence of His Excellency the Administrator of the Government, who was one of the Governors of the corporation of McGill College, it became incumbent on him to make a few remarks on the present occasion. He would, however, first state that he was commissioned by His Excellency to express his regret that in consequence of the very late arrival of the April and May mails he was unable to leave Quebec in time to assist at the ceremony of promulgating the charter which had been conferred on the College. His Excellency in his letter was pleased to add that he would not fail to use all his exertions to promote the Institution. Having fulfilled this duty, the Lord Bishop begged to observe that the bequest which had been made in favour of this College by the late Hon. James McGill consisted of the valuable estate of Burnside, comprising the building in which they were then assembled, and the garden and grounds adjoining, together with the sum of £10,000, in furtherance of his benevolent intention. This liberal bequest was made in 1811 (two years previous to the death of Mr. McGill), in trust to a corporation called the Royal Institution which was contemplated by an act passed in 1801. This Institution was to transfer the bequest, when a College, in pursuance of his views, was established and bearing his name. To this most benevolent legacy, he could not help referring as characteristic of its liberal donor, with whom he had the honour of an acquaintance, and as furnishing an example which he hoped to see more frequently followed in the Province. The late Mr. McGill, who had assumed a very considerable fortune within the country, did not, like many others, leave the Province and spend his money in some other part of the globe, but having no direct heirs, he had left a very handsome legacy for the laudable purpose of commencing a University in a country where such an establishment was very desirable. The Institution was to bear the name of its excellent founder, and he firmly hoped that it might prove a blessing to many generations yet to come, that it might tend to immortalise his name, and be the best monument that could be erected to his memory. The Royal Institution was incorporated in 1818 and through their instrumentality, this College was in pursuance of the will of Mr. McGill incorporated in 1821 by a charter which would be

read to them.   Under that charter the Governors
of the College were the Governor and Lieutenant-
Governor of Lower Canada, the Lieutenant-Governor of Upper Canada, the Chief Justices of Montreal and Upper Canada, the Bishop of Quebec and
the Principal of the College.   It would be needless
for him to refer to the detentions and obstacles which
had hitherto prevented the College from going into
operation; it was known that they arose from the
residuary legatee under the will of Mr. McGill dis-
puting the legality of the bequest, and carrying his
opposition through all the Courts of the Province,
till His Majesty in his Privy Council had finally
given the decision in favour of the Institution, whose
duty it had become to prosecute for the recovery of
the bequest.   The suit in relation to the money bequeathed to the College was still before the Council,
but he was happy to say that that unfortunate dispute
would soon be terminated as it was understood the
residuary legatee intended to withdraw all further
opposition.   It was the intention of the Royal Institution to transfer to the Governors of the College
the property of Burnside, and on the part of the
Governors, he was authorised to say that they were
willing to accept of it.   A majority of them were
either now present or consenting, for he was charged
with the consent of the Governor of this, and the
Lieutenant-Governor of the adjoining Province, both
of whom had expressed a desire to attend on the
present occasion, and it was known that there was
now no Chief Justice in Upper Canada.   On the
part of the majority, he accepted from the Royal
Institution the Charter which the Secretary of that
body would now read.

"The Rev. Dr. Mills, Secretary to the Royal Institution for the Advancement of Learning, then read at length the Charter of the College.

"The Lord Bishop then again rose and said that he was authorised on the part of the Governors of the new College to state it to be their intention as far as it was in their power to carry into effect the liberal intentions of the late Mr. McGill. It was not a work in which they themselves were solely interested, but it was an institution which concerned every inhabitant of the Province, and under such feelings the Governors were determined that no obstacles should deter them from following up and prosecuting the views of the testator. He deemed it unnecessary for him to exhort them upon the advantages of education, as he was sure they were all of opinion that a moral and religious education on Christian principles, and a scientific course of studies on a true philosophical system were what it was their bounden duty to promote. The Governors in assuming the Charter hoped that their exertions would meet with the co-operation of every individual within the Province.

"The Venerable Archdeacon Mountain then rose, and stated that as the individual named to fill the honourable office of Principal of the new College, it became his duty now to say a few words. He could not but express his sense of his own unworthiness for such a distinguished office, and he firmly hoped that he would be succeeded by a long line of eminent and learned principals. He had it in charge for his colleagues to state their anxiety to put the College into immediate operation, and he might urge as a proof of their wish that they had not been idle in

this respect. With the assistance of the Honourable
Mr. Cochran then present, they had been engaged
in preparing and modelling a constitution and rules
for the government of the Institution. Although it
was not necessary to detail at present their precise
nature, yet he could take upon himself to state that
they were liberal in every sense of the word, impos-
ing no test upon Professors or Students. In thus
applying the term liberal he wished it distinctly to be
understood that he was not conveying the charge of
illiberality against those noble and venerable Institutions of the Mother Country, in which a test was
properly exacted of conformity to the National Religion, but there were local circumstances which
required local adaptation; and according both to the
terms of the will and the provisions of the Royal
Charter, all offices whatever in McGill College were
left freely open either to Protestants or Roman Catholics, and Students of all denominations would be
permitted to attend. He deemed it necessary for
him to explain how the present Professors happened
all to be members of the Church of England. When
found necessary to name Professors in virtue of the
Charter of the College, his late father, then Bishop
of the Diocese, had submitted several names to His
Excellency the Earl of Dalhousie for these offices,
among which those of the Rev. Archdeacon Strachan
and the Rev. Dr. Harkness, having been proposed
as eligible, either one or the other, to the same
Professorship, His Excellency, whether swayed by
a feeling of delicacy and desire to avoid the appearance of partiality, on account of his being himself
a member of the Church of Scotland, or from whatever cause, decided in favour of the former gentle-

man. This circumstance was mentioned in proof
that the original as well as the present intention of
the Governors was in all respects to shew due respect to the intentions of the will of Mr. McGill
and the terms of the Charter. It had been deemed
necessary for the present to declare that the Professors should be graduates of some British University, but that a preference should hereafter be
shown to those who had graduated within its walls.
The Governors would feel it to be their duty under
all discouraging obstacles to push on the great undertaking, and never to cease in their exertions for its
prosperity. They hoped they would meet with general support and they trusted with confidence that
they would be assisted by all, when the very liberal
terms of the will and Charter were considered. It
would be necessary for them to make a strong and
powerful appeal to the Mother Country, and they
also expected great pecuniary assistance from those
resident near the establishment, and more directly
interested in its prosperity. They would as soon as
possible establish a system of collegiate education,
and there was a predisposition to engraft upon the
College the well-known and respectable Medical
Institution now in existence in the city. The door
of the building was at length open, and it was the
duty of all to proceed with vigour. They might at
first complain of a great want of means for such
an Institution, for it required much to place it on a
respectable footing, but while they thus looked forward with confidence, they should not be unmindful
that the Province was highly indebted to the very
liberal disposition of Mr. McGill, who had set such
a praiseworthy example to his fellow-citizens, whose

duty it now became generally to aid his work and follow up his munificent views. The Archdeacon concluded his address by expressing his conviction that all who were present felt alike the dependence of every human undertaking for its success upon the blessing of Divine Providence, and would therefore be unanimously ready to join in the religious services with which it was proposed to conclude the business of the day; and in which he accordingly proceeded.

"The 8th chapter of Proverbs, which had been selected as appropriate to the occasion, was first read; after which the following verses selected from different Psalms were repeated in the way of alternation, the responsive part being sustained by the other Clergy of the Church of England who were present.

" 'The Lord hath been mindful of us and shall bless us: even he shall bless the house of Israel; he shall bless the house of Aaron.

" 'He shall bless them that fear the Lord both small and great.

" 'The Lord shall increase you more and more, both you and your children.

" 'All the whole Heavens are the Lord's: the earth hath he given to the children of men.

" 'The lot is fallen unto me in a fair ground: yea, I have a goodly heritage.

" 'Lord, thou art become gracious unto thy land: thou sendest a gracious rain upon thine inheritance, and refreshedst it when it was weary.

" 'O pray for the peace of Jerusalem,—they shall prosper that love thee.

" 'Peace be within thy walls, and plenteousness within thy palaces.

" 'For my brethren and companions' sakes, I will wish thee prosperity.

" 'Yea, because of the house of the Lord our God, I will seek to do thee good.

" 'Except the Lord build the house; their labour is but lost that build it.

" 'Not unto us, O Lord, not unto us, but unto thy name give the praise; for thy loving mercy and for thy truth's sake.

" 'Glory be to the Father, and to the Son, and to the Holy Ghost.

" 'As it was in the beginning, is now and ever shall be, world without end. Amen.'

"The Archdeacon then proceeded with the following prayers:

" 'O blessed and eternal God, who by wisdom hast founded the earth and by understanding hast stretched out the Heavens—Father of Light and Author of every good and perfect gift, from whom we receive all that we have, and all that we are made capable of performing—upon whose pleasure both we, and our works, and all creation depend—look down from the habitation of thy holiness and glory, and favour the undertaking which is here before us; let thy blessing rest upon it; let the cloud and pillar of thy presence go with us; establish the work of our hands upon us, yea, the work of our hands establish thou it. Our hope is in Thee and thou art able to do for us, in things temporal as well as spiritual, exceedingly abundantly above all that we can ask or think. Raise us means, we beseech thee, to provide for the wants of this Institution: dispose the hearts of men and order the course of events favourably towards it: shed down the spirit of wisdom and of patient continuance upon those who plant and those who water, and do thou give the increase from on high. Sanctify all the instruction which shall hereafter be given and all the studies which shall be pursued in this Institution, and render them subservient to thy glory and the good of mankind. Grant that all the stores of knowledge and science, which shall be here opened to the minds of youth, may form them to the greater love of thy holy name, and lead them to magnify thee in thy wonderful works. O righteous Father, who hast hid the highest of all knowledge from the wise and prudent of this world, and revealed it unto babes, grant that none may be here spoiled, through philosophy and vain deceit, nor lifted up in hearts through the opposition of science falsely so called, but give them grace to cast down imaginations and every high thing which exalteth itself against the knowledge of God, and to bring into captivity every thought to the obedience of Christ. Yet, O Lord, while they are subjected to this gentle and blessed yoke, enrich this Institution, we pray thee, with ample streams of all sound learning and science; and as we are taught in thy holy word that the Lawgiver of thy ancient people was learned in all the wisdom of the Egyptians, and the blessed apostle St. Paul, profited above his equals, as well in the studies of his time and people, as in the learned lore of the ancients at large—and as thou didst miraculously supply to the first planters of our holy faith that knowledge which, under thy blessing, must now be acquired by labour and length of time— grant that all beneficence and industry may be exerted in the endowment and enlargement, the furtherance and prosperity of this Institution; grant that the grain of seed which is here sown may become, in process of time, a great and goodly tree; that Science and Literature may spring up and flourish upon this dedicated spot, and bear fruit a hundred-fold.

" 'With these our prayers, O Father of Heaven and Earth, we offer up our humble thanksgiving for all thy mercies manifested to us, and especially for that thou didst put it into the heart of thy servant, the Founder of this Institution, to provide, out of the means which thou hadst given him, for so needful a work. And, alike in thanksgiving or prayer, we approach thy Throne in the prevailing name and through the powerful mediation of Jesus Christ, whose own holy words also we couple still with our imperfect address.' The Archdeacon here repeated the Lord's Prayer.

"Then followed the Prayer for the Church Militant, from the Liturgy, with some adaptations to render it immediately applicable to the local authorities and to the occasion of the day. The assembly was dismissed by a blessing pronounced by the Bishop.

"Before closing this subject, we deem it but justice to the Venerable Archdeacon Strachan, to state, that to that Reverend gentleman the Province is greatly indebted for McGill College, as to his suggestions on this subject, his friend and relative the late Mr. McGill lent a ready and willing ear, and was induced to frame the bequest, which is now about to be employed according to the intentions of its donor. To that gentleman, we understand, is also due the very liberal arrangement which was announced by the Principal, with regard to the total absence of any tests for the admission of Professors or Students. . . ."

When the ceremony of formally opening the College and establishing the Faculty of Arts, "as a place of liberal education," was ended and the gathering dispersed, the Governors of the College met in the late afternoon for the transaction of business. They received the Lecturers of the Montreal Medical Institution, who formally placed before them the plans for "engrafting upon the College the well-known and respectable Medical Institution" as already indicated in the report above. The scheme was acceptable to the Governors and the Montreal Medical Institution became part of McGill University. The Governors' Minutes of the meeting contains the following entry:

"The public business having been closed, the Governors of the Corporation held an interview with the members of the Montreal Medical Institution, who had been requested to attend the meeting for that purpose. During this interview it was resolved by the Governors of the Corporation that the members of the Montreal Medical Institution (Dr. Caldwell, Dr. Stephenson, Dr. Robertson, Dr. Holmes) be engrafted upon the College as its Medical Faculty, it being understood and agreed upon by and between the said contracting parties that until the powers of the Charter would be altered, one of their number only should be a university professor and the others lecturers; that they should immediately enter upon the duties of their offices. All of which arrangements were agreed to."

The Montreal Medical Institution owed its origin to the Medical Staff of the Montreal General Hos-

Andrew Fernando Holmes, M.D., LL.D.
1798-1850

pital, which was opened to patients in May, 1822. At that time there were no opportunities in Canada for the obtaining of medical education. Realising the existing and urgent need for such training, certain members of the Hospital Staff gave courses of lectures to students during the winter of 1822-1823. Later, a memorial was forwarded to the Lieutenant-Governor setting forth the necessity for the foundation of a permanent school of medical education, and outlining plans for the establishment and incorporation of the proposed Medical Institution. The reply to this memorial stated that an endeavour would be made to give assistance to a Medical School, and as a result the Montreal Medical Institution was organised. It was opened in October, 1824. Efforts were then made to secure its incorporation, and in 1826 a Charter was drawn up and forwarded through the Lieutenant-Governor to the Solicitor-General for opinion or approval. A delay of several months followed, and it was not until 1828 that a reply was received. The reply was not favourable to the Institution. The Charter was refused for the reasons that the School was not connected with any Seminary of Learning, and that it had no foundation or endowment. No degrees could therefore be conferred and the Institution had no standing in law. Meanwhile the Privy Council had given judgment in favour of the Royal Institution in the first Desrivières suit in connection with the Burnside Estate, as already recorded, and it was clear that a similar judgment in the second suit in connection with the endowment fund was but a question of time. The establishment of McGill College was assured, and arrangements for its opening had already been announced. It naturally occurred to those interested in the Medical Institution that their problems of University connection and of endowment referred to by the Solicitor-General could be solved by "engrafting" the Institution on the proposed McGill College. They accordingly forwarded a memorial to the Government, suggesting that the Lecturers in the Institution be appointed "professors of the University to be established at Burnside near the city." The Government referred the suggestion to the Board of the Royal Institution to whom formal application was then made by the Medical body. A committee of the Board was appointed to consider the question. The Medical Institution pressed for a decision, and on February 16, 1829, the Secretary wrote to Dr. Holmes, of the Hospital Staff, stating, "The Committee to whom was referred the communication from the Montreal Medical Institution have not, I am sorry to say, yet made their report; but I trust the business will be proceeded in very shortly, and I shall not fail to inform you of the result without delay. Of this be assured that there is every desire on the part of the Board to meet the wishes of the Institution as far as it may be found practicable to do so."

The Board had in 1824 appointed Dr. Fargues of Quebec Professor of Medicine, but he expressed his willingness to resign in order to leave the Board free to negotiate with the Medical Institution. On April 10th, 1829, the decision of the Board was conveyed to Dr. Holmes, in the following letter:

"Referring to a former communication upon the subject, I lose no time in transmitting to you the following Extract from the Report of a Committee

of the Royal Institution, to whom it was referred to
consider what measures it may be necessary for the
Board to take, on having now obtained possession
of the Estate of Burnside.

"The Medical Institution at Montreal, connected
at present with the Montreal Hospital, having solicited the aid and protection of the Royal Institution, and expressed a desire to become a branch of
McGill College, it is conceived that the gentlemen
of that Institution might be willing (in consideration
of being so associated with a legally constituted establishment) to execute gratuitously the duties of
one or more Professorships in the College, connected
with the Faculty of Medicine. The Professorships
being limited to *four,* it is obvious that there can be
only *one* Medical Professor, and I am happy to inform you that Dr. Fargues, having been solicited to
resign, has consented to do so with the utmost readi-
ness, and it is accordingly open to the gentlemen of
the Montreal Medical Institution to recommend for
the consideration of the Governors of the College
any one of their members, being a graduate in Medicine, as his successor."

As a result of this decision the Governors of the
College agreed to appoint one of the Lecturers in
the Montreal Medical Institution to the Professorship of Medicine vacated by the resignation of Dr.
Fargues. Meanwhile there was a misunderstanding
between the Governors and the Board over the number of Professors already appointed in 1824. The
Charter provided for a Principal and four Professors; the Governors made these appointments, but
also made the Principal Honorary Professor of
Divinity. The Board contended that five Professor-

ships had thus been created and filled, contrary to the provisions of the Charter. On April 22nd, 1829, Dr. Stephenson wrote to the Board on behalf of the Medical Institution urging that the number of Professorships in the College be increased to enable all the Medical Lecturers to be attached to McGill College. The Secretary replied on May 19th, 1829, as follows:

"Your letter of the 22nd ult., was duly submitted by me to the Board of the Royal Institution, and I am directed to inform you in reply, that the Board having carefully considered the subject, are of opinion that, as the matter actually stands at present, it is not in their power to procure an augmentation of the number of professorships. They conceive, however, that the Medical Professor of the University might deliver Lectures in one particular branch of the Science, and that the other Departments might be conducted by gentlemen, who should be named Lecturers in the College, as is the case with respect to the different branches of Learning and Science, which are taught in the Colleges of the Universities at home. The words of the Charter are evidently restrictive. The College shall 'consist of a Principal and four Professors,' and in this view of the subject the Board are supported by high legal authority. This limitation, for which it is difficult to assign an adequate reason, is much to be regretted. The Governors of the College have committed an oversight in some way or other. It had not escaped the previous notice of the Board. The Bishop, the Archdeacon and myself intend visiting Montreal next month, when we shall have an opportunity of discussing the subject at full length. I have only now

to add that we all of us, both as a body and as individuals, feel interested in the success of the Montreal
Medical Institution, and that we shall be most happy
if it can be in any way promoted by a connection with
McGill College."

After the College was formally opened it was
necessary for the Governors and the Board of the
Royal Institution to wait for the final decision of the
courts on the possession of the endowment fund,
which was still held by the Desrivières heirs. No
money was available for salaries; no building on
the estate was suitable for classes. It was therefore
considered impossible, for the present at least, to
undertake actual teaching in the College. But meanwhile the Montreal Medical Institution had received
from the Royal Institution the "aid and protection"
it required, and it continued to carry on its work and
to give instruction to students as before, but with a
definite connection with the University as one of its
Faculties. Pending the securing of the endowment
fund which would make possible the putting in operation of the College proper, as provided for in the
will, the Governors of the College therefore decided
to appoint, temporarily, and without remuneration,
the lecturers in the newly formed Medical Faculty
to the four professorships at their disposal, in
order that degrees in at least one department of the
University could be conferred. To make this possible the Professors who had already been appointed
in the Faculty of Arts, and whose duties could not
yet begin, willingly consented to resign. But before
degrees could be granted it was necessary, under the
terms of the Charter, to draw up statutes for the
government of the University, such statutes to re-

ceive the approval of the Crown. The Statutes, Rules and Ordinances for the Medical Faculty were agreed upon by the Governors; and were submitted to the Colonial Office by Lord Aylmer on March 8th, 1832. The Royal approval was forwarded to the Lieutenant-Governor of the Province in a despatch dated May 2nd, 1832, together with the confirmation of the appointment of William Caldwell, John Stephenson, Andrew F. Holmes and William Robertson of the Medical School to the four University professorships, "without specifying at present the precise nature of each Professorship." They received no remuneration from the College. Later, Dr. Stephenson acted for a brief period as supervisor of the Burnside Estate.

The Home Government's knowledge of the exact circumstances and terms and even the making of the Montreal Medical Institution into a Faculty of McGill seems afterwards to have been somewhat hazy. On August 20th, 1834, the Colonial Office wrote to Lord Aylmer, the Lieutenant-Governor, saying, "It would appear from Sir James Kempt's Despatches of 1830, that it was contemplated to incorporate with the College an association of Medical Practitioners but that difficulties arose as to the selection of the Governors . . . but I do not gather from your despatch whether the incorporation of this association is still desired." He asked for a report on the question—a question that had been decided five years before. It was pointed out in reply that the Montreal Medical Institution no longer existed independent of the College and that the several Lecturers in that school now occupied all the four Professorships provided for by the Charter. There was misunderstanding, too, as we shall see, between the Governors of the College and the Royal Institution with reference to the temporary or the permanent nature of the above appointments, three of which the latter Board had never ratified, and of which they were apparently not informed. For several years the tradition of a distinct Institution, as it had already been known, continued. The Medical Faculty carried on its work more or less independently of the College, although it was incorporated with it and was legally a part of it, but because of tradition it was not always regarded as an integral part of the University. It was looked upon as a well established teaching body now linked up with the new College. The Rules and Ordinances of the University did not apply to the Medical Faculty, and for several years after the actual erection and opening of the College buildings the students of the Medical School were not included in the statement of enrolment annually sent to the Home Government by the Visitor to the University.

On the 24th of May of 1833, four years after the opening of the College, the first University degree awarded was conferred in the Faculty of Medicine on William Logie. On May 7th, 1833, Dr. J. Stephenson, Secretary of the Medical School, wrote to Principal Mountain with reference to the conferring of this degree:

"I am directed by the Medical Faculty of the University to inform you that Mr. William Logie of Montreal, after having produced to the Secretary of the Faculty credentials entitling him, was examined, as the Statutes, Rules and Ordinances of the College direct, touching his Classical knowledge and then got a general examination on all the branches of Medical and Surgical Science. The Medical Faculty found him well qualified to practise Medicine and Surgery and accordingly have announced to him that they will forward his name to the Governors to obtain the Degree of Doctor of Medicine and Surgery.

"In consequence I am directed by the Faculty to address you on the following points:

"1st. That we will, with your approbation, have our Gowns made as that of a Bachelor of Laws except the Cowl.

"2nd. That we will have the Theses printed by Mr. Armour of Montreal.

"3rd. The Faculty desire to know how the degree will be conferred on the 24th of May and the tenor of said Degree that they might be getting it ready."

Under the rules of that time, it was necessary for a student proceeding to a degree to defend before the members of Faculty a Thesis on some previously approved topic. The Thesis was printed at the expense of the student. The rules provided, too, that "the student be required to attend the Hospital during the time required by the Statutes, and to receive clinical instruction from the Professors at the bedside of the patients." The legal power of the University to confer degrees on the graduates of the Medical Faculty was questioned by rival authorities, and was later tested in the courts, but the legality of the degree and the privilege of the holder to practise Medicine in the Province was upheld.

The Governors now decided that an effort should be made to begin actual teaching in the liberal Arts and Sciences as called for in the will of the founder. They determined to appoint professors and to con-

duct classes, temporarily, in Burnside House. At a
meeting of the Governors held on the 4th of January,
1834, at which were present Lord Aylmer, Governor
in Chief, The Lord Bishop of Quebec, and the Principal of the College, it was decided to ask that the
Charter be amended, and that the Governing Board
of the College be changed to consist henceforth of
the following: The Governor in Chief, the Lieutenant-Governor or person administering the Government; the Lieutenant-Governor of Upper Canada;
the Lord Bishop of the Diocese; the Chief Justice
of Montreal; the Chief Justice of Upper Canada;
the Speaker of the two Houses of the Provincial
Parliament of Lower Canada; the Senior Executive
Councillor residing in Montreal; the Archdeacon of
Quebec; the Solicitor-General; the Principal of the
College; the Rector of Montreal; together with four
other Governors to be named by the Governor in
Chief, the Lieutenant-Governor or the person administering the Government under a power to be
introduced into the Charter to that effect. Efforts
were made afterwards to have the Minister of the
Church of Scotland added to this list, ex-officio, but
it was pointed out in reply that he was "not conceived
to have any perpetual capacity in law and thence cannot be an ex-officio Governor." It was decided also
that His Excellency be requested to recommend to
His Majesty's Government that power should be
given in the amended Charter to the Governors
of the College to establish additional professorships
from time to time, at their discretion, according to
the exigencies of the University and the means at
their command.

It was further resolved that in the meantime until

endowments for Professorships were available from the McGill bequest, "gentlemen resident in Montreal qualified to give lectures should be appointed on the same footing as the four Professors in the Medical Faculty and that they should receive fees from their students . . . with the duty annexed of delivering occasional lectures, fees being paid by those who will attend them according to a regulated scale, there being at present no means of endowing Professorships with salaries." Professors were recommended for the following subjects: Classical Literature and History; Natural Philosophy and Mathematics; and Hebrew and Oriental Languages—all to be appointed on the same footing as provided for by the foregoing resolution. At this meeting, too, a recommendation was made that a Vice-Principal should be appointed—or that one of the Professors be empowered to act as Vice-Principal—because of the frequent absence of the Principal on other duties. Later, the Chair of Natural Philosophy was separated from that of Mathematics. As a result of the Governors' decision an amended Charter was drawn up for submission to the authorities, providing, among other things, for an increased number of Professorships. It was prepared by the Professors of the Medical Faculty, but it was greatly altered by the Governors at a meeting called to consider it. The Colonial Office to whom it was forwarded would not approve of it, and even the consideration of it was very long delayed. The question was debated until January, 1837, when the Colonial Office declared that it was impossible further to discuss it.

In April, 1834, the occupation of the House and Premises of Burnside as a "Classical School" was approved. But it was to be conducted by the Professors in their private capacity and no provision was made for their maintenance, and the occupation of the premises was to be subject to the conditions imposed by the Governors and the Royal Institution acting conjointly.

The Principal, Archdeacon Mountain, now expressed his desire to retire from office. Other duties were calling for his attention. Indeed, at intervals for several weeks in succession he had been obliged to take little part in the management of the University, for his presence as Archdeacon of Lower Canada was required in many places. Frequently, too, it was necessary for him to be absent from the Province for a considerable length of time. He felt, also, that he had been appointed Principal mainly for the purpose of putting the College in operation and that his work was now done. The Governors then decided to offer the Principalship to the Rev. S. T. Wood of Three Rivers, and if he declined to accept it, to offer it to the Rev. Thomas Littlehales of Christ Church College, Oxford. But neither of these men would agree to occupy the proffered post; indeed, the former entirely ignored the Governors' letter. Archdeacon Mountain was induced to remain some months longer, or until a competent successor could be found. The Professorship of Classical Literature was offered to the Rev. James Ramsay, a graduate of Trinity College, Dublin; that of Mathematics and Natural Philosophy to Mr. Alex. Skakel of King's College, Aberdeen; and that of Hebrew and Oriental Languages to the Rev. E. Black, of the University of Edinburgh. Difficulties resulting from the Charter prevented these appointments from being

actually made at that time. Because of irritating
delays, the somewhat hopeless situation brought
about by the refusal of the Home Government to
permit the increase of Professorships, and numerous
other differences of opinion, trouble was now growing between the Governors and the Crown. At a
meeting of the former held on November 14, 1834,
at which were present Lord Aylmer, Governor in
Chief, the Chief Justice and the Principal, the Governor was asked to bring to the notice of the Secretary of State "the great inconvenience which it is
feared may result from the necessity of referring to
His Majesty's Home Government, as required by
the Charter, every appointment of a Professor or
even of a Principal." This was the beginning of a
bitter and prolonged controversy which did not end
until 1846, and which involved the College in perhaps the gravest difficulty and uncertainty of its
history.

Meanwhile, the case against the Desrivières heirs,
James McGill Desrivières, Henri Desrivières, Francis Desrivières, and Alex McKenzie, had proceeded.
Every effort was made to have the suit settled. On
December 21, 1833, the Governors authorised the
Medical Professors to join them in a Memorial on
the subject to the Home Government. The Board
of the Royal Institution persistently urged haste,
but delay followed delay. At last, on February 7th,
1835, the Order in Council deciding the case in
favour of the Board was issued, but it was not forwarded until the 21st of May. But notwithstanding
the decision of the Privy Council the heirs of James
McGill were slow to accede to the demands of the
Royal Institution. On March 8th, 1836, the Secre-

tary of the Board wrote "as to Burnside we are extremely perplexed by the pertinacity of the heirs in resisting and threatening further resistance to the payment of any money on account of the debt due to the Royal Institution unless terms are granted them . . . which . . . members of the Board think that we could not accept without rendering ourselves personally liable if any further loss should accrue thereby to the College. I should be strongly disposed to try and borrow money to begin with, if I knew what tangible security we could offer." A further delay resulted, and even after the suit was settled the executors of the will hesitated to transfer the money to the Board or the Governors until the Home Government fulfilled certain promises which they understood to have been made. It was not until October, 1837, that the case was brought to final conclusion. As a result of delays, negligence, and unsatisfactory communications, the Governors appointed a special agent in London to conduct their business, with the frank comment, "If documents are sent through the Public Offices to Great Britain by way of the Colonial Office, there will be no end to the delay."

In July, 1835, two months after judgment was given in favour of the Board, Principal Mountain retired from office in order to proceed to England. Now that the possession of the endowment fund was assured he believed that the College would soon be without difficulties and that its infant days of helplessness had passed. The Principalship was offered to the Rev. S. J. Lockhart, M.A. (Oxford), Chaplain and Secretary to the Bishop of Quebec. He seems to have accepted the post, but he never assumed the duties of his office. A meeting of Governors was held in Quebec on November 18, 1835, attended by Lord Gosford, who had meanwhile become Governor in Chief of Lower Canada, the Lord Bishop of Quebec, and the Chief Justice of Montreal. It was there resolved "that the Rev. John Bethune, Rector of Christ Church, Montreal, be appointed Principal of the College *pro tempore;* and that it be conveyed to him that his appointment shall not interfere with any future appointment which the Governors of the College may see fit to make." The office of Principal was accepted by Mr. Bethune on November 24th, 1835, in the following letter:

"I cordially accept the appointment which the Governors of McGill College have done me the honour to confer on me, of Principal of the Institution *pro tempore,* under the explanation given to me by the Chief Justice of Montreal of the following passage in your Lordship's communication 'that the appointment shall not interfere with any future appointment that the Governors of the College may see fit to make,' viz., that if the funds of McGill College should at any future period enable the Governors to offer the Principal a sufficient emolument to secure his exclusive services to the Institution the present nomination shall not interfere with any such future appointment—but that the present nomination is not to be cancelled to make room for any future *pro tempore* appointment."

During the six years that had passed since the formal opening of the College definite progress had been made. But apart from the activity of the Medical School, which did not owe its origin to the University and had merely changed its name, the progress was connected only with laying plans for the future and with securing adequate resources and a definite habitation. The Governors were harassed by litigation and by not a little uncertainty; they were dismayed at times by the evident lack of sympathy and the discouraging indifference of officials of the Home Government. But they did not cease to hope, and they did not dream of abandoning their educational scheme. They would struggle on to the fulfilment of the founder's vision. It was the task of the newly appointed acting-Principal to carry out these plans and to take up the administration of the University in one of the most difficult and critical periods of its existence. The years that followed were to be troubled years of poverty, anxiety and controversy, not unmixed with bitterness, during which, at times, extinction and oblivion threatened the University's life.

CHAPTER V

ANXIOUS YEARS

THE Rev. John Bethune, appointed acting-Principal of McGill in temporary succession to Principal Mountain on November 18th, 1835, was a Canadian by birth and education. His father, the Rev. John Bethune, a native of the Island of Skye, Scotland, and a graduate of King's College, Aberdeen, emigrated to America before the War of Independence. At the beginning of the Revolution he served as Chaplain of a militia regiment fighting in the Carolinas on the British side; he was taken prisoner by Republican troops, and after his release by exchange he moved with other British Empire Loyalists to Canada. He lived for a short time in Nova Scotia, became Chaplain again of a Highland Regiment fighting in defence of Canada against Montgomery's Army, and when the War ended he settled in Montreal. Here he organised, as we have seen, the first Presbyterian Congregation in the City, and ministered to it from March, 1786, until May, 1787. He then removed to Williamstown in the county of Glengarry, where he became minister of the Church of Scotland.

The future acting-Principal of McGill, the Rev. John Bethune, the younger, was born at Williamstown, Glengarry County, in January, 1791. He received his education at the school of the Rev. Dr.

Rev. Dr. John Bethune
Actg. Principal of McGill University
1835-1846

John Strachan at Cornwall, already referred to. After serving in the War of 1812, he entered the ministry of the Church of England, possibly through the influence of his former teacher, who left a deep impression on the minds and lives of all his pupils, and in 1814, he was ordained by Bishop Mountain at Quebec. He was stationed for a time at Brockville and vicinity, and in 1818 he was made Rector of Christ Church, Montreal, where he remained for more than fifty years, eventually becoming Dean of the diocese. He was acting-Principal of McGill from November, 1835, until May, 1846. He died in August, 1872.

Soon after his appointment, the acting-Principal entered into negotiations with the Board of the Royal Institution on the question of the erection of a suitable building on the Burnside Estate for the reception and instruction of students, as required by James McGill's will. The Medical lectures, the only lectures given in the name of the College, were given in a building far removed from the College property. The College authorities did not even pay the rent of the building nor did they pay the salaries of the Professors, and the School, except in name, and for its own protection and the privilege gained thereby for the conferring of degrees, was still, to all intents and purposes, a private institution. Technically, it was contended, it was not a part of the University at all. It was not situated on the Burnside Estate as the will of the founder required, and it could not therefore be considered as fulfilling any of the provisions of the bequest. Even the legality of the degrees conferred had been questioned, and had been accepted on the basis

of equity and intention rather than on that "of justice and of fact." The Principal and Governors
realised the force of these arguments, and the necessity of removing the cause. The situation could only
be met, they believed, by the erection of a building
or buildings on the Burnside Estate, as the terms
of the bequest demanded, and the Governors urged
immediate action. They pointed out that "without
provision for resident students very little good can
be expected to result from the opening of the College, and without residence within the College for
one or more professors it cannot be expected that
resident students will be obtained." The acting-
President of the Royal Institution for the Advancement of Learning, A. W. Cochrane, wrote to Principal Bethune on January 11th, 1836, stating "with
respect to the measures proper to be taken towards
the speedy erection of a College on Burnside property, it was my intention to have submitted to a
meeting of the Royal Institution which was fixed
for Thursday next a proposal to advertise for plans
and estimates of a suitable building. . . . My own
opinion is that a new building calculated for 40 students (*intimus*) with a suitable public apartment and
accommodation for two professors would be sufficient for the present demands of the country (perhaps even beyond what is necessary) and that at all
events it would not be justifiable to exceed the expenditure of £4000 or £5000 out of the bequest for
such a purpose at the outset. The present building,
Burnside House, might be adapted to the residence
of the Head of the College." He added that, as
promised in 1801, the Crown should give an endowment for general education in the Province, in a way

that would not rouse political or sectarian feelings. "I should not," he said, "wish to see the question connected with the proceedings of any political association. If taken up in this general way, I think that some public movement at Montreal in favour of it would not fail to have a good effect; but great caution and moderation are requisite." But the Board and the Governors could not agree on the kind of building required and over a year passed without any action on the part of either body.

Further difficulty arose in connection with the amended Charter of 1834, which had not received the approval of the authorities. Until it was given confirmation no additional professorships could be appointed. That it did not conform to the ideas of the Board of the Royal Institution is evident from a letter written to Principal Bethune by the President in June, 1836. Objection was taken to making the Governors a self-elective body, and the necessity of making it essential that the Governors or a majority of them should be of the Protestant faith was also insisted on. That the discord between the Governors and the Board which led in the end to unfortunate bitterness and disaster, was then developing is also apparent in this letter. The President of the Board wrote: "Whatever changes are proposed to be made in the existing Charter must, I should conceive as a matter of course, be submitted for the consideration of the Royal Institution, the Visitatorial body who are bound to see that the views of the founder of the College are not defeated." The Governors then decided to submit new amendments, and at a meeting held on November 14th, 1836, attended by the Lieutenant-Governor, the Chief Justice and the Principal, the Charter recommended in January, 1834, was changed to read as follows: "The Governors of the College shall consist of the Governor in Chief of Lower Canada; the Right Rev. Charles J. Stewart, Lord Bishop of Quebec and his successors, Bishops of Quebec; the Right Rev. George J. Mountain, Lord Bishop of Montreal and his successors, Bishops of Montreal; the Rector of Christ Church, Montreal, and his successors of the said Church; a minister of the Church of Scotland resident in Montreal, to be selected for the purpose by the Presbytery of Montreal to be perpetually succeeded by a minister of the Church of Scotland chosen in like manner; the Principal of the College; the Hon. James Reid; the Hon. George Moffat; the Hon. Peter McGill; William Robertson, M.D.; William P. Christie; Samuel Gerrard and John Samuel McCord." Authority was given to fill all vacancies by a majority vote of the Governors, seven to constitute a quorum. It was stipulated that all Governors of the College must henceforth be residents in the district of Montreal. The Chief Justice and the Principal agreed to the above changes in the Charter, but the Governor of the Province "declined under existing circumstances to give any opinion on the subject, and his vote was not recorded." It was also decided at this meeting that the rents from the Burnside Estate be expended on repairs and that the premises be placed in the occupation and charge of the Principal for the time being, he to keep them in a good state of repair. This latter decision was not approved by the Royal Institution and it gave rise to further controversy. Without the approval of the Board of the Royal Institution the Governors forwarded their amendments to the Governor-General for transmission to the Home Government, but at the request of the Board he stayed proceedings.

Meanwhile, the ultimate possession of the endowment fund was causing anxiety. The case was settled in favour of the College in 1835, but the Governors were unable to secure the money. The Desrivières heirs who were in control of the legacy demanded terms as we have already seen, but their terms were refused. When the Executors at last secured possession of the funds they declined to convey them to the Royal Institution until certain promised conditions were fulfilled by that body acting for the Home Government. On November 10th, 1836, a memorial on the subject of the legacy was forwarded to the Colonial Office by Dr. Strachan, one of the surviving Executors of the will of James McGill. He pointed out that the original bequest had increased by the accumulation of interest to £22,000. This amount together with the Burnside Estate would, he said, be transferred to the Royal Institution when two conditions were fulfilled—first, the contributing by His Majesty's Government towards the erection and endowment of the proposed University, and second, the carrying out of the intention of the testator, to which Dr. Strachan stated himself to be a living witness, that the proposed College should be essentially Protestant. To this Memorial the Colonial Office replied that the will did not stipulate for a contribution from His Majesty's Government towards the proposed University, and added "nor can we perceive any disposition on the part of the testator to impress on the Institution to which he so liberally contributed a character of religious exclusiveness. . . . The testator did not in his will either directly or indirectly introduce such a condition, and adverting moreover to the even-handed liberality with which his bequests were distributed between the poor Catholic and Protestant inhabitants of Montreal, we apprehend it would be impossible to impose such a restriction founded on mere verbal testimony as to the intention of the testator. . . . His Majesty's Government cannot now advise His Majesty to reconsider it for the purpose of narrowing the Charter of 1821." In November, 1836, the Board conveyed to the Governors of the College the possession of the Burnside Estate, subject to the Board's subsequent approval of all decisions affecting it. But the controversy between the executors and the Colonial Office over the conveyance of the funds, which the heirs had not yet given up, continued for several months. It was not until October 20th, 1837, that the litigation finally ended. In December following, a transfer of all monies, investments, etc., was obtained by the Trustees of the Royal Institution, estimated at the value of £22,000, the amount of the legacy and accrued interest, and yielding an income of between £800 and £900. But in the meantime the College suffered and its progress was retarded.

There were other worries than those of buildings and charter and endowment fund. Since the College was opened in 1829 no repairs had been made on the Burnside property. The buildings and fences were rapidly falling into decay; the neighbours were complaining that the fences of Burnside had disappeared and that through the property cattle wandered at will to their lands and gardens, and the farmer who had leased the premises "on the halves" had neither the money nor the inclination to effect a remedy. There was also a demand for streets or roads through the estate. The Governors had no money at their disposal; they must beg every cent expended from the Royal Institution. The situation was incongruous. On December 17th, 1836, Principal Bethune wrote to the Secretary of the Board informing him that "there is a demand on the part of the neighbours for fences, which on a close inspection are found to be unserviceable with the exception of 170 cedar rails or rather logs which will serve by being split into two for rails." The neighbours, he said, preferred "a fence 10 feet high, but they will be satisfied with one 6 feet high." He also advised that the Royal Institution should join in the proposal of one of the neighbours, Phillips (who is remembered in the present "Phillips Square"), "a man difficult to deal with if thwarted by delay," for opening streets through the estate of Burnside.

As a result of this appeal the Board granted £75 to be expended on the buildings and fences. The expenditure of this sum created further friction between the Governors and the Board. The latter body was not informed until February, 1837, of the Governors' decision at their meeting on November 14, 1836, to put Burnside House and premises into the occupation and charge of the Principal of the College. When they received the information they wrote to the Principal asking him what use he intended to make of the estate. The Principal in his reply questioned the authority of the Board, and said: "With regard to the use intended to be made by the Governors of the House, the Governors do not conceive themselves in any way accountable to the Board in this respect . . . yet they feel no objection to communicating it for the information of the Board." To this letter the Secretary of the Board replied: "The Board was only originally induced to make the grant of £75 on the 14th of November last, for the repairing of the Burnside House and fences in the expectation that the same would be made tenantable and be let to the advantage of the Trust, and have learned with much dissatisfaction that the House is to be occupied by the acting-Principal without any advantage to the Trust; and a personal interest thereby given to him to prevent the College going into speedy operation; and that the Board do also think it necessary to record their opinion that as the Visitors of McGill College they are at all times entitled to inquire into the management of the Burnside property, especially when a demand is made upon the Board for a grant of money to be laid out on the said property. It was ordered [by the Board] that Mr. Bethune be further informed that under the circumstances disclosed to the Board for the first time in his letter, the Board cannot feel themselves justified in advancing any further sums for the repairs on the Burnside property." The Principal answered that the Board had no right to act in any matter affecting the College without consulting the Governors; that "the Governors cannot recognise the Visitatorial powers of the Board to the extent claimed"; and that the Board was "illegally and unjustly detaining the funds." He emphasised his desire "to effect a restoration of harmony and unanimity between all the parties"; but it was clear that because of the rapidly growing friction and misunderstanding a crisis was not very far off.

For several months thereafter no meetings of the Governors were held. The Rebellion of 1837 and the struggle for Canadian autonomy required all the attention and the energy of the Provincial authorities, and the subject of Collegiate education was again somewhat neglected. But in May, 1837, the Royal Institution announced to the Principal that they were about to erect buildings for the University, and they asked for suggestions which might guide them in calling for plans. But the Principal and Governors declined to make suggestions. They denied the right of the Royal Institution to undertake the erection of buildings, and they contended that the whole property and management of the affairs of the College devolved upon the Governors. They would therefore not surrender into other hands what they conceived to be their own vested rights. They pointed out, too, that the case between the executors and the Royal Institution for the possession of the funds was not yet settled. The Board replied that until a College was actually erected they were in control, under the terms of the will. They were somewhat inconsistent in their attitude. In the first suit against the Desrivières heirs for the possession of the estate they had pleaded that by the mere obtaining of the Charter the College was to all intents and purposes "erected and established." The courts sustained their plea. Now, however, they repudiated their own former contention; they maintained that the College had not yet been "erected and established"; and that until buildings were actually constructed they had the sole authority!

Discord continued to characterise the relations of

the two bodies. The Governors' meetings were usually attended only by the Principal and the Chief Justice. The former had a double or casting vote in case of dispute. He was virtually in control. The Board of the Royal Institution declared that he did not represent the views of the Governors. Apart from the disagreements arising from a dual management, other causes contributed to the bitterness of the controversy. The period was not conducive to harmony. Downing Street was not a name to conjure with, and "Downing Street rule" had become in Canada a synonym for indifference or coercion. The suspicion that the Royal Institution was but the mouthpiece, or at least the meek and unprotesting agent, of Downing Street only added to the irritation. The suspicion was not well founded, for the Royal Institution did not willingly submit to dictation from the Home authorities. But a new and sturdy Canadian spirit was evident in education as well as in politics. It was apparent as early as 1815 when Dr. Strachan outlined his plan for a University and expressed his doubts on the suitability of English methods in Canada. It had grown rapidly since that time. The year 1837 was a year of turmoil, with a cry for the privilege of solving Canadian problems in a Canadian way by those who were familiar with the requirements and conditions, and were not dwelling thousands of miles away. In such a period, aside from the waste of time, it was doubly distasteful to the Governors and to those interested in education to have to submit all appointments and all plans to the Home Government for ratification. The friction was, on the surface, between the Governors and the Royal Institution, but its roots lay deeper. Its cause was not far removed from the cause of the political rebellion of the hour.

After several months of somewhat discordant discussion the Principal finally agreed to submit to the Board suggestions on the proposed buildings, and on June 30th, 1838, he forwarded an outline of what he believed the College should include. He suggested that it should provide "(1) Accommodation for 100 students, namely, 100 sleeping rooms, and 50 sitting-rooms, two students in one set of apartments; (2) apartments for the Principal, and Vice-Principal, and family, and for four other Professors. The present house of Burnside might, he said, be adopted for the residence of the Principal; (3) a College Hall which for the present may be used both for lectures, exercises and refectory; (4) a Library; (5) a Chapel; (6) Steward's apartments." As an alternative to (3) he suggested three lecture rooms with some adjacent small apartments. It was proposed that prizes should be offered for the first and second best plans with specifications and estimates, not only for the buildings, but also for the laying out of College grounds on the northwest side of Sherbrooke Street "in avenues and ornamental and kitchen gardens." It was pointed out that this land consisted of about seventeen acres, and was considered sufficient for the College grounds, and that the upper side of Sherbrooke Street, which was then being opened to the width of 80 feet, was considered the best site for the College, as it was the most elevated land on Burnside and had the best approach. It was desired that the Building should include "a large room for the business of the Professor of Latin and Greek which might also be appropriated

to many general purposes; a room for the Professor
of Mathematics, Natural Philosophy and Astronomy
with suitable adjacent apartments for his apparatus;
a room for the Medical Department with suitable
adjacent apartments for Chemical apparatus." The
Professorships proposed to be established in the first
instance were four: that of Divinity and Moral
Philosophy to be occupied by the Principal; that of
Medicine, with a suitable number of Lectureships
in the different departments of Medical Science; that
of Mathematics, Natural Philosophy and Astronomy; and that of Latin, Greek and History. It was
pointed out that "in the present state of the College
funds the greater number of these Professors can
have little more allowed them than the fees derivable
from pupils and that their salaries will therefore be
uncertain."

The Royal Institution refused, however, to proceed at that time with the erection of buildings on
so large a plan as suggested. On August 1st, 1838,
they announced their intention to "proceed immediately on such an extent as the limited resources at
their command will justify." They agreed to call
for plans for a building containing lecture rooms and
a public hall, but no apartments for students or
professors, the building to cost not more than £5000.
They contended that all the money in their possession
was required to endow professorships and that they
could not therefore make so great an expenditure
as the large building suggested by the Governors
would entail. They stated, too, that only three professorships could at present be established, those of
Classical Literature, Mathematics and Natural
Philosophy, and Metaphysical and Moral Philoso-

phy, on the understanding that when the charter was changed to permit it, each of these professorships should be divided into two. They pointed out that their University scheme "in the absence of the long hoped for assistance from Her Majesty's Government will not embrace either Theology, Law, or Medicine." It was stipulated that the .Principal should be also one of the Professors. An interesting condition with reference to the teaching of Theology was also set forth by the Board in the following resolution:

"That it is not expedient that a Professor of Divinity be appointed under the Charter, but that it be intimated to the Right Reverend the Lord Bishop of Montreal on behalf of the Church of England in this Province and to the Reverend the Presbytery of Quebec or the Synod of Canada on behalf of the Church of Scotland that Lecture Rooms will be set apart and that application will be made for such an alteration in the Charter as will give all rights and privileges of the University to such Professor or Professors as they may appoint and endow, or procure endowments for, for the instruction of students of Divinity of their respective churches; and that the authorities in both churches be respectfully requested to recommend or to enforce on their students attendance on the classes of general education in the College."

It was later decided that the Board of the Royal Institution and the Governors of McGill should write a memorial to Her Majesty's Government asking for the means of endowing at least four Medical Professorships; that a similar memorial be prepared with respect to a Professorship of Law; and that until such Professorships be established, every facility be given within the College to Lecturers in the various branches of Medical and Legal Science. These memorials had no response.

Another effort was now made by the Governors to secure the passing of the new Charter as amended in 1834 and 1836, which had been ignored by the Home Government. But Lord Gosford, the Lieutenant-Governor, refused to give it his sanction. Application was then made to Lord Durham, but no answer was received from His Lordship, who declared that he was "too busy to consider the question."

The correspondence during this period indicates that the Board and the Governors were working in harmony. But the peace was not of long duration. It lasted but a few days. It was, however, of sufficient length to permit of temporary agreement on the kind of building required. As a result, plans for the laying out of the grounds and for the erection of buildings were at last called for by the Board of the Royal Institution, and the following advertisement appeared in the *Mercury* and the *Official Gazette* on the 16th of August, 1838, and in the *Quebec Gazette* on the day following:

TO ARCHITECTS

Office of the Royal Institution for the Advancement of Learning

Quebec, 16th August, 1838.

By order of the Principal and Trustees of this Board, Public Notice is hereby given that they are desirous of obtaining plans, specifications, and esti-

mates for the erection of suitable buildings on the
estate of Burnside, near Montreal, for the McGill
College; and that the sum of fifty pounds currency
will be paid for the plan which shall be accepted by
the Board as the best plan; and twenty-five pounds
for the plan which shall be adjudged as second best.

The said plans to provide:

1ST.   Apartments for 100 students: to consist of 50
        sitting rooms and 100 sleeping rooms.
2ND.   Apartments for a Vice-Principal and family,
        and for 4 Professors.
3RD.   College Hall.
4TH.   Library.
5TH.   Chapel.
6TH.   Steward's Apartments.

With a connected plan for the distribution of the
ground on the northwest side of the continuation of
Sherbrooke Street in avenues—with ornamental and
kitchen gardens.

The said plans to provide for the erection in the
first instance of such portions of the building as are
specified below to be hereafter incorporated with the
general design when completed; the sum at present
disposable being limited to about £5000.

1ST.   Two large rooms, each calculated for separate
        classes of 50 non-resident students.
2ND.   Two rooms available for medical students,
        chemical apparatus, etc.
3RD.   College Hall.
4TH.   Library.
5TH.   Steward's Apartments.

Information respecting the proposed site and

grounds, with other particulars, can be obtained on
application to the Rev. Dr. Bethune, Principal of
McGill College, Montreal, to whom the plans are
to be delivered on or before the 1ST of October next.

WILLIAM S. BURRAGE,
For the Rev. R. R. Burrage,
(Sec'y to the Board of R. I.)

Plans were accordingly submitted by several archi-
tects, and were forwarded by the Board to the Governors of McGill for their comments. The Governors pointed out that even in the best and most suitable plan submitted "no provision was made for
retiring rooms for Professors!" The plans provided
for a Post Office at the entrance to the grounds, a
Botanical Lecture-house and "ornamental bridges"
over the stream that ran through the grounds near
the present University Street. The Board of the
Royal Institution declined to accept any of the plans
submitted on the ground that they involved too great
an expenditure, and building operations were again
indefinitely delayed.

The Governors continued to urge with vigour the
immediate erection of a building. They tried to
force the Board, for no apparent legal reason, to
have the building completed before the 29th of
June, 1839, the tenth anniversary of the opening
of the College, and in October, 1838, the Principal
wrote to the Board: "I am well informed that it is
the intention of the heirs Desrivières, should not a
College be erected on Burnside property within ten
years from the period of possession thereof by the
Royal Institution, to sue for the recovery of the
whole bequest. No legal advice has been taken on

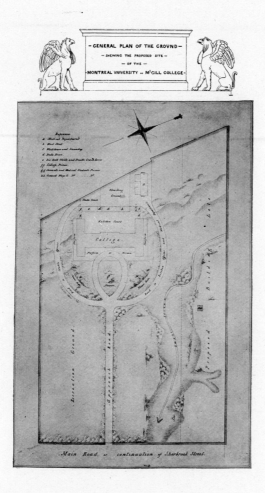

The Plan of the
Proposed University

the subject, but we think it prudent to avoid the
contest." The Board sought legal advice on the
latter question and were assured that there were no
grounds whatsoever for such an assumption on the
part of the heirs, and that such a contention could
not be defended in law. No attempt indeed was
made to put forward such a plea, and it is very
doubtful if such an attempt was ever contemplated.

But that the Board feared this possibility is evident from their determination speedily to establish
the College on a more real basis. They decided to
begin instruction in Burnside House. Difficulties,
however, were in the way. The Principal was occupying the dwelling house, and although he had
taken possession of it without the Board's approval
they could not well compel him to leave. Moreover,
he had expended a considerable sum from his own
private funds on repairs to the estate. He had submitted a bill for the amount to the Board, but the
Board declined to pay it as they had not authorised
the expenditure. They contended, too, that he could
reimburse himself from the products of the farm.
The situation was a delicate one, and gradually the
evils of a dual control were being disclosed. The
Board knew that the Principal would not vacate the
building in which they wished to begin instruction
until his bill was paid. On November 21st, 1838,
they voted: "that a communication be made to the
Governors of McGill College that it is in the opinion of the Board expedient that a permanent Principal and Professors be appointed and the actual
working of the College commenced as speedily as
possible in Burnside House till such time as more
convenient buildings be erected, by which means the

wishes of the Governors to have the College established and in operation before the 29th of June next
will be met, and that the Board will take into consideration the claim of Dr. Bethune arising out of expenses incurred by him on the estate of Burnside
while in his possession on his vacating the premises
and rendering an account." Meanwhile the Governors' meetings had dwindled to two, and sometimes to one member. There was criticism that
their meetings were no longer representative, and
to these statements, because of their own objection
to the alleged Downing Street methods of the Royal
Institution, the Governors were sensitive. To meet
this criticism they established the "Corporation" of
the College, to include not only the Governors, but
a number of the members of the teaching staff, and
certain citizens selected because of their interest in
education. The first meeting of this body was held
on November 27th, 1838. There were present Sir
John Colborne, the Governor-General; the Principal; Drs. Robertson, Stephenson and Holmes of
the Medical School, and the Hon. George Moffatt.
It was at this meeting that the resolution of the
Board above referred to was considered.

The resolution was not received with applause nor
with delighted approval. The Governors doubted
the efficacy of the plan. The Principal was not
eager to vacate Burnside House. The Professors
in the Medical School resented the suggestion that
the "actual working of the College" had yet to be
commenced. In answer, it was resolved that "in the
opinion of Corporation it is expedient that a College
be *built* before the 29th of June next on the Burnside Estate as the surest means of securing the be-

quest of the late Mr. McGill." But the bequest
had already been secured; it had been paid over to
the Royal Institution in December, 1837! Notwithstanding the Board's decision, the Governors insisted
on the erection of a building before the 29th of the
following June. The amended Charter had not yet
been approved. There was still provision only for
four professorships, and these had been filled by
the members of the Medical School. Only one of
them was now vacant. Until the Charter was approved, then, and provision made for the appointment of more professors, the building erected could
only be occupied mainly by Medical teachers. In
December, 1838, the Royal Institution again recorded their opposition to the Governors' desire for
"the hasty erection in a few weeks of a building
adapted only for instruction in Medical Science."
They expressed their belief "that the first proper
and most pressing measure to be adopted in execution of the plain expression of the testator's will
and of the Charter is to commence forthwith a
course of general instruction in the ordinary branches
of a learned Collegiate education in the buildings
now erected on the Burnside Estate." They added
that "they see no difficulty in accomplishing this object before it would be possible to commence the erection of a new building, and they are of opinion that
it would be a nearer approach to a real performance
of the testator's intentions than the attempt to run
up a new building before the 29th of June, next,
which even if it could be finished by that time would
not deserve the name of a University." They did
not consider that the terms "erect" and "establish"
used in the will "could with any propriety be inter-

preted as meaning the erection of a material building." They declared that it was undoubtedly the
testator's intention to establish an institution for
collegiate education; they expressed their determination to apply the funds first of all to the payment of
"a Principal and of such Professors as may be
required, and to proceed in due course with the erection of a more extensive building than even that
suggested by the Governors."

To this the Governors would not agree; they
urged that a decision on the Charter be obtained at
once. On February 5th, 1839, the Board again
expressed their views. They were sensible, they
said, of the necessity for the appointment of additional professors, but they emphasised the folly of
waiting for this permission before erecting a College
building. Approval of the amended Charter might
be postponed indefinitely, and the present Charter
provided for a building for collegiate education.
They added: "The Board are not aware of the
circumstances under which the *Medical Faculty of
Montreal* became possessed of all the Professorships
of the College but they must suppose that it could
only have been a temporary arrangement, without
remuneration, adopted with such precautions as not
to allow the present holders of Professorships setting
up the pretension to continue to fill them to the exclu-
sion of other branches of knowledge. The existing
arrangement appears to the Board to be clearly liable
to the objection that it is contrary to the terms of the
Charter and the intention of the founder since an
institution of which the offices are so filled for the
purpose of one science alone cannot in law or in
common parlance be considered as a University where

all the branches of literature are or may be universally taught, and such an Institution is erected by the Charter according to the express will of the testator."

Their plan was to appoint a permanent Principal who should be required to lecture in some branch or branches of knowledge, and to establish temporary Lectureships which could be changed to Professorships when the amended Charter, permitting an increase in the number of Professorships, was approved. Under this plan they saw "an easy means of opening at once a course of public instruction which would meet the present wants of the Province and be capable of future extension." They would devote the endowment fund, they said, to the payment of Professors' salaries. The house on the Burnside Estate was sufficient, they thought, "for the limited purpose at present contemplated," and "in that building, if nowhere else, a College should be put in actual operation," for by so doing "an effective answer would be afforded to any demand or pretension that might be raised to obtain the forfeiture of the property bequeathed on the pretence of the College not being in operation." They promised to proceed to the erection of a building "with all despatch consistent with due caution. But at least a year from next summer must elapse before a building suitable to the purpose of a University can be prepared for occupation." They therefore urged the use of Burnside House for the present, at least.

In answer to this letter the Medical Professors contended through the Principal, that their appointment was not a temporary arrangement and that it was not their intention to resign their commissions.

The Governors stated further, that they could not feel themselves justified in pressing for the resignation of any of these Professors, who were receiving no salary, but who "now had a near prospect of reaping some advantage from their appointment." They condemned the Board for unnecessary delay in erecting a building in which to hold classes and their letters did not add to the harmony so desirable in that critical period. The Principal and Governors did not approve of using Burnside House for lecture rooms, because, in their opinion, it was unfit for such a purpose "except on such a scale as would entitle it only to the name of a Grammar School; because they believed a suitable building could be erected within a year; because it was intended to be the residence of the Principal; and because they could not see that any object would be attained by such a temporary, insufficient and unsatisfactory arrangement." They stated further, with some suggestion of defiance, that they would be prepared to open the College with suitable teachers as soon as the necessary building or buildings were erected "on the most extensive scale and in the most efficient manner which the funds that may be at their disposal will admit of, and that until such a building was provided no instruction would be given."

The Royal Institution seems to have desired harmony and to have been willing to meet the wishes of the Governors at least half-way. At a meeting of the Board on February 20th, 1839, it was decided to call again for plans to be submitted before the 10th of May following. It was resolved at this meeting "that the accommodation of the Medical Faculty be limited to two rooms for class rooms, these to form part of the general building unless separate accommodation in detached buildings could be obtained for them within the limits of the £5,000 allotted for the whole edifice, and without interfering with or embarrassing the general plan; and that if the Medical Faculty required other or larger accommodation than was consistent with these conditions they must be left to their own resources to obtain it, the Board, however, being willing to allow them to build on some part of the grounds of Burnside if they found funds for doing so." They had meanwhile petitioned the Lieutenant-Governor, Sir John Colborne, and Council, for a Provincial grant to aid in the construction of the building, but their appeal had no success.

The Governors of the College then decided to agree to the erection of a smaller building than that at first requested. The Medical School, too, for various reasons concluded that they did not desire accommodation in the new building. The Governors wrote to the Board stating that they would be satisfied with the erection of a building for 60 students, without sitting rooms; necessary class rooms; College Hall; Library; Steward's Apartments and accommodation for the Principal and two Professors—which could be built for £6,000. They pointed out that in this estimate there was no provision whatever for the Medical Department "nor perhaps will such provision be at all necessary. The present Medical Professors are now of opinion that the situation of Burnside is too remote from the centre of the population for this department, because, besides the inconvenience to the Professors themselves, the attendance there of Medical Students who will be generally resident in the Town at 4 or 5 different Lectures daily will be attended with very serious inconvenience if not insuperable difficulty. They would therefore much prefer that a sufficient allowance should be made for renting a building in Town for the Medical Department. To meet their views in this respect the House on Burnside (which will not be required for the residence of the Principal if accommodation be provided for him within the walls of the College), together with that portion of the premises on the southeast side of Sherbrooke Street, might be let for a sum fully adequate to the expense of renting sufficient accommodation for the Medical Department in Town."

To this latter suggestion the Board agreed. They were still determined that pending the completion of the proposed building, Collegiate teaching should be undertaken at once in Burnside House. But it was first necessary that the Principal give up the house. A dispute then arose between the Board and the Governors with reference to the responsibility for the repairs to the estate. More money had been expended than the Board had authorised. The Board contended that the Principal should make an allowance for rent of the house, which he had occupied for nearly two years, and they refused to pay the account submitted for the expenses incurred. The Governors declined to admit the justice of this claim. The Principal had already written to the Board in January, 1839, stating that he would "keep possession of Burnside until his full account was paid, and that he would vacate the premises when required to do so by the Governors."

The Board then agreed to pay to the Principal the whole amount claimed by him, "however liable to objection, with whatever deduction for rent he himself should agree to," if he would consent to vacate Burnside House. The Principal, in a somewhat scornful reply, declined for two reasons, first that this proposal implied the necessity of bribing him to vacate the premises; and second that by accepting it, he might be considered as selling for the settlement of his account the possession which the Governors held of the premises by reason of his occupancy. But he again stated that he would vacate the premises when ordered to do so by the Governors. The result was a protracted and bitter discussion between the two bodies, with many recriminations on both sides and more frankness than tact. The Lord Bishop of Montreal, the Rev. Dr. G. J. Mountain, who was Principal of the Royal Institution and formerly Principal of McGill, naturally interested himself personally in the discussion. On February 25th, 1839, he wrote to the Principal, saying, "I will tell you unreservedly what I think, which is that . . . you are apt to give colour to the transactions in which you are engaged. . . . I say this without reserve because if you will receive it in good part I think it may be of use to you and save upon occasion hard constructions being put upon your proceedings. . . . It is very unwillingly indeed that as Principal of the Board, I have been drawn into any sort of collision with you."

To this the Principal promptly replied, accusing the Board of gross neglect and unnecessary delay. "Indeed," he said, "their zeal for the interests of the College has for some time past chiefly manifested itself in their efforts and schemes for dislodging me from Burnside and in their proceedings they seem to have adopted the favourite peroration of Cicero which may be freely translated thus, 'and Bethune must be ousted.'" He added: "I can afford to forgive the Board for any hard constructions they put upon my proceedings; they may be necessary for their own justification." To this Bishop Mountain replied: "I have had quite enough of this painful collision."

The Principal declared his intention of remaining in possession of Burnside House, and he wrote to the Board that "no precise period is fixed for my vacating the premises." The Board contended that they "desired an amicable adjustment of such differences as had unfortunately existed"; but for several years no adjustment was made. It is unnecessary to enter here into the details of the subsequent dispute between the Board and the Principal and Governors over the occupancy of Burnside House. It was but one of many unfortunate disagreements in which each side contended for what they believed to be just. The Principal's account for repairs to the property was in the end paid and in November, 1839, he vacated Burnside House. But the controversy between the two bodies did not then end.

In the summer of 1839, the Governors decided to ignore the Board and to seek direct aid from the Provincial Government. They asked for a grant of £5,000 for building purposes and £5,000 for the purchase of philosophical apparatus, furniture and books for a Library. They included also £100 a year for a Professor of Classical Literature and £100 a year for a Professor of Mathematics; £50 each for two Divinity Lecturers, one of the Anglican Church and one of the Church of Scotland; £50 each for three Medical Professors; and £50 for a Professor of Law "much wanted." They expressed their desire, if the building fund was granted, to rent Burnside House and with the proceeds therefrom to pay for a building in town for the Medical School. "The Medical Faculty," they said, "could then go into immediate operation, and all the other Professors, with the exception of the Principal, could also commence instruction at their respective residences." Apparently it was their opinion that the Medical School had not yet begun to operate as an integral part of the University. For obvious reasons the above appeal failed. The Government declined to interfere. The grant was not made and the Governors of the College turned again with reluctance to the Royal Institution.

There was likewise further difficulty in connection with the amended Charter, which the Home authorities had not yet ratified. The Board of the Royal Institution had been asked by the Governor-General for their detailed opinions and suggestions on necessary amendments. The Board was slow to answer. The delay was preventing the appointment of Professors and the growth of the College. The hands of the Governors were tied. On August 11, 1839, the Principal wrote to Sir John Colborne, the Governor-General, protesting against the continued failure to decide the issue. "When I agreed to the appointment of another Principal in my room," he said, "it was in the confident expectation that the amended Charter would have been in our possession before this period. By that Charter I should retain my office of Governor of the College even if vacated by my resignation of the Office of Principal, but as ob-

stacles are thrown in the way of a speedy accomplishment of the wishes of the Governors in respect of the
amended Charter, I feel myself constrained to retain
the office of Principal until the Charter shall have
been procured." He also objected on behalf of the
Governors to the appointment of any Professors
and to the opening of the College, except the Medical
Department, until approval was given to the Charter.
Possibly the fact that the amended Charter permitted
the acting-Principal, after his retirement, still to be
a Governor of the College as Rector of Christ
Church, Montreal, influenced the Board in their dis-
approval of it. For the quarrel was not always
above personal prejudices, to which the advancement
of the College was often unfortunately sacrificed.

On August 17th, 1839, the Board at last broke
their silence, and in a letter to Sir John Colborne
they gave utterance to their reasons for opposition.
They blamed the Governors for not having first
submitted the Charter to them before sending it to
the Colonial Office,—and in this they were well
within their rights. They had not, they said, even
seen a certified copy of the document. They now
agreed, however, that the existing Charter required
alteration. They suggested that all the Governors of
the College should be residents of the Province, but
they objected to giving the Governors power to fill
vacancies as they occurred, as this would lead in the
end to a clique or cabal rule which would lead to
abuses in the management of the Institution. The
number of Professorships should, they thought, be
left unlimited, at the joint discretion of the Governors and the Board. The Governors were to be
subservient in power to the Board, and all appoint-

ments were to be ratified by the Crown. There should also be permission given for the granting of Honorary degrees. The Visitatorial duties and powers of the Royal Institution should be more clearly defined. "The Board," the letter stated, "also think it important, seeing that the declared object of the Royal Charter was the promotion of true religion, that the body of the Governors should be Protestants, and they beg leave also to call the particular attention of your Excellency to the necessity of introducing some provision into the amended Charter for requiring not only the Principal, Vice-Principal and Professors, and all others engaged in the instruction of youth in the University, but also the Governors themselves before being admitted to office, to make and subscribe a declaration of their belief in the Holy Scriptures as the Word of God, and in the doctrine of the Trinity of persons in the Godhead, as held by orthodox Protestant Churches."

To the majority of these suggestions the Governors agreed. But they denied the right of the members of the Board to exercise so great a power as such suggestions, if carried out, would give them. They protested against the necessity of having appointments ratified by the Crown. There was a rapid cross-fire of correspondence to the Governor-General, in which the various suggestions were presented and answered by each of the contending parties. But into the details of this long-continued and at times bitter correspondence it is unnecessary here further to enter. Meanwhile the Charter waited.

In the autumn of 1839, the Medical School was in need of funds. They appealed to the Governors.

The Governors had no money, but they voted £500, and on September 19th, they applied to the Royal Institution for a grant of that amount "in order to enable them to commence a course of Medical Instruction." The Board refused in the following letter forwarded on October 12th: "The Board resolve with regret that they cannot give sanction to this vote of the Governors, as they conceive themselves bound in the first instance to apply the means at their disposal for purposes of general instruction, and those means are so limited as to render it impossible to grant the sum demanded by the Medical Faculty without sacrificing general to one branch of professional education. . . . The Board are, however, fully aware of the advantages to McGill College and to the public generally which the proposed course of Medical lectures cannot fail to be attended with." They hoped at a later date "to be able to entertain the application," if the appeal for funds recently made to the Government should succeed.

Principal Bethune desired to procure a legal decision before a competent tribunal on the Board's refusal to make the above grant. The Governor of the Province was appealed to, but as he was about to leave Canada at the end of his term of office he again declined to interfere. He felt, too, with reference to a Provincial grant that he was only authorised to issue from the funds of the Province such a sum as was absolutely necessary to carry on educational work until a meeting of the Special Council could make provision for such an object and also for the voting of "a sum of money towards the erecting of McGill College." The discussion was finally closed by a resolution of the Board on the

4th of April, 1840, in which they said that in addition to having voted £8,000 for the erection of a building they had provided for the establishment of three Professorships with £300 a year for each chair, and an additional £100 for the Principal. "In these arrangements," they pointed out, "the Board did not lose sight of the necessity of subsequently providing for the instruction of students in the Medical and Legal professions, but they were clearly of opinion that in the actual state of the funds, these objects, however desirable, must be postponed for the opening of the Institution in the other branches of general education. To these arrangements the Governors offered no material objection and it was obvious that the resources at the disposal of the Board did not warrant any material increase of expenditure." With reference to the requested grant for the Medical School, they expressed surprise that such a demand should be made on their scanty and already inadequate resources, and they declared that they "would not be justified in the administration of their trust, in suffering their resources to be diminished for any object however desirable or important but that which they conscientiously judged the most desirable and important and primarily contemplated in the will of Mr. McGill,—which was the providing of collegiate education." There the discussion ended. The Medical School continued to be regarded as an independent institution, under the protection of the McGill authorities for the purpose merely of legalising their degrees. The Board had won in their contention, and the question was temporarily dropped.

In the meantime, during the brief armistice be-

tween the Governors and the Royal Institution, plans
for the College building had been agreed upon and
the contract had been let. The original plans had
been greatly modified so that the expenditure might
be in keeping with the funds available. But even
with many changes the first estimate of £5,000 was
soon found to have increased in fact to between
£10,000 and £12,000. One of the original plans
herewith reproduced, and typical of all the plans
submitted, called for a large building in the form of
the letter H. The two main wings looked east and
west, instead of north and south as at present, and
between them was a connecting structure. Rooms
were provided for 100 students. The Medical
building was to be separate. The College building
was to have a Chapel, but it was also to have a large
"cellar for beer and wine." Certain sections attached to the building were distinctly classified and
designated "for Professors," "for McGill students,"
and "for servants and Medical students." It was
found that such a building would entail too great an
expense, and the plans were changed to provide two
buildings, the present Central Arts Building and the
present East Wing, or Administration Offices. The
latter was intended to contain the Principal's apartments and rooms for Professors, and there the Principal subsequently dwelt for several years. Between
the two buildings provision was made for a covered
passage.

It was soon apparent that the cost of the new buildings would be greater than estimated. Before June,
1840, a sum of £2,783 had been expended and provision had to be made for the payment of a further
sum of £5,000 in the following January. In order to

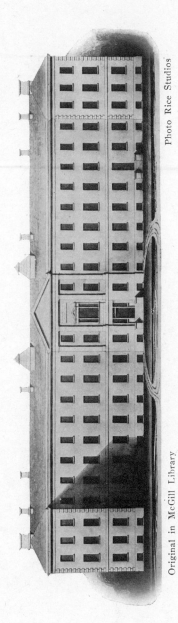

Photo Rice Studios

Original in McGill Library

The Proposed McGill College Original Building

secure this amount it was decided to advertise for sale certain lots adjoining the College site on Burnside Estate, and to procure plans for the laying out in building lots of all the land not in use. This was the beginning of the disposal of the unused part of the estate, a sacrifice which relieved the College from temporary financial embarrassment but which in later years, when real-estate increased in value, greatly depleted its revenue. The funds at this time were so low that the Governors could not pay a watchman or caretaker and the Board wrote to the Governors in October, 1840, asking, "Is any suitable person known to you who would consent to have charge of them [the buildings under construction] without remuneration, on condition of the requisite fuel being provided?" The gross annual revenue from the McGill properties vested in the Board for the support of the College was only £559. 6. 8. The Board again appealed to the Government for a grant of £5,000 to finish the building, also for "a very moderate sum to purchase the large collection of books formerly belonging to the late Mr. Fleming, the greater part of which would form a suitable foundation for a Library." This appeal was again unsuccessful.

During the summer of 1841, amidst many discouragements and financial worries, the erection of the buildings went forward. On October 21st, 1841, the Principal, who was one of the building committee, notified the Board that they were nearly ready for the reception of pupils. But their completion was for various reasons delayed several months. The Governors then decided to apply to the Legislature for a grant of £1,500 a year for current expenses

and £5,000 for Philosophical Apparatus, the rudiments of a Library, and furniture; to ask also for
the passing of an act repealing the Act of 1801, and
vesting the McGill bequest in the Governors of the
College; and to request that the Chief Justice and
the Principal be authorised to communicate with the
Royal Institution and to take steps to carry out this
resolution. This application was again without avail,
and the submitting of it was obviously not conducive
to harmony and peace.

Arrangements were now completed for the sale of
lots from the Burnside Estate. In all 25½ acres
were offered in small sections "as soon as Mr.
Phillips' consent could be obtained to give one-half
of the ground required for a proposed street," and
negotiations were entered into for the leasing of any
of the land left unsold. The Governors demanded
that the Royal Institution should transfer to them
the entire property, but the Board refused, claiming
that they were prohibited from so doing by the terms
of the will.

The Governors then devised an ingenious scheme
to secure possession of the premises. The Principal
proposed to the Board in May, 1842, that they lease
the estate to the Governors for a period of 99 years.
This the Board refused to do. They had obviously
no desire to allow the Governors to get control. An
endeavour to secure a lease was then made by a
Mr. Pelton, and his application was recommended
by the Principal. The Board replied that there were
legal and insuperable objections to the granting of
such a request and that they had no power under the
law to give a lease for a longer period than 21 years.
They agreed to give Pelton a lease for that period,

and they guaranteed "that the same shall be renewed for each subsequent term until the whole period of 99 years shall be accomplished." The lease seems to have been actually entered into, but because of difficulty over the security offered, combined with legal obstacles, it was cancelled soon afterwards. It transpired later that Pelton was merely the agent of the Governors and that in order to secure possession of the property, they had engaged him to act on their behalf, on the understanding that he was to transfer the lease to them when he received it.

Of the Governors' connection with this plan the Board was obviously not aware at the time. The details were frankly and clearly outlined in an interesting letter written by acting-Principal Bethune to the Hon. R. A. Tucker, Principal of the Royal Institution, on November 4th, 1845, when Pelton tried without success to establish a claim to some of the property. Extracts from this letter give further indication of the bitterness and hopelessness of the controversy:

"After the sale of the 99 years' lease had been advertised, it occurred to me that a good opportunity was thereby afforded to the Governors of the College for getting the management of the property into their own hands, by purchasing the lease. I need hardly say that the difficulties which had occurred between the late Board of the Royal Institution and the Governors of the College with regard to the right of possession naturally led to such a desire. Being the only Governor then resident in Montreal, and His Excellency, the late Sir Charles Bagot, having left the management with reference to that sale to me, I took upon myself the responsibility of making the purchase for the Governors;—but I felt convinced that if I did so in my own name, the Board of the Royal Institution would throw difficulties in the way. I therefore employed Mr. Pelton to purchase the property for me, and he did so on the perfect understanding that the property should, in the first instance, be conveyed to him, and afterwards by him to me, as he supposed, but really to 'the Governors, Principal and Fellows of McGill College.' In that transaction therefore Mr. Pelton acted as my agent; and continued to do so, placing only such tenants on Burnside as were approved by me, and collecting the rents for and paying them to me until the 1st May, 1844, after which he refused to continue to pay them to me. Immediately after the adjudication of the property, a correspondence took place with the Royal Institution about security for the payment of the rents, before it was discovered that a 99 years' lease could not be granted, and Mr. Pelton took upon himself without consulting me to offer security, which he said was accepted by the Board; and then, knowing that I had not offered any security, proposed to me to let him be the *bona fide* purchaser; but I refused, saying that I supposed the same person who was willing to be security for him would also be security for me. It was immediately after this discovered that the Royal Institution could not grant a lease for a longer period than 21 years, and the whole affair was considered by me as at an end, that is, that it was no sale, because the Royal Institution could not be expected to do that which they had no legal authority to do. . . ." The lease was subsequently cancelled, and it was shown that Pelton had no legal claim upon the property.

When the College buildings were nearing completion, towards the end of 1842, the Board prepared the necessary documents for the transfer of the Burnside Estate to the possession of the Governors of the College. But they took care to safeguard their own powers. They retained the right to inquire from time to time into the management and administration of the University, to remove officers of the College for misconduct, to examine into the compliance of the Governors with the Charter, and to establish statutes and by-laws for the government of the College. In short, the Governors, although they were at last to obtain possession of the property, were still to be subservient to the Board.

This was naturally not satisfactory to the Governors. In accordance with the resolution passed on August 8th, 1842, they drew up a bill the object of which was "to abolish the Royal Institution, and to provide for the better government of McGill College." It stipulated that all the monies, goods and chattels of which the Royal Institution was possessed under the will of James McGill should be vested in the Government of the University. The Principal went to Kingston to endeavour to have the bill passed during the following session of Parliament but the abrupt ending of the session prevented even its introduction. He went to Kingston again in 1843, but he was frustrated by a similar cause. Against the bill the Board emphatically protested. They declared it to be an attempt to overthrow the plainly expressed intentions and directions of the testator, and an action "as unexampled in the history of British legislation as it is contrary to the first principles of law, justice and reason." They stated further that "they

have executed the intentions of the testator diligently, faithfully and efficiently, so far as they have
not been obstructed in doing so by the acts of those
whose duty it was to have facilitated their proceedings." The bill was not passed. It helped only to
shatter whatever hopes may have existed for the
ending of the quarrel between the Governors and the
Board as then constituted. It made it plain that
there was now no possibility of an amicable
agreement.

In the spring of 1843, the buildings were completed
as far as the funds available would permit. Because
of lack of money, the Board did not feel justified in
making any outlay on the College grounds. Meanwhile, however, they had increased the value of the
estate by giving to the City of Montreal the continuation lines of Dorchester and St. Catherine
Streets on condition that the additional fences required on opening these streets should be erected at
the expense of the city.

In June, 1843, it was decided to open the buildings
for the reception of students in the first week of the
following September. To this the Board and the
Governors, strangely enough, agreed, but the agreement was only momentary. The Board asked the
Governors for an estimate of the amount required
for furniture for the buildings. The Governors refused to make an estimate. They were unable, they
said, to do so; they desired a covering grant of £500
to buy what they needed. The Board suggested with
some touch of sarcasm that they should get "a carpenter or a tradesman" to make an estimate if they
could not make it themselves, but the Governors
again declined. The Board contended that they

could not make a grant unless they previously knew precisely the details of the proposed expenditure; and the Governors answered that they would borrow £500 if the Royal Institution would not give it to them. The Board then asked for an accounting of the money "already received and expended by the Principal in connection with the rents and products of the Burnside Estate." The Secretary was instructed to reply that no account would be submitted as the Governors felt that any money so received was but a very small remuneration for services rendered by the Principal. To this the Board rejoined with bitterness that the Principal had not been regularly appointed, that he had done no duty as Professor, that they had never authorised his taking possession of Burnside and that the products from the farm should provide for him more than a sufficient remuneration; they were determined, they said, to pay no salaries unless accounts were rendered to them and approved. Such, at this critical period, was the co-operation arising from a dual control!

On June 21st, the opening of the College in the autumn was approved by the Governor General. The Rev. F. J. Lundy (a graduate of Oxford) had been appointed Professor of Classical Literature in November, 1842. He had received, with the Principal, one of the first D.C.L. degrees conferred by McGill in the spring of 1843. In addition to his duties as Professor he was now appointed Secretary of the College, and was later made Vice-Principal. His appointment to the Faculty of Arts was not ratified at once by the Board of the Royal Institution, and they intimated that they would not pay his salary. The Governors voted £300 a year and fuel for a Professor of Mathematics. As a result of the Board's contention that the Principal had not been regularly appointed, a commission or warrant of appointment was issued by the Governors on July 12th, and on the following day the Principal was appointed to be also Professor of Divinity, at a salary of £250, "as soon as funds derived from the property shall admit of it." A Bursar, Secretary and Registrar was appointed at a salary of £100 a year and fees, to be later sanctioned, and a Beadle was selected at £30 a year and fees and board.

A Code of Statutes, Rules and Regulations for the government of the College was now prepared by the Governors. Without the approval of the Board it was forwarded to the Governor-General for submission to the Crown for ratification. Six years passed before these Statutes, with slight alterations, received Royal sanction, with the result that the College opened without definite rules for its guidance. The reasons for this delay will be outlined elsewhere. It is only necessary to mention here that the first difficulty in connection with the Statutes arose from requirements connected with religious instruction in the University. Two of these, which were later disallowed by Her Majesty's Government, provided first, that "no Professor, Lecturer or Tutor shall teach in the College any principles contrary to the doctrines of the United Church of England and Ireland," and second, that "on every Sunday during the term, all the resident members of the University under the degree of B.C.L. who have not obtained a dispensation to the contrary, shall attend the morning service in the Protestant Episcopal Parish Church of Montreal." It was also stipulated that "the prayers in the College Chapel shall be said in rotation by such officers of the College as shall be in Holy Orders of the United Church of England and Ireland." These provisions, together with the fact that the acting-Principal, who was also Rector of Christ Church, had just been appointed Professor of Divinity, gave rise to critical discussion, and made Lord Metcalfe, the Governor-General, pause before advising the Colonial Office to obtain the Royal ratification of the Statutes. He wrote to Lord Stanley, "The main point involved in these questions is whether the Religious Instruction to be given at McGill College shall be exclusively that of the Church of England. . . .

"The grounds on which the Governors have adopted the affirmative of the proposition, and appointed a Divinity Professor of the Church of England, are ably stated in their letter to me. On the other hand, there are strenuous remonstrances against this arrangement on the part of the Ministers of the other Protestant persuasions in the Province, and a strong feeling against it in the community; and the design manifested to connect the Institution, in that respect, exclusively with the Church of England will most probably deprive it of that support from the Provincial Legislature without which it will necessarily be crippled. The opinions on this subject, understood to be prevalent in the Province, are likely to lead to discussions in the Legislature; and it may become necessary to modify the Institution so as to make it more suitable to public expectation and general utility. If, therefore, it rested with me to determine on this reference, I should be disposed, either to disallow the Professorship of Divinity, or to suspend the decision until it could be seen that the Institution can stand on the footing on which the Governors have placed it.

"I am, by the Charter, a Governor of the Institution, but have not acted in that capacity; at first, simply because more urgent business prevented my going to Montreal to take a part in the proceedings of the Governors; but subsequently, on reflection, for the following reasons:—I doubt the expediency of the Governor-General's taking a part as one of the Governors of an Institution in which he may be overruled by a majority, and apparently sanction measures which he disapproves. The perusal of the correspondence between the Governors of the College and the Royal Institution of Quebec satisfied me that I ought not to place myself in a position which would render me liable to become a party concerned in such a correspondence, and subject to the assumed authority and control of another Institution. The Income of the Institution having become a bone of contention between the Church of England and the other Protestant Churches, it appears to me to be right that I should perform my part as Governor-General without being embarrassed by proceedings to which I might be a party as a Governor of the College."

The action of the Governor-General was approved by Lord Stanley and consideration of the Statutes was consequently postponed.

In shaping the policy of the University the place of religious instruction and theological training received earnest consideration. On the necessity of including it in the College curriculum the Governors of the College and the Board of the Royal Institution agreed, but they differed on the nature of the instruction and on the theological creed which should dominate or dictate such teaching. It was recognised as a vexed question. The Governors attempted to explain and justify their attitude of alleged religious "exclusiveness" referred to above in Lord Metcalfe's despatch, and to give reasons for the Statutes already mentioned. The following extracts from a long and somewhat laboured letter forwarded by the Governors to Lord Metcalfe on July 15, 1843, are of interest. The arguments advanced in the letter and the frequent "begging of the question" need no comment. The Governors still pleaded for a Provincial grant, but they wished part, at least, of that public grant devoted to one exclusive form of theological teaching, and they were not averse to giving to the entire University a distinctively sectarian character.

"Another reason which compels us," they said, "to commence on a scale so limited, is the scantiness of our means. At present, the resources of the College, arising from the property bequeathed by the founder, supply only an annual income of £560 Provincial currency, and that not clear of deductions. The Legislature has occasionally appropriated £500 annually, in aid of these funds, and though we trust there can be no danger of this assistance being withdrawn, after the College shall have begun to be more extensively useful to the Province, yet, it is incumbent on us, to consider that even this small aid is not permanently assured to the University, and that to enable us to go beyond what we have now proposed, it will be necessary that the funds should be very considerably increased. . . . To meet the exigency of the present moment, we earnestly hope that the liberal suggestion, in which the late Governor-General concurred, will be acted upon with effect by Your Excellency and the Legislature, and with as little delay as may be consistent with the unspeakable importance of the object to be obtained. In Lower Canada, which is supposed to contain a population of not less than 800,000 souls, there is at present (except in regard to the Medical Faculty) no seat of Learning, either Catholic or Protestant, in which a Degree can be conferred in any Art or Science. This is a defect which, we believe, has not existed since the era of civilisation among so large a community of British subjects, and we very anxiously hope that from this moment no time may be lost in establishing McGill College upon such a footing as may command the confidence of the country, and enable the Institution, though indeed too tardily, to answer the purposes contemplated by its munificent founder. . . . There is one point (and it is the last) upon which, from the interest naturally and properly attached to it, we are aware much discussion may arise, and upon which, from its paramount importance, we desire, above all things, to be open and explicit.

"It will be found, on examination of the Statutes now submitted, that no test of a religious character is requisite, either from the Teachers or Scholars. Persons of any religious creed may, therefore, dispense instruction or receive it, except as regards religion itself, the College being equally open to all. But it will be found also that it is proposed to be distinctly made a Statute of the College, that no Professor, Lecturer or Tutor shall teach within it any principles contrary to the doctrines of the United Church of England and Ireland.

"We have not been able to bring ourselves to take part in the establishment of an Institution for the education of youth without making provisions for their Religious Instruction, and for inculcating as a duty the worship of their Creator. We have therefore made certain Statutes respecting the performance of, and attendance at, Divine Service, and we have established, so far as our power extends, a Professorship of Divinity in our College.

"Taking these provisions in connection with the Statutes which enjoins that nothing contrary to the doctrines of the United Church of England and Ireland shall be taught within the College, it follows obviously (and this we wish to be plainly understood) that the Divine Service to be performed, and the Professorship of Divinity to be established, will be of the Church of England, and of no other. But we have been careful at the same time to exempt from any necessity of attending Divine Service, or of being present at the Lectures on Divinity, all such Scholars, being members of other Religious Communities, as may desire a dispensation.

"Knowing the diversity of opinions entertained respecting the footing on which religious instruction should be placed in Seats of Learning, and how futile have been the efforts made to reconcile them, we came to the consideration of this subject with a dire sense of its difficulty, and with much anxiety that we should ourselves arrive at the soundest and best conclusion, and that our conclusion may, for the sake of the Institution and of the Province, be sanctioned by that authority to which under the Statutes it must be submitted. We offer no further arguments for the propriety of not leaving religious instruction and public worship unattended to, or inadequately provided for, in a College which is destined to conduct in a Christian country the education of youth at a period of life when they are most exposed to temptations, and when, if ever, the attempt should be made to furnish them with the highest and most sacred motives to the discharge of their religious and moral duties.

"We do not believe that there is, rationally speaking, a choice between the two alternatives, of omitting wholly to establish any system of religious instruction and public worship in the College, or of providing for it by placing the Institution in strict and acknowledged connection with some one recognised Church or form of doctrine. Not assenting to the former course, we have unanimously agreed on the latter, and we have in favour of the course we have adopted the examples of the Universities of the Mother Country, which have been for ages looked up to with undiminished confidence and respect. We have also in its support the acknowledged favour of an experiment made in England under many advantages to recommend it to public favour, an University established on other principles; and we have, in addition to this, the very strong arguments to be derived from the well supported and most useful Institutions of learning established in Lower Canada in strict connection with the Roman Catholic Church, and from the efforts made by the Roman Catholics, the Church of Scotland, and the Methodist Society to found Colleges in Upper Canada as closely connected with their respective religious bodies,—Colleges in which there is not only nothing taught contrary to their respective Creeds, but in which the whole government and business of the Institution is carefully confined to those who profess the one form of Doctrine.

"We have considered, too, that while these Religious Bodies, comprising together the great bulk of the population, have given this strong and plain evidence of their conviction that this system is the soundest, they have not thought it unreasonable to solicit the aid and countenance of the Government and the Legislature towards the establishment of such Colleges, and have not found their solicitations hopeless. So far as regards our Roman Catholic fellow-subjects, who form a great majority of the population in this portion of Canada, we do not apprehend that we shall be offending any prejudices of theirs, for we believe they would be as unwilling to throw impediments in the way of Institutions of Learning not intended to belong exclusively to their Church, as they would be reluctant to admit the interference of others in the management of their own valuable Seminaries where the exclusive maintenance of one form of doctrine and worship tends to secure in all respects the advantages of unity and peace.

"It then only remains, in the view which we have taken on the subject, that we should state shortly the reasons which have led us, where we thought a connection with some one Church should be established and acknowledged, to make that Church the Church of England.

"They are these:—1st. The founder, Mr. McGill, is silent in his will upon the subject of religion, and gave no direction to which these Statutes will be repugnant. He was himself a member of the Church of England, in communion with that Church.

We do not feel at liberty to imagine that he desired religious instruction to be excluded, and we think it reasonable to believe that in selecting some Church whose ministration should be recognised in the College which he intended to found, he would naturally have desired the choice to fall on that Church of which he was a member.

"2nd. The Charter which appoints us to be Governors declares that His Majesty desired the erection of this University in order to provide for the instruction of youth in the principles of true religion, as well as in the different branches of Science and Literature; and whatever may be the honest convictions of opposing Churches and Sects, we think it right to assume that when the Sovereign speaks of the principles of true religion, he means that which is the prevailing National Religion of the British Empire, and which he must himself have solemnly professed. We consider, therefore, that in placing McGill College on the footing proposed, we have taken the only course which we could satisfactorily account for, whatever may be the opinions or acts of others, whom it does not rest with us to control.

"3rd. While other religious communities have their separate Colleges closely connected with their form of doctrine and worship and partaking of public support, there is none in the Province of Canada which is bound by plain and acknowledged ties to the Church of England. We have felt it not to be unjust or illiberal to allow to the members of that Church this advantage so desirable to themselves in an Institution founded by the munificence of one of their communion while the youth of all other religious bodies may, in the discretion of themselves and their parents, resort to it for instruction in the several branches of Science, with the assurance that no attempt will be suffered to be made to bias their religious belief; and with the satisfaction at the same time of knowing, that whenever instruction in Religion may be desired, it cannot be uncertain in what form it will be conveyed.

"We hope that our fellow-subjects of all persuasions will view, without jealousy or alarm, the provisions which we have proposed to make on this subject, and that they will carry their liberality so far as to give efficient aid to an Institution, founded, as we believe, on the only principles of which reason and religion can approve,—namely, the principle of giving it a known and acknowledged religious character. At all events, we have not refrained from adopting that course which our judgment has led us to prefer; we have had no difficulty in resting in the conclusion which we have come to, and no difference of opinion among ourselves. It now rests with Her Majesty to dispose of these measures, which we humbly submit to the Royal consideration."

Her Majesty's Government, however, on the advice of the Governor-General, ultimately withheld their assent from the controversial clauses referred to.

Before the College was opened the Governors made a final effort to curtail the powers of the Board of the Royal Institution. They considered that with the erection of College buildings the duties of the Board in connection with the McGill bequest were at an end and that with any other buildings which might later be erected the Board was not concerned. They wrote to the Royal Institution and to the Governor-General setting forth their views. "If the Board's power is what is stated and assumed," they said, "it will not be possible for the Governors to attain the object of the Charter." They deplored the spirit in which the authority of the Board had been exercised. They assumed that James McGill intended his bequest to be administered by the Board only until buildings were erected and a Charter granted to a Corporate body, for the Board's control was primarily over grants from the Crown and not from private individuals. The Board had now, therefore, no legal existence, for the objects for which it had been created were gone. It was clearly apparent, in their judgment, that when he gave control of his bequest to the Board, James McGill thought public funds would be added to his gift; this, they believed, was proved by the stipulation of "ten years" after his death as the required term for the erection of the College; hence he had given his bequest to the Board simply and solely because they controlled public funds given for education. But practically no public funds had been regularly given; hence the Board's control automatically ceased.

It is unnecessary to follow here the Governors' subtle reasoning. They seem to have forgotten the Provincial funds granted from the Jesuits' Estates, and to be unmindful of the fact that they were at that very moment still pleading for a Provincial grant, as indicated in the letter quoted above. They justly emphasised, however, the necessity of providing a convenient power of management within the College itself and the ending of the dual control. It was absurd, they rightly contended, that every cent expended for a piece of stove pipe or a chair should be first approved by the Board. The Governors resented, too, the visitatorial power of the Royal Institution. "In what spirit," they asked, "and for what purpose do they carry out the right of visitation?" Such power was useful, they declared, only for the purpose of interposing in the minutest details of the management of McGill College, although a Corporation and a board of Governors existed for that purpose; the Royal Institution, in short, was, in its connection with McGill, nothing more than "a source of interference and impediment," and the Governors asked that the Legislature should investigate the whole situation with a view to remedying it. This appeal, like the others, failed to make any impression on the authorities, and the causes of friction were not removed.

In this atmosphere of discord and dissension and disputed powers the College buildings were opened on September 6th, 1843, and collegiate instruction was at last commenced in accordance with the founder's bequest. Twenty-two years had passed since the College had been established by Charter, and fourteen years had gone since its actual opening. They were years of doubt and uncertainty, of protracted litigation and differences, even of virulent wrangling and bitter strife. But amidst it all and in the face of all its obstacles, the College had gone slowly but steadily forward. Its sign-posts had pointed onward. Reading to-day the troubled pages of its early story revealed in a mass of musty documents written by hands long since folded, or dictated by voices long since stilled,—which then helped to shape its destiny,—we wonder how it survived. The explanation lies in the fact that the men who guided it, whether

of Governors or of Royal Institution, were men of
unfaltering faith; they believed in the future of Mc-
Gill; amidst their disagreements and their contro-
versies, they never lost sight of the founder's hope
although their ways for the fulfilment of that hope
lay often painfully apart.   From the struggles of its
early years McGill now emerged to be an established
fact.   The first of its buildings, the present Arts or
Centre Building, had been erected and opened.   The
College had at last an actual home.   But the days
of its travail and its worry, its poverty and its depression, its fight for life itself, had not yet passed.

CHAPTER VI

The College in the First McGill Buildings

THE original College buildings were opened for the reception and instruction of students on September 6th, 1843. Only twenty regular students were in attendance during the first session, seventeen of whom took the Classical course and three the Mathematical course. Steps were at once taken to provide an adequate collegiate education as called for in the founder's will, and to organise the teaching and administration on as extensive and sound a basis as the available funds would permit. A few books and some scanty school equipment were received from the Normal School recently closed. The fees of students were fixed at £5 a year, of which £1 13s. 4d. was assigned to the Senior Professor as his portion, 6s. 8d. to the Bursar, and the remaining £3 to the "House Fund." In addition, each student paid to the Registrar who was also Secretary and Bursar, a matriculation fee of 10 shillings which that official was allowed to keep for his own use. The fees were reduced a few months later to £3, of which the House Fund received £2 13s. 4d., and the Bursar 6s. 8d. Students under fourteen years of age and over eighteen were not allowed to matriculate into the ordinary classes except in very exceptional cases. The matriculation examination was at first mainly in Latin and Greek

Grammar and the 1st Book of Cæsar's Commentaries. Students who failed to pass this examination were allowed to enter the College and were formed into a separate class. They paid an additional entrance fee of 10 shillings and an annual fee of £2, for which they were not to expect the attention given to other students. Students over eighteen were permitted to enter as "Fellow Commoners," and were allowed the special privilege of dining at "the high table." They paid a double matriculation fee, and their ordinary fee was twenty-five per cent higher than that of other students. For a brief time only there was a common dining-room, but because of financial storm and stress and the necessity for additional room this was in the end abandoned and the students boarded with the professors who had rooms in the College. Indeed, the willingness to accept students as boarders seems, in some cases at least, to have been a condition of appointment, and little choice in the matter was left to the professor. It was decided that all examinations for degrees should be held "within the walls of the College in the presence of all the officers of the University and College," and that every candidate for a medical degree "must forward his inaugural dissertation to the Principal before the last day of March."

Soon after the opening of the building, Principal Bethune and the Governors looked about for additional professors or instructors or tutors. In negotiating with prospective tutors it was pointed out that "no gentleman would be elected to a Tutorship who was not able to translate fluently the works of Horace, Xenophon, and Heroditus, together with the other Classical authors of that stamp; and that an examination of all candidates would be held." One candidate inquired about rooms in the College for himself and his wife, but the Vice-Principal replied, "I must inform you that there will be no accommodation for your wife in the College at present, but that you will yourself be expected to reside within the College. The Tutor is not allowed his board during the long vacation." In February, 1844, William Wickes, M.A., a graduate of Trinity College, Cambridge, was appointed Professor of Mathematics and Natural Philosophy. He was promised £20 to defray his travelling expenses "as soon as it can be paid." Mr. E. Chapman was appointed Tutor, at a salary of £100 a year payable, it was hoped, from students' fees, and his board and lodging; and the Rev. Dr. Fallon was appointed Lecturer in Divinity.

Because of the shortage of funds it was decided that no further appointments could then be made and that only absolutely necessary expenses should be incurred. A valuable lot of scientific instruments, which would be of use in the Natural Philosophy classes, was offered to the College "for £70 if paid in six months, or £81 4s. 6d. if paid after that time." The Secretary replied that "they would take the instruments but they could not name any period of payment." The Governors were sorely pinched for funds during this first year, and the anxieties of poverty pressed hard upon the College authorities. In January, 1844, the Governors made a formal demand for the payment of expenses incurred by them amounting to £1,736, and also for the payment of all monies in the Board's possession. The Board had but little money at their disposal and they refused to grant the Governors' request. The gross annual income was then scarcely more than £500, while the salaries and fixed charges amounted annually to £730. The Board accused the Governors of having made "wasteful and extravagant expenditures without precedent or principle," some of which did not appear to have any connection with the opening or the carrying on of McGill; many of these, they said, were wholly unnecessary, and had never been authorised by the Board, whose consent had not even been asked.. The expenditures for contingencies alone, it was pointed out, amounted in five months to more than the total income of three years. "It is obvious," the Secretary added, "that the Governors and the Board entertain views entirely opposite as to the nature of the trust committed to the Board and to the duties which that trust imposes. . . . There can be no proper understanding between the Board and the Governors until it can be authoritatively settled which view of the duties and the functions of the Board is right according to law. The Board has no desire to retain funds to which they have no right." In November, 1844, application was accordingly made to the Law Offices of the Crown for a decision, but as usual the decision was slow in coming. But pending the decision the Board agreed to liquidate the legal debts as far as they were able and they did so to the extent of £1,550. By so doing the Board reluctantly sacrificed a part of the capital of the trust and thereby diminished by £90 the annual income, which was already insufficient. But this payment was only a temporary relief; the debt was in reality over £2,500; other and larger accounts remained unpaid, and liabilities continued to increase.

In May, 1844, in order to make the academic

management of the College more democratic, the Governors made provision for the formation of a College Board which should hold weekly meetings. As early as 1841 the Board of the Royal Institution had recommended the formation of a College Council "for the ordinary exercise of discipline," consisting of the Principal, the Vice-Principal and Professors, the Rector of Christ Church, Montreal, and the Minister of the Church of Scotland, Montreal. This recommendation was not considered, pending the actual opening of the College buildings. The College Board now formed consisted of "the Principal, the Vice-Principal, Professors, and (until the whole number of Professors in the University be increased to six) the Lecturers in the Faculties in Divinity and the Arts, not under the degree of M.A., and of the person holding the office of Secretary, Registrar and Bursar, provided he shall be a graduate of some University in the British Dominions and not under the degree of M.A." This Board was called "the Caput"; two of the members, with the Principal or Vice-Principal, constituted a quorum. Its duty was to frame rules and regulations for the discipline and internal government of Lecturers, students and "inferior officers" of the College, to supervise the system of living within the College, and to consider applications for degrees, except honorary degrees. It had no jurisdiction over the Medical School.

The period that followed was a period of critical wrestling with financial troubles. The College was suffering from lack of funds. Part of the cost of the erection of the buildings was yet unpaid. An action was instituted against the Governors on ac-

count of the College furniture, the payment for
which was long in arrears. Tradesmen and work-
men were pressing for a settlement of their bills,
and lawyers' letters threatening suits were daily coming in. The salaries of Professors were not paid,
and in January, 1845, only £250 was given by the
Board to pay the combined yearly salaries of Professors, Tutors and Bursar. The Vice-Principal's
allowance of fuel for the entire year was reduced to
"30 cords of maple wood and 2 chaldrons of coal."
Frequently appeals were made to the Home Government for assistance, but the authorities disagreed in
their opinions on the actual state of the College.
They had little first-hand knowledge of the facts,
and their attitude was one of indifference or at least
delay. Lord Stanley wrote from the Colonial Office:
"I cannot but regret that the circumstances of this
Institution should have hitherto prevented the Province from deriving the benefit which its founder
contemplated; and as the chief obstacle at present
consists in the want of funds, I am of opinion that
measures should be taken to procure the requisite
assistance from the Legislature." On the other
hand, Lord Metcalfe, the Governor-General, replied,
"The financial prospects of the Institution appear to
be more promising than was formerly anticipated."
There the matter for the time ended, and while the
authorities waited and differed, the future existence
of the College was in grave doubt.

It was apparent, too, that internal dissension was
growing within the College itself. Charges in connection with the administration and with the Principal's management were laid before the Royal Institution by the Vice-Principal, who seems to have

had the support of certain other College officers, including Professor Wickes, and the Tutor, Chapman. As a result of these charges, combined with the hopeless financial situation in which the College was floundering, the Board of the Royal Institution determined to exercise their visitatorial power and to make an investigation. They would examine the entire working of the College, its discipline, its administration and also the methods of collecting and expending the rents and profits of the Estate of which no adequate accounting had for some time been received. The visitation was made on the 13th and 14th of November, 1844, and the meetings, not always peaceful, were held in the council-room of the College. The Visitors found that there were five Professors or Instructors, while only nine students were enrolled in the college, that there was a lack of harmony among the College officers, "some of whom were not on speaking terms with each other," and that the outlook was not promising.

The following official report was forwarded to Lord Metcalfe, the Governor-General, by the Lord Bishop of Montreal, the Rev. Dr. Mountain, Principal of the Royal Institution, on December 11th, 1844:

"The Board of the Royal Institution, at the request of Professor Lundy, Vice-Principal of McGill College, and in consequence of a variety of circumstances leading them to believe such a step expedient and necessary, met at Montreal on the 14th November, and, as Visitors of McGill College under the Royal Charter, entered into an examination of the whole affairs of that Institution.

"The general result of their investigation they are

now desirous to lay before Your Excellency, both because it is to Your Excellency's interposition that the Board look for obtaining certain important measures, which appear to them indispensable to the prosperity of the College of which they are Visitors and Trustees.

"When the visitation of McGill College took place the Visitors found in it nine students (fewer by half than at the same period last year, and these, with one or two exceptions, boys) under the tuition of a Principal, who is also Professor of Divinity, a Lecturer on Divinity, a Vice-Principal, who is also Professor of Classical Literature, a Professor of Mathematics, and a Classical Tutor; the establishment having also the services of a Bursar, a Beadle and others. The regular expenditure for the College Establishment in salaries and contingent charges is twofold of the income applicable to it; and the Governors have contracted a debt of £1,550 in opening the College, the various items of which expenditure appeared to the Board to be on a scale of extravagance and wastefulness entirely unsuitable to the pecuniary resources of the Institution. There is a great want of cordiality and harmony among the Professors and Officers of the College; some not even speaking to others. There are no Statutes in operation which are binding in Law.

"The Principal refused to acknowledge the authority of the Visitors, or to furnish them with any information. The united testimony of the College Officers induces the Board to believe that one main reason of the College having received so little support is that the acting-Principal does not enjoy that confidence on the part of the public of which an individual, standing in his position, ought to be possessed. . . .

"The Board also had the testimony of the College Officers that the inefficiency and unpopularity of the College are also, in part, owing to the general want of confidence, rightly or wrongly entertained, in the Vice-Principal, Professor Lundy.

"The Bursar is the Rev. Mr. Abbott, who has a Salary of £100 a year, and is permitted to do his duty by Deputy. He does not, he says, understand accounts; nor do those of his Deputy appear to be regularly and correctly kept.

"There are only two Governors resident in Montreal—the Chief Justice of the District, and Dr. Bethune, who is a Governor in consequence of his holding the interim appointment of Principal. The other Governors, who occasionally act, are the Chief Justice of Upper Canada, and the Bishop of Montreal, both too distant from the College to take much part in the management of its affairs, and the latter having only very recently a title to do so. The Chief Justice of Montreal is unwilling, as a Roman Catholic, to interfere more than he can avoid in the government of a Protestant Institution; and the practical result of this state of things in the governing body is to throw almost the whole management of the Institution into the hands of Dr. Bethune, the acting-Principal. Both the resident Governors resisted the authority of the Visitors, and refused to co-operate with them.

"Between the Governors and the Board of the Royal Institution certain differences do also exist in respect of the possession of the funds of the College, now held in trust by the Board. The Governors are of opinion that such funds should be unreservedly handed over to them. The Royal Institution, acting on the opinion of eminent Counsel, and holding that in this course they are supported by manifest expediency, as well as Law, decline to make such transfer. The knowledge of the Public that such differences exist is also stated as one ground of the want of public confidence in the Institution.

"A more full and accurate account of the whole investigation, contained in the Minutes of the Board, is herewith respectfully submitted for Your Excellency's information; but such, we have to state to Your Excellency, is generally the disorderly and inefficient state of an Institution from which the public looked, and were justly entitled to look, for great benefits.

"The remedy for existing evils is, it appears to the Board of Visitors, to be sought in various quarters. In part, it rests with the Board itself to apply a remedy; and, in so far, they are prepared to act without delay.

"The differences between the Board and the Governors may be settled by an amicable suit in a Court of Law; or by the opinion of the Law Officers of the Crown. The Board have repeatedly expressed to the Governors their desire to have the matter so decided.

"And the debts of the Institution the Board are also prepared to liquidate, though in doing so they must of necessity trench deeply on the capital in their possession.

"And the changes of the Institution itself, which the Board consider necessary, and which it is more immediately the province of the Governors to effect, are these:

"1st.   To obtain the services of an able and efficient Principal, possessing the public confidence, who should reside in the College, and take an active part in the education of the students.

"2ndly. To dispense with the Office of Vice-Principal altogether, which, in that case, would be unnecessary, and to confine Professor Lundy's duties entirely to the work of Classical Instruction.

"3rdly. To dispense with the Office of Bursar, and require the nowise onerous duties thereof to be performed by some of the Resident Officers of the College.

"4thly. To dispense with the services of a Classical Tutor till the attendance of students render them necessary, which, at present, is manifestly not the case.

"Preparatory, however, to these changes, and without which, indeed, they cannot be carried into effect, there needs, the Board would humbly represent, an interposition of Her Majesty's Government for the removal of the present Principal, and for an addition to the number of Governors resident in Montreal.

"The Board of Visitors believe they are by Law entitled to remove the Principal from his Office on the sole ground of his contumacy in refusing to appear before them; and they have restrained from depriving him of his Office by their own authority, simply by a consideration of the still greater disorder which must have been the result of the College.

"The Board of Visitors would, however, represent

to Your Excellency that, in their judgment, such removal is indispensable to the well-being of the College; and that as Dr. Bethune was never appointed, except temporarily, and his appointment has never received the necessary sanction of Her Majesty's Government; if that sanction were refused, the office would be forthwith vacant, and it would be competent for the Governors to appoint an able and efficient Principal in his stead.

"Even such removal, however, would serve but little purpose, greatly as the Board believe it would contribute to restore public confidence, unless an addition were made to the number of Governors resident in Montreal. If three or four enlightened and intelligent men were united in the government of this institution, who, from their residence in Montreal, could give a fair share of their attention to its interests, the most beneficial consequences might be expected; and the public confidence would be greater if, in the selection of these Governors, regard should be had to different Protestant bodies in the Provinces, none of which (except by such limitation as may be conceived to be included in the words 'sound religion') are, by any Clause, either of Mr. McGill's will, or of the Royal Charter, excluded from the Offices, Honours, or Benefits of the College.

"May it therefore please Your Excellency to use your influence with Her Majesty's Government to refuse to sanction Dr. Bethune's appointment, and to give, as speedily as possible, a Supplementary Charter, making an addition to the number of resident Governors in Montreal. The Board are persuaded that the result of such action on the part of Her Majesty's Government would be to rescue the College from its present disorderly and inefficient state, and to render it, according to the intentions of the benevolent founder, a public benefit."

Against the justice of this report the Governors entered a vigorous and emphatic protest. They denied the right of the Royal Institution as Visitors to investigate College conditions. They contended that McGill University was a private foundation, and as such might only be "visited by the legal representatives of James McGill and not by the Sovereign Lady the Queen, her heirs or successors, or by any person or body appointed by the Crown as supposed and assumed in the Royal Charter incorporating the College." As the Statutes had not yet been approved, they forwarded at the same time a resolution to the Colonial Office declaring that "the College being a private foundation has the undoubted right and power as such to make its own Statutes, Rules, etc.," and that they would therefore no longer wait for the Royal sanction. They also made representations to the Legislative Assembly asking support for their contention that "the provision of the Charter by which the right of the Crown is reserved to disallow the appointments made by the Governors is an assumption of power inconsistent with the very nature of the Foundation and is absolutely null and void in Law." They sought legal means for obtaining from the Royal Institution all rights and titles to the properties and monies in their possession belonging to McGill University. Their main argument was that the University was a "private institution." But their protests were of no avail.

The Governors then summarily dismissed the Vice-Principal and Professor of Classics, the Rev.

F. J. Lundy, mainly because of the allegations he had made before the Royal Institution. His dismissal caused further trouble, not, however, without its lighter side. Dr. Lundy appealed to the Royal Institution from the Governors' decision. In his petition he suggested that the Governors who dismissed him were not a representative body and that their action was illegal. He stated that "the Chief Justice of Montreal and the Rev. John Bethune, *two* of the Governors of McGill College, did proceed to hold a special meeting in the parlor of the residence of the Chief Justice and not at the College; that . . . without previous summons or notification he was there informed . . . [on being called in] that his further services were not required in the College, and that he was accordingly dismissed . . . without any semblance of a trial or investigation. . . . That on asking for an explanation he was informed that no explanation would be rendered and that he would not be allowed a hearing in the matter." With his appeal the Royal Institution, in the absence of Statutes and Rules, was powerless to deal. Dr. Lundy was dismissed on the 4th of January, 1845. He was allowed to retain his rooms in the College until May 1st "because of the inconvenience to his family of moving in winter," but he was considered "as removed on and after the day of his dismissal." In June he was still occupying his College rooms, and he was told by the Governors to vacate them or he would be ejected in fourteen days. In July he was still there, and the Governors again told him that if he was not out at the end of two days they would remove him, "using no more force than might be necessary for that purpose." He went; and the controversy ended.

Professor Wickes then became Vice-Principal, but he retired two years afterwards. Chapman, the Tutor, became Lecturer in Classics, but he retired a few weeks later. His salary was long in arrears and he could not collect it, and when he left he had to be content with a return of the money he had expended "in making a window into a door in his room." The Beadle was also dismissed, and the entire personnel of the College officers was soon changed. Other appointments were made and were approved by the Royal Institution. In making the appointments provision was made for "a Librarian," and the Rev. Joseph Abbott was selected as the first Librarian of McGill at the beginning of 1845. The Royal Institution considered the Governors' actions to be growing daily more drastic and intolerable, and they urged the Home Government to take steps to end the struggle between the two bodies. On January 13th the Lord Bishop of Montreal, the Rev. Dr. Mountain, who had meanwhile become one of the Governors of the University, again wrote to the Governor-General, Lord Metcalfe, as follows:

"It is with extreme unwillingness that I obtrude upon Your Excellency, with the purpose of their being submitted if you should see fit, to Her Majesty's Principal Secretary of State for the Colonies, any representation relating to the affairs of McGill College, in addition to those which are already before you from other quarters; and it is with feelings of a nature more seriously painful that I find myself compelled to state to Your Excellency the conviction at which I have arrived, of its being inexpedient for me to take my seat at the Board of Governors of that institution so long as the Rev. Dr. Bethune, in virtue of his acting as Principal of the College, is also a member of the Board.

"Your Excellency will readily believe that unless I had strong and what I conceive to be imperative grounds for my proceeding, one of the last things which I could possibly be prompted to do would be to bring under the notice of Her Majesty's Government any disadvantageous exhibition of the management of important public interests in the hands of one of my own Clergy, and one who occupies so prominent a position in the Canadian Church as the Rector of Montreal.

"I have, however, long felt that the College could never prosper while presided over by Dr. Bethune. And I should have been impelled before this day officially to submit my views upon the subject to Your Excellency had it not been that I had no seat among the Governors till after the passing of the Act of the last Session, which confers upon me, as Bishop of Montreal, all the legal powers vested in the Bishop of Quebec; and, moreover, that having all along regarded the appointment of Dr. Bethune simply as an ad interim arrangement (in which I believe there are abundant means of showing that I was perfectly correct) I anticipated that his retirement would have taken place in time to save me from the necessity of making official statements, from which it is sufficiently obvious that I must desire to be spared.

"When, however, I consider the general character of Dr. Bethune's proceedings in those matters con-

nected with McGill College which it has devolved
upon him to conduct, or in which he has taken a leading part, and more especially in the intercourse of
business with the Royal Institution for the Advancement of Learning; when I consider again his too
evident deficiency in very important points of qualification for his office, such as academical experience
(for he never studied at any University), actual
classical attainments of the nature and extent which
the case requires, and I am constrained to add, such
temper, such discretion, and such weight of personal
influence and possession of public confidence, as must
be necessary on the part of the Principal, to preside
with effect over an infant University in a country
like this, or to execute his part in recovering it from
the utterly inefficient and discreditable condition in
which it now lies, I am brought to the unavoidable
conclusion not only that his appointment ought not
to be confirmed, but that every delay in the disallowance of it opens a door to some new mischief within
the Institution; more particularly as the powers committed to the body of Governors, in something more
than their mere ordinary exercise, are, from peculiar-
ity of circumstances, in a manner left in his hands.
The long continued ill health and infirmity of the
Chief Justice of Montreal, the consequent seclusion
in which he lives, and the fact of his not having either
the sort of interest in the Institution or the opportunities of familiarly knowing the relations subsist-
ing between Dr. Bethune and other parties concerned
which he would naturally have if he were of the
Protestant religion, appear, I may venture to say it,
to justify the conclusion that the proceedings of the
Governors resident at Montreal are to be regarded

as little or nothing more than the decisions and acts of the individual filling the office of Principal, at the same time that they have in several instances involved a result of which I can hardly be persuaded that two Governors were sufficient to dispose. These proceedings have been recently crowned by the summary dismissal, without a hearing, of the Vice-Principal and Professor of Classical Literature, under circumstances with which Your Excellency, as I am informed, has recently been made acquainted. I feel that I am now called upon to state to Your Excellency both as the Head of the Body of Governors, whenever you may see fit to take part in their proceedings, and also as the Head of the Government, that till Dr. Bethune shall cease to occupy a place at the Board of Governors I must abstain from attending it, persuaded as I am that I cannot do so either with the hope of advantage to the public or with comfort to myself.

"With reference to the question intimated above, respecting the competency of two Governors to dispose of some matters such as have actually been disposed of by that number only, Your Excellency is aware that the number to whom the wisdom of Government had originally within their particular province confided the interests of the College was seven, and comprised the highest functionaries of Upper and Lower Canada : and I conceive it to be necessary for those interests, not to say for the very existence of McGill College, that an efficient Body of Governors should, as soon as possible, be given to the Institution.

"I have only to add, although it is not within the more immediate scope of the representations here

submitted, that the observations which I have made
with reference to the inexpediency of Dr. Bethune's
retention of the office of Principal, will manifestly
suggest reasons of at least equal force against the
confirmation of his appointment to the Professorship
of Divinity."

This communication was forwarded by the Governor-General to the Colonial Office, but over a year
passed before definite action in connection with it
was taken by the authorities.

Meanwhile the Governors carried on the work of
the University, harassed always by debts and by
insufficient revenue. The Medical School now sought
a closer union with the University. Its connection
with the College since the latter's establishment had
been more or less nominal; it was at least indefinitely
hazy, other than in the mere fact that it was "engrafted," and in the imprimatur of its degrees.
Since its request for a grant from University funds
six years before was refused, there was little actual
intercourse or connection between the two bodies.
They worked, on the whole, independently, although
the legal incorporation of one with the other was
recognized. The Medical School had carried on its
work in temporary quarters. It had begun its work
in 1824 in a building at 20 St. James Street, on Place
d'Armes. Its Statutes, Rules, etc., had been approved, as already seen, in 1832. About a year later
the School was moved to a larger building near the
present Bank of Montreal, where it remained for
more than two years. It then was again moved to
a building on St. George Street, not far from the
corner of Craig Street. In 1843 the Medical Faculty
applied to the Governors for a piece of ground on

the Burnside Estate, near the recently erected Mc-
Gill buildings, "for the purpose of erecting lecture
rooms." The request was granted and the giving of
sufficient ground was approved by the Royal Institution. But like the College, the Medical School had
no funds. The grant asked for from the Provincial
Government by the Board of the Royal Institution to
help "in bringing the Faculties of Law, Theology and
Medicine into actual operation," and partly promised, had in the end been refused. The Royal Institution, as we have seen, did not feel justified in giving
the Medical School assistance from the funds already
inadequate to provide for Collegiate education, as
called for in the bequest. As a result, although
ground for a building was willingly given, the erection of a building had to be indefinitely postponed.
The Medical Faculty then applied for permission to
use any rooms that might be available in the College
buildings. On September 16th, 1845, the Governors
agreed—and the Royal Institution later approved
their action—to give the Medical School the refectory or dining-room for its exclusive use—as the
students were now for the most part boarding with
Professors or outside the College—together with the
southwest lecture-room as a lecture-room and museum, the private room of the Bursar for the Professors' office, and two small adjoining rooms "for
anatomy and dissecting rooms." Medical students,
too, were to be permitted to reside in the College,
on condition that they were to be under the same
discipline as the College students. The Medical
Faculty accordingly moved to these rooms provided
in the McGill buildings, and a closer contiguous connection with the University was thereby established.

There the Faculty remained until 1851, when because of its growth and the inconvenient distance from the city and the Hospital, it moved to the building at 15 Cote Street, erected for its use by three of the members of its staff.

Efforts were made to increase the attendance in the College and students from the French-Canadian Colleges were admitted to equal standing with McGill students. The need for funds became gradually more acute. The Royal Institution would not listen to the Governors' demands for the payment of salaries and contingent expenses. In December, 1845, they again appealed to the Governor-General, Lord Metcalfe, but he declined to interfere, pointing out that the Royal Institution were the trustees of the Trust; that all the Statutes, Rules, etc., of the College should be confirmed by Royal authority before they became law; and that as the statutes under the authority of which debts had been contracted by the Governors of McGill had never received Royal sanction, these debts had no effect in law. The Governors were therefore themselves liable. But the Governors had already borrowed £500 from the Bank of British North America to meet necessary and vital requirements. That amount had not yet been paid off, and they naturally were not disposed to assume the responsibility for further personal indebtedness.

All the correspondence in connection with the whole situation, in addition to the various petitions and appeals, was forwarded to the Colonial Office, with which the Rt. Hon. W. E. Gladstone had meanwhile become connected as Secretary of State for the Colonies. It was hoped that Mr. Gladstone would display more interest and energy than his predecessors, and that a decision would soon be reached. The College authorities expected that the Provincial Legislature would be asked to make an investigation by Committee. Accordingly, on April 15th, 1846, they issued instructions "forbidding officers and members of the College from answering any summons from a Committee of the Legislative Assembly acting on the petitions of Chapman, Wickes or Lundy." The excuse for not answering was that "McGill College was a private foundation and was therefore not liable to the action of the Legislature." But their expectations were not realized and no investigation was held by the Assembly.

It was clear, however, that action was soon to be taken by the Colonial Office; the Governors were not aware of the precise nature of the action, but they felt that the Home Government would support the Royal Institution. Before the decision was received, a final effort was made to give to the University a more pronounced character of "religious exclusiveness," a tendency which the Governor-General had already deplored. In October, 1845, this desire had been indicated by the making of a rule requiring that prayers in the College were to be said "by a College Chaplain appointed by the Governors, or by any other person appointed or approved by the Principal, he to be a member of the Church of England"; a sum of £50 was voted for such Chaplain. On April 25, 1846, at a meeting attended by two Governors—the Chief Justice of Montreal and the Principal, and two Fellows—the Rev. J. Ramsay and the Rev. J. Abbott, it was resolved on motion of the Principal to ask that the

Charter be amended in the following particulars:
"That the Governors of the College consist henceforth of all the clergy of the Church of England
now holding or who may hereafter hold preferment
in the Parish of Montreal, and of a certain number
of laymen of the Church of England resident in the
aforesaid Parish to be named in the Charter. That
vacancies occasioned by the death, resignation, etc.,
of any of the lay Governors shall be filled up from
time to time by the majority of the Governors present at a meeting. That the Bishop of the Diocese
shall be the Visitor of the College. That appointments to office in the College are not to be subject
to disallowance by any other authority than that of
the Governors. That the Statutes, Rules, and Ordinances made by the Governors are to be in full
force and effect until disallowed by the Judges of the
Court of Queen's Bench for the District of Montreal. That a committee be appointed to draft a
petition to Her Majesty the Queen with reference
to this resolution, the Committee to consist of the
Principal, the Vice-Principal, and the Professor of
Classical Literature." The Professor of Classical
Literature was then the Rev. W. T. Leach, who had
been appointed on April 4th preceding. The Vice-
Principal was the Rev. J. Abbott.

A few days later, and before this resolution could
be acted on, however, Mr. Gladstone's despatch
disallowing Principal Bethune's appointment and
asking for his retirement was received. In forwarding it to the Secretary of McGill on April 24th, 1846,
the Civil Secretary wrote: "I have only to add
the expression of the hope that the Governors will
forthwith proceed to replace Dr. Bethune and that

in so doing they will anxiously endeavour to secure the services of a man in all respects qualified for such important posts." Mr. Gladstone's despatch, which embodied in the main the suggestions of the Lord Bishop of Montreal, the Rev. Dr. Mountain, quoted above, was written on April 3rd, 1846, and was as follows:

"I have had under my serious consideration your Lordship's confidential Despatch of the 19th of February, on the subject of McGill College at Montreal, and in connection with it I have reviewed the copious correspondence which passed between your Lordship's predecessor and Lord Stanley on this question. I have observed with great regret the state of disorder and inefficiency in which the Institution appears to be.

"The question which has appeared to me to call for my immediate decision is that of the continuance in the office of Principal of the College, and in the Professorship of Divinity, of the present holder, the Reverend Dr. Bethune, whose appointment it is still competent for the Crown, according to the Charter of the College, to disallow.

"It is with regret that I have come to the conclusion that it is my duty to recommend to Her Majesty to disallow this appointment.

"Into the various and somewhat complicated charges which have been brought against Dr. Bethune, in his capacity of Principal of the College, I do not find it necessary to enter; nor do I wish to state at the present moment any decided opinion as to the extent to which the present condition of the Institution is owing to the character and position of its Principal. My decision is founded upon rea-

sons which are not open to dispute; the first, the
weight of the Bishop's authority, together with your
own, independently of any reference to that of the
Board of Visitors, which may be considered to be to
some extent at this moment in dispute; next, the fact
that Dr. Bethune did not himself receive an University education, which I must hold to be, unless
under circumstances of the rarest occurrence, an indispensable requisite for such a position as he occupies. To these I am disposed to add, although I
express the opinion without having had the advantage of learning what may be the view of the Lord
Bishop in this particular, that I cannot think it expedient that the offices of Principal and Professor
of Divinity in McGill College should be combined
with that of Rector of Montreal. This latter circumstance is not much adverted to in the papers before me; but I am strongly impressed with the incon-
gruity of this junction of important collegiate
appointments with a no less important pastoral
charge in the same person; either the former or the
latter of which, especially considering the large population of the Town of Montreal, I must, as at present
advised, hold to be enough to occupy his individual
attention.

"I have, therefore, felt bound to advise Her
Majesty to disallow this appointment in both respects, in pursuance of the power vested in her; and
have only to add the expression of my hope that the
Governors will forthwith proceed to replace Dr.
Bethune, and that in so doing they will anxiously
endeavour to secure the services of a man in all
respects qualified for such important posts.

"With regard to the general position of the College, there are indeed many points as to its Constitution, its Laws, its Revenues, and its Administration which obviously require a careful consideration and an early and definitive settlement; among which perhaps the most prominent is the confirmation, or otherwise, of the Statutes which have for some time been awaiting the decision of the Crown. But adverting to the course adopted by Lord Stanley, and to the information received from your Lordship's predecessor, with particular reference to the Despatches noted in the margin, I have resolved to suspend any active measure on my part, at least till the conclusion of the present session of the Canadian Legislature, thinking it not improbable that the proceedings of that body may tend to throw some light on the questions connected with the College, by which I may be guided in the consideration of my own course in this important matter."

As a result of the above despatch, Dr. Bethune retired from the acting-Principalship in May following. On July 3rd he protested in a memorial to the Colonial Office against the legality of the act of the Home Government in the disallowing of his appointment, but no action was taken by the authorities, and there the matter dropped.

Dr. Bethune did not give up the acting-Principalship, which he had filled for eleven years, without the regrets and the tributes of men who had been closely associated with him during his term of office. The Chief Justice of Montreal, the Hon. James Reid, one of the Governors of the College, had already written to him on February 13th, 1845, not long before his death:

"I am enabled to say that after your appointment

From Painting in McGill Library   Photo Rice Studios

Venerable Archdeacon Leach
D.C.L., L.L.D.,
Vice-Principal of McGill University
1846-1886

as Principal the interests of the College, which had previously been much obstructed and delayed, were more closely pursued and attended to, principally by your exertions, your declared object being to bring the College into operation as soon as possible, and to render all the means belonging to it available for this purpose."

On May 11th, 1846, after Mr. Gladstone's despatch had been received, and Dr. Bethune was about to leave the College, the Rev. John Abbott, the Vice-Principal and Secretary, and E. Chapman, formerly Lecturer in Classical Literature, whose relations with the Principal had not always been harmonious, wrote as follows:

"We, the undersigned Officers of the University of McGill College, from our personal knowledge, as far as we have been respectively connected with it, do hereby certify that the Reverend John Bethune, D.D., has performed the duties of his Office of Principal of this Institution with a zeal, ability, and moderation only equalled by his patient and enduring perseverance, under circumstances of great and harassing difficulty; and that the opening and establishing of the College, and consequently its very existence, are mainly to be ascribed, as we verily believe, to his active and indefatigable exertions."

To this letter the Rev. W. T. Leach, who had been appointed Professor of Classical Literature on April 4th preceding, added:

"My connection with McGill College has been of very recent date, and I have no objection to add my testimony to the above."

It was also certified by the Bursar, the Rev. John Abbott, that the Principal was jointly responsible with the Chief Justice of Montreal for £500 borrowed from the Bank of British North America, and for £100 for outbuildings; that he was personally responsible for a debt of £120 for fuel, which "by his own individual means and credit he had obtained and provided for the College while the funds belonging to it were withheld during a considerable period." These liabilities, however, were all liquidated later by the Royal Institution.

The eleven years that had passed since the acting-Principal assumed office were among the most critical in McGill's history. They were fraught with a hopeless misunderstanding arising from a dual control, the causes of which have been made sufficiently clear in the documents quoted. The Governors resented the interference of the Royal Institution, which in those days of advocacy of political autonomy and sensitive abhorrence of Downing Street coercion they could not easily tolerate. It was contrary to the spirit of the age. Whether the Governors helped their cause by their attitude or by their attempt to give to the College a character of sectarian exclusiveness need not be here discussed. They had, however, urged the actual erection and equipment of a College, and it was in a large measure because of their persistence and their faith that the original buildings were so early constructed. They had the good fortune to see the buildings actually opened, students enrolled and collegiate instruction commenced in accordance with the will of the founder. They saw, too, the Medical School made an integral part of the University.

And the controversy in which they had so prominent and at times so painful a part, although unfor-

tunate in many ways, had at least one good result—
it showed plainly and unmistakably the hopelessness
of dual supervision and divided authority.   Nevertheless, by the dissension of those bitter years of
storm and stress the College had been brought financially, at least, to a feeble and uncertain state, and
many who watched its progress were wondering if
it could still endure.   But again it struggled forward.   Those who were really interested in its existence never doubted its ultimate concord and prosperity and growth.   But to bring it to its destined
place of usefulness and power it needed unfaltering
strength and unwavering faith to guide it through the
troubled period that lay yet before it.

CHAPTER VII

THE STRUGGLE FOR EXISTENCE

ON July 7th, 1846, the Governors of McGill met at Government House to appoint a Principal to succeed Dr. Bethune. The meeting was attended by the Lord Bishop of Montreal, the Rev. Dr. Mountain; the Chief Justice of Upper Canada and the Governor-General. The seriousness of the situation that had developed was indicated by the presence of the two last named members, who had not attended a meeting for several years. It was resolved that pending a decision on the former acting-Principal's memorial to Her Majesty's Council, protesting against the disallowance of his appointment, a temporary appointment of Principal be made. The choice was Edmund A. Meredith, B.A., LL.B., a graduate of Trinity College, Dublin. He was at once informed of the Governors' decision; he accepted the post and took his seat at the meeting. He was to receive no remuneration for his services. The condition of the College was reviewed by the Governors and was found to be critical. Dr. Holmes of the Medical School reported that no degrees had been conferred in the spring "in consequence of the disallowance by Her Majesty of the former election of Principal." The Governors therefore changed the date for the conferring of Medical degrees from the 25th of May, previously fixed, to "a date to be

Edmund A. Meredith, L.L.D.
Principal of McGill University
1846-1849

agreed upon by the Governors on application from the Medical Faculty," and the deferred Medical degrees were given at a convocation held on December 17th, following. It was found that the liabilities of the College amounted to over £3300, made up of £2300 for old unpaid bills and over £1000 for arrears of Professors' salaries. The revenue of the College was shown to be only about £900 a year, and the current expenses, exclusive of salaries, about £500 a year. The financial outlook, considering the large liabilities, was therefore not encouraging.

The new Principal, Edmund A. Meredith, was the son of the Rev. Thomas Meredith, D.D., a Fellow of Trinity College, Dublin, and a mathematician of distinction. His mother was a daughter of the Very Rev. Richard Graves, also a Fellow of Trinity, Dean of Ardagh, and a theologian of note. He graduated in 1837 from Trinity College, Dublin, where he won the second classical scholarship, the prize for political economy, and the graduation medal in science. He then began the study of law, but before his course was completed he came to Canada in 1843. Here he resumed his legal studies, and on fulfilling the requirements he became a member of the Bar in both Upper and Lower Canada. When he was appointed Principal of McGill he was a lawyer in active practice in Montreal. In scholarship he was well qualified for his duties, as Lecturer in Mathematics and as Principal of the struggling College in which courses had to be arranged and the whole academic policy reformed. He was possessed, too, of unusual administrative ability and of legal knowledge of great value in that time of College chaos and disagreement; and he displayed un-

common tact and abundant patience and energy in
his efforts to solve the delicate problems with which
the University was then confronted. It was largely
through his initiative that the movement was undertaken for the securing of a new Charter. In 1847
he accepted the post of Assistant Provincial Secretary, but as the seat of Government was then in
Montreal he still remained Principal of McGill.
After the burning of the Parliament Buildings and
the violence in connection with the Rebellion Losses
Bill, when the seat of Government was moved to
Toronto, Mr. Meredith tendered his resignation as
Principal on October 26, 1849. He was induced to
retain the Principalship, however, although living in
Toronto, until a successor could be found, and it was
not until 1851 that he finally withdrew. His name
appears as Principal in documents of that year. In
recognition of his services the University conferred
on him the honorary degree of LL.D. in 1857.
When Thomas Workman gave the workshops to the
Faculty of Applied Science he directed that a sum
of $3000 be paid to the former Principal, Dr. Mere-
dith, "inasmuch," he said, "as I have long been
convinced of the value of the services rendered to
the University of McGill by Edmund A. Meredith,
LL.D., during a very critical period of its history."
Dr. Meredith afterwards became Under-Secretary
of State for Canada, and he was connected with the
Civil Service until 1878.

The nine years between 1846 and 1855 were years
of continuous financial perplexity during which the
Governors had great difficulty in keeping the College
in operation. There is little else to record than a
discouraging battle with poverty and want. But in

this period hope for ultimate success was not abandoned. The new Board of Governors had first to reorganize the teaching staff and make new appointments. In addition to his other duties the Principal undertook to conduct, as Lecturer, the classes in Mathematics and Natural Philosophy. The Professor of Classical Literature, the Rev. W. T. Leach, was made Vice-Principal in September, 1846. It was also realised that in a country of two languages instruction in French was an absolute necessity. No funds were available for the purpose, but Monsieur L. D. Montier accepted the position of Lecturer in return for lodging and fuel and a portion of students' fees, on the understanding that he was to receive a salary of £30 a year as soon as money was available. But students' fees, because of the small number in attendance, gave but little reward, and as a result the new French Lecturer was apparently not always as zealous and enthusiastic in his unremunerative labours as the Caput desired. It frequently happened that for several days he gave no instruction, and soon after his appointment the Caput censured him for neglecting his work and for "conduct highly reprehensible and subversive of all College discipline." In recognition of his services, however, and perhaps to keep him from becoming weary in well-doing, the Governors allowed him half an acre of land "in the northeast corner of the College grounds, to pasture his cow and make a garden," from the products of which they hoped he might receive some slight return for his work. The Rev. G. F. Simpson, Headmaster of the High School, consented to act as Lecturer in Mathematics without any salary or fees. In March, 1847, the Hon. Justice Badgley, LL.D., was appointed Lecturer in Law without remuneration other than fees, and instruction in Law which later led to the establishment of the Law Faculty was commenced during the following term. In July, 1848, a Lecturer in Hebrew and Oriental Languages was appointed without salary. It was decided not to appoint a Professor of Divinity in succession to Dr. Bethune, not only because of the lack of funds, but because the clauses in the Statutes bearing on the nature of the theological instruction to be given had not yet been agreed upon by the Home Government.

But the gravest and most important duty of the new administration was in connection with the serious financial condition of the University, and with efforts to improve the situation. When the Governors met in July, 1846, the Professors and Lecturers, some of whom had already retired because of resignation or dismissal, appealed to them for payment of their salaries. They had worked without pay for several months, and in some cases for a year and a half. It was even difficult for them to obtain fuel and candles. The Governors expressed their "sympathy with them in their embarrassment and distress," but regretted that they were unable to relieve them. The Vice-Principal was given land behind the College to enable him to make a garden, "on condition that he would not interfere with the Bursar's garden." The Governors and the Board of the Royal Institution were unwilling to encroach upon the meagre capital to pay for ordinary running expenses. They believed that if the burden of debt which the College carried could be removed they could meet in some way all current obligations, and that there would be no doubt about the future success of the University. In liquidating the debt they hoped for assistance from the Government. In November, 1846, the Secretary of the Governors wrote: "The prospects of the College are now in so promising a state as to lead the Governors to entertain the most sanguine hopes, if they would but be relieved from their present embarrassments, of succeeding in carrying into full effect the great object its benevolent founder had in view." But their hopes for direct assistance from the Government or the Home authorities were not early fulfilled.

It was soon evident that the removal of the burden of debt without Government assistance would be an arduous task uncertain of accomplishment, and that a problematical period doubtless lay ahead. Many of the debts were of ten years' standing. Some of them had been incurred with mechanics and tradesmen in connection with the construction of the College buildings. Professors had long been unpaid. Since July, 1845, no money had been placed at the disposal of the Governors to meet expenses. The Statutes for the government of the College were still unsanctioned by the Crown, and this fact and the dispute between the Board of the Royal Institution and the Governors continued to furnish an excuse, whether valid or not is questionable, for paying no money for several months out of College funds. The Governors had borrowed from the Banks on their own personal security, and had obtained small sums at different times on their own personal undertaking to pay for fuel and to meet the most pressing demands made by absolutely necessary contingencies. Were it not for this timely assistance it is probable that the College would have been closed; its fortunes at best were precarious.

The Royal Institution had meanwhile concluded to transfer to the Receiver-General of the Province all sums paid to them on account of the College. But the Receiver-General would not pay them to the College authorities, pending the Crown's decision on the Statutes. The Governors urged the Royal Institution to a hasty consideration of their embarrassment. They did not blame or censure the Board for the extraordinary situation in which they found themselves. In the question as to the cause of the situation they were not primarily interested. Debating on the responsibility for it and on bygone disputes would not improve it. The fact was plain that the College's existence was in the balance because of financial conditions, and that this fact must be faced. "The buildings are becoming dilapidated and useless," they wrote, "and those who inhabit them will be frozen or starved unless the Governors contribute from their private means." They likewise vigorously called the attention of the Home Government to their incongruous and lamentable plight. "We desire earnestly," they said, "to impress upon Her Majesty's Government that the attainment of the benevolent and noble object of the founder of McGill College has been unfortunately if not culpably delayed." Yet they insisted that the present problem "will work out and the whole income will soon be available for expenditure." There would then be no difficulty, they thought, "in maintaining the College on a scale large enough to be of use in a colony of a million people without means for obtaining education for youth." And they declared with astonishing optimism, "the Governors have great hopes that when once fairly put in action this Institution will speedily attract patronage and support and will expand with the wealth of the country." This note of courage and faith is all the more remarkable when we realise the exact condition of the University, without money, without Statutes, a fact which was used as an excuse for withholding funds, with but little sympathy from Provincial Government or Home Government, with its few Professors unpaid and pleading even for fuel and light, with unfinished and poorly equipped buildings falling rapidly into decay, with grounds uncared for, and with a very small enrollment of students.

The Governors were determined, however, not to decrease the capital funds of the College and that payments, if any, must be made out of surplus revenue. In this they had the approval and co-operation of the Board of the Royal Institution. Nor did they wish to dispose of any of the land until it was absolutely necessary to do so, and then only with a unanimous consent. They made an effort first to increase the value of their real estate. A large portion of the land had been let for pasture and for grass, but the leaseholders were slow to pay the rent and many of them were several months in arrears. The Board of the Royal Institution now endeavoured to collect all rents promptly when due. They decided to discriminate between their own various debts. They would pay tradesmen first, in the order of the age of their bills. When the tradesmen had all been paid they would then pay the Professors, but not until all other debts had first been liquidated. The Professors must wait. An agreement was then entered into with the various creditors to pay their debts off in installments. In order to secure more revenue the students' fees were increased. They had already been raised from £3 to £4 6s. 8d., of which £2 13s. 4d. went to the House Fund, 6s. 8d. to the Bursar, the same amount to the Library, and £1 to the servants. The fees were now advanced to £10. Every matriculant was also to pay £1 5s. to the Bursar for his use and benefit, and all students were to deposit 10s. "caution money," to cover breakages and damages to furniture, this deposit or the portion of it not used to be refunded in the spring. Expenses during this period were reduced to a minimum. In 1845 the large dining-hall or refectory had been given over to the Medical Faculty, and one of the small rooms had then become the dining-room. In 1847, however, because of the financial loss incurred even the small dining-room was closed and, as we have seen, the students boarded with Professors. In 1848, when Law students were first permitted to reside in the College, it was on the express condition that "Professor Leach would board them."

The necessity for much needed repairs to fences and buildings and for fuel for the College rooms called urgently for funds. But there was no money to provide these necessities. Permission was asked and received by the Governors to pull down and remove an old wooden hut on the College grounds, "which had long been considered an unsightly object and a nuisance fast falling to decay." It was arranged that "the boards of the roof and floor would mend fences and that the old logs would be used for fuel." It was later decided to sell the surplus furniture in the College, scanty enough at best, and also the sand that had been taken from the excavations for the buildings, the money from the sales to be put to "repairs to the spouts of the buildings and to the fences, also to bring water from the spring near the bridge [in the present "hollow"], to put a railing on the bridge, and to make passable the road between the College and Sherbrooke Street." But in the midst of all their financial worries the determination of the College authorities to encourage students is evident from their establishing two exhibitions of the value of £10 each, to be awarded yearly to the two students standing highest in the matriculation examination. Professors might starve or freeze and creditors might wait, but ambitious and meritorious students must be practically encouraged.

The Governors were at last given some slight relief by the receipt of over £1400, on account, from the Receiver-General, to whom the revenues arising from College funds and properties were being periodically transferred by the Royal Institution. Of this amount only £50 was voted for current expenses; the remainder was used to pay off a portion of the debts, among them the amount borrowed from the Bank by the former Principal and the Chief Justice of Montreal. A further sum of £280 was received by the Governors from rentals, of which £100 was paid to the Vice-Principal, £100 to the Bursar, Registrar and Secretary, £50 to the Professor of Mathematics and £30 to the Lecturer in French, in part payment of their long overdue salaries. But it was decided that in consideration of these payments "no fuel could be provided for the present for any College officer."

The relief resulting from the above receipts was

of but brief duration. In November, 1848, the Governors had only the sum of £54 at their disposal. They divided it between the Bursar and the two Lecturers in proportion to the amount of salary in arrears, and as a result the Lecturer in French, M. Montier, received £2 14s. as his share from January 1st, 1848, to November 29, 1848. That was the full amount of salary received by him during the year; but he still had his cow and his garden! As if to increase the worries of the College authorities the College buildings caught fire on January 24, 1849. Fortunately the damage was only small, but any damage, however trifling, could at that time be ill-afforded. To add to the embarrassment, several of the few students enrolled failed to pay their fees, and the Bursar could not collect them. In February, 1849, he was in urgent need of funds, and on the 13th he sent out to the student debtors appealing letters of which the following is typical: "I beg that you will pay your fees this week if possible, as I have a heavy College claim to meet on Saturday without the wherewithal to pay it." He supported this appeal by letters to parents, "I beg that you would be good enough to pay your son's College fees on or before Saturday next, as I have a heavy College debt to pay on that day and not sufficient funds to meet it." These appeals were not always successful, and the revenue from this source remained indefinite. In the spring the students who had paid their dues were not given back the caution money they had deposited because "no funds were available." There is a record of one student, more persistent than the others, who was difficult to placate. He was finally promised that his "caution money would be refunded when possible," and he was assured that "funds would soon be available because the Statutes would soon be ratified."

The gross revenue available to the College in 1849 was £494, made up of £70 from the rent of Burnside House, £274 from rents of building lots and other lands, and £150 from the rent of a large stone building known as the King's Arms or Mack's Hotel, situated on Jacques Cartier Square, formerly Nelson's Market. The rent of this latter building was first £250 a year, but from depreciation in value because of the removal of the Market it had decreased by £100. After deducting the amounts required for insurance, etc., the net revenue was only about £440. Only thirteen students were in attendance; two of these had obtained exhibitions and were admitted free, and the income derived from the fees of the remaining eleven was £110. The salaries, which, however, were several months in arrears, amounted to £292 a year. The Principal received no remuneration. The salary of the Rev. W. T. Leach, Vice-Principal and Professor of Classical Literature, was supposed to be £100; that of T. Guerin, Lecturer in Mathematics and Natural Philosophy, £50; the Hon. W. Badgley, Lecturer in Law, received no stated reward, but he was entitled to a fee of £2 per term from each student attending his lectures; the Rev. J. Abbott, Registrar, Bursar, Secretary, and Lecturer in Ancient and Modern History, Geography and Logic, was supposed to receive a salary of £100, and in addition several small fees from students, which amounted the previous year to only £4 5s.; L. D. Montier, Lecturer in French, received £30 a year, and the Beadle, F. Hewitt, was

given £12; the Lecturer in Hebrew, the Rev. A. De-
Sola, received no salary.   Later in the year a lecturer
in Botany was appointed "without remuneration for
the present."

The Board of the Royal Institution endeavoured
earnestly to relieve the financial situation of the
College, and they requested the Receiver-General to
make all possible payments to the Governors.   But
the liabilities far exceeded the assets.   In January,
1850, the College officers urgently pleaded for their
overdue salaries.   It was decided to pay them 2s. 9d.
in the pound.   Accordingly, Vice-Principal Leach received £55 of the £404 in arrears; L. D. Montier,
the Lecturer in French, was given £4 of the £34 due
him, and the others were paid very small amounts in
proportion for a year or, as in the case of the Vice-
Principal, several years of work.   A grant of £25
was asked for by the College authorities to purchase
books for students, but it was of necessity refused.
The supply of fuel for the year was reduced to "ten
cords of maple wood," and altogether the outlook
of the College was not promising.

Meanwhile the Statutes, Rules, etc., which had
been forwarded to the Colonial Office for Royal
sanction in 1843, had been approved with some alterations, and the Royal confirmation was announced
in a despatch from Lord Grey to Lord Elgin, the
Governor-General, on September 27th, 1848.   The
Home Government had delayed their approval of
the Statutes because they were not sure of the attitude of the Provincial Legislature towards the College.   Remembering the political events of 1837 and
realising as a result Canadian resentment of any
semblance of dictation or coercion, they decided to

proceed with caution.   In this they followed the
advice of the Governor-General, Lord Metcalfe,
who, as we have seen, strongly urged delay and a
careful consideration of the clauses bearing on religious instruction, in his despatch of September 6,
1843.   To this despatch Lord Stanley replied from
Downing Street on October 13, stating his approval
of the suggestions and expressing his desire to meet
first the wishes of the Provincial Assemblies.   "It is
evident," he said, "that these questions cannot be
decided without the intervention of the Legislature
of Canada and that it must rest with the Provincial
Parliament to determine whether pecuniary aid shall
or shall not be afforded to the College. . . . It could
answer no useful purpose, but may lead to a most
embarrassing controversy if, by the confirmation of
those Statutes . . . Her Majesty should hazard a
collision on such topics as these, between the Royal
Authority irrevocably exercised and the future recommendation of both or either of the Houses of
local Legislature.   Consequently, until I shall be
apprised of the results of their deliberations, the
decision of the Queen will be suspended."

There were rumours that a bitter attack against
the College, its administration and its religious exclusiveness would be made in the Legislature, and
that a Bill would be introduced which might possibly
lead in the end to its abolition.   Lord Metcalfe
feared such a possibility.   But no attack was made,
and on January 17, 1844, the Governor-General
wrote to Downing Street: "No attack was made on
McGill College in the shape of a Bill during the late
Session.   The Institution perhaps owes its escape to
the prudence of the French Canadian party, who,

having several Roman Catholic Colleges that are exclusive, are not disposed generally to join in attacking
other Institutions on account of their exclusiveness,
lest the same weapons should be turned against their
own.   Under those circumstances McGill College
being in Lower Canada appears to be in a safer position than it seemingly occupied before the late Session; and I do not consider the expediency of withholding confirmation of their Statutes to be so urgent
as I then conceived it.   Nevertheless, it is not certain
that the Institution may not be attacked in any future
Session, for the Presbyterians and Dissenters of all
classes are bent on destroying the exclusive character
which it has acquired in the hands of the Church of
England." Efforts were now renewed by the Royal
Institutions to have the Statutes, in part at least, approved, but the Board was informed by the Colonial
Office that "it does not appear to Her Majesty that
the College has the means of sustaining itself on a
reasonable scale of efficiency."   The closing of the
College was looked upon by the Home authorities as
a mere matter of time!

After much discussion and delay, when it seemed
probable that the College would weather the storm,
the Statutes were finally in part approved in the
autumn of 1848.   The time for action had come
and the Home authorities realised that "further delay might issue in the ruin of the College."   As we
have already seen, the clauses relating to the sectarian character of theological instruction and of
the College prayers were not confirmed.   In giving
reasons for the vetoing of these clauses, Lord Grey
wrote that in his opinion, based on the advice of
Lord Metcalfe, "aid would not be granted [to the

College] if the Royal confirmation of the Statutes should first have impressed indelibly on that Institution a character of exclusiveness in whatever relates to Theological degrees and studies and to the public worship of the place. . . . The Will and Charter are both silent on the subject of the peculiar religious tenets or ecclesiastical principles to be inculcated at the College, a silence very significant in the case of a Testator who was himself the member of a Christian Church, a silence not less significant in the case of the Sovereign . . . a silence not to be explained by any supposed forgetfulness or intentional omission of the subject, since the inculcation of 'the principles of true religion' is expressly provided for by the Charter; a silence, therefore, apparently indicating a design that Christianity should be taught, not in any single or exclusive form, but in any and in every form in which its great fundamental truths and precepts could be imparted to the students. . . . The questions respecting the religious and ecclesiastical principles to be inculcated in the College will, therefore, for the present rest in the same state of indecision as that in which the Will of the founder and the Royal Charter have left them."

With the approval of the Statutes, the Governors made an effort to reorganise the College on a better working basis. In December, 1849, the Principal forwarded to the Board of the Royal Institution suggestions for amendments to the Charter in order to provide a greater freedom of action which might render the management more efficient. This step resulted largely from a report sent to the Governors by the Board of the Royal Institution, setting forth the latter's observations on conditions found during

their official Visit in 1848, and including an outline
of the remedies they thought should be applied.   The
Board approved of their suggestions and urged immediate consideration of the question.   Three months
passed without action.   Meanwhile a peculiar situation had developed.   The Principal of the College
had desired in October, 1849, to resign, as he was
about to move to Toronto because of the change in
the seat of Government.   He was now Assistant
Provincial Secretary.   But as no successor was available he was persuaded to retain the office for the
present, although no longer able, because of his residence in Toronto, to take a very active part in College affairs, or to exercise any direct supervision over
the administration.   The remaining Governors consisted of the Lord Bishop of Montreal, who resided
at Quebec; the Chief Justice of Upper Canada, the
Hon. J. Beverley Robinson, who, like the Principal,
dwelt in Toronto; and the Governor-General, Lord
Elgin, who, after he had been attacked by a mob in
1849 as a result of his attitude on the "Rebellion
Losses Bill," no longer resided in Montreal.   None
of the Governors was therefore able to exercise any
oversight of the College of which they were the
legal guardians.   In April, 1850, a Committee of
the Board of the Royal Institution was appointed to
suggest a solution of the peculiar problem.   They
wrote to the Governor-General, setting forth the ab-
surdity and the hopelessness of a condition which
permitted the College to be controlled by Governors
no longer resident in Montreal, and emphasising the
necessity that existed for "a prompt application of
remedies to relieve the College from its present
unfortunate state of depression."   They urged an

amended Charter as the first requirement. A long
correspondence followed between the Board and the
individual Governors, relating to the details of the
Charter. In June the Board's Committee wrote
again to the Governor-General, stating that if the
Charter were amended according to the draft prepared "McGill College would speedily be relieved
from the difficulties by which it has been so long
surrounded."

The Board desired to amend the original Charter
rather than to abrogate it in order not to raise any
question of the tenure of the estate through a lapse
of possession. They feared that between the brief
period of time which would necessarily intervene
between the annulment of the old Charter and the
passing of the new, the heirs-at-law of James Mc-
Gill might, even at that late date, claim that the
College no longer existed in fact, and that they were
entitled to the estate. They therefore preferred an
amended Charter, even if more cumbersome. One
of the amendments provided that the members of
the Board of the Royal Institution should henceforth
be the Governors of the College, the members still
to be appointed by the Crown. The number of
Governors was left indefinite, but the Board suggested strongly that "the number should not be less
than thirteen, and that they should be selected from
the different Protestant denominations in the city
and district of Montreal." Later they suggested
that the number should be nine or eleven, exclusive
of ex-officio members. They pointed out that "so
long as the Board of the Royal Institution and the
Board of Governors are composed of different bodies
of men exercising a co-ordinate and uncertain juris-

diction over matters very ill-defined . . . it is impossible to expect either unanimity in the bodies themselves or harmony in the system. . . . The only means of imparting to these bodies unity of action and design will be found in making them identical." Such an amendment would forever end the dual control which had brought about in the past disaster and depression.

Other clauses in the amendment provided that all Statutes and Rules of the College could be approved by the Governor-General at his discretion without transmission to England; and that the visitatorial power be transferred from the Royal Institution and vested in the Governor-General. The purpose of the amendments was to simplify the government of the College and to secure an efficient administration. The suggestions with reference to numbers and to the selecting of the Governors from the different Protestant denominations were not followed by the Government. There was much correspondence between the Board and the Governor-General and his Council over the proposals. But it was on the whole amicable. The objections of one side were always met with reasonableness by the other, and a harmonious agreement was finally reached. The Governor-General forwarded the amended Charter to the Colonial Office with his approval and his advice that it should receive Royal sanction. The Board of the Royal Institution, realising from past experience the slow methods of Downing Street, appointed an agent in London to hasten the passage of the Charter through the different offices of the Imperial Government. It was not until August, 1852, however, that the amended Charter was finally approved.

Between 1849 and 1852 very few meetings of the Governors were held, owing to the absence of the Governors from Montreal. The affairs of the College were largely in the hands of the Vice-Principal and his assistants. Conditions gradually became graver. The Lecturers in French and Mathematics were dismissed because no money to pay them was in prospect. By 1851 the buildings, which had not been completed and were uncomfortable at best, had fallen into a dilapidated state. Rain and snow fell freely through the cracks in the roof, and leaked to the rooms below. Windows and doors, which in the course of time had been shattered, were still unrepaired. There was not enough fuel to heat the broken and damaged structures, for an allowance of "ten cords of maple wood for the winter" was not sufficient to bring warmth. The College grounds were uncared for. Students who dwelt in the city tramped through snowdrifts to the cold College classrooms. Because of the discomfort, the lack of adequate accommodation, and the inconvenient distance from the Hospital and the city, the Medical classes, which had been held in the Centre building since 1845, were removed in 1851, as already recorded, to the building on Coté Street, built by three members of the Medical Staff, Drs. Campbell, MacCulloch, and Sutherland, and leased to the Faculty. A year later the City began excavations for the reservoir in rear of the College grounds. The blasting in connection with this work did not add to the peace or the safety of student life in McGill, and later

serious breaks in the buildings were caused by heavy
stones falling on the roof. For these various reasons
it was ordered by the College authorities that all
occupants except the Vice-Principal should withdraw
from the College buildings. The chief excuse given
was economy, but the real reasons were not then disclosed to the public. The Arts classes were afterwards carried on in part of the building used for
the High School. The McGill buildings were abandoned, except by the Vice-Principal, and it was not
until 1860 that they were reoccupied by the Faculty
of Arts.

Several changes now took place in the administration of the College. In 1851 Principal Meredith resigned. His resignation was followed the next year
by that of the Rev. John Abbott, who had been Secretary and Bursar and Registrar for several years.
The Hon. Judge Charles Dewey Day was now
President of the Royal Institution for the Advancement of Learning, and as such he assumed, in con-
junction with Vice-Principal Leach, direction of the
College management.

Charles Dewey Day was a native of Bennington,
Vermont. While he was still a boy he moved with
his parents to Montreal, and there he received his
education. He studied law, and in 1827 he was
admitted to the Bar. Ten years later he was made
a Queen's Counsel. When the Rebellion of 1837
ended he was appointed Deputy Judge Advocate-
General, and he consequently had an active part in
the courts-martial appointed for the trial of accused
insurgents. He was made Solicitor-General in 1839.
At the election of 1841 he was chosen to represent
the County of Ottawa, but he retired from political

life in the following year and accepted a Judgeship
in the Court of Queen's Bench.   In 1849 he was
elevated to the Superior Court.   He was later appointed a member of the Royal Institution for the
Advancement of Learning, of which he became President, and after the amended Charter of the University was approved in August, 1852, he became
in virtue of that position a Governor of McGill.   In
1857 he became Chancellor of the University, a position which he occupied until his death twenty-seven
years later.   He filled many important offices.   In
1859 he was one of the Commission entrusted to
prepare a Civil Code for the Province of Quebec;
he subsequently served on Commissions appointed at
different times to determine the amount of the Provincial debt to be assumed by the Dominion; to investigate the details of the Pacific Railway scandal;
and to settle the amount of subsidy which should be
paid to the railroads for carrying the mails.   He also
helped to prepare Canada's case in the negotiations
for the Webster-Ashburton Treaty, and after his
retirement from the Bench he assisted in prosecuting
the Hudson Bay Company's claims against the United States under the treaties of 1846 and 1863.
After his appointment as a Governor of McGill,
Judge Day took a deep and earnest interest in the
activities of the College.   He devoted his energy
and his time to advancing the College's welfare, to
removing the causes of its many troubles, and to
giving it a place of power and usefulness in Canada.
He died in 1884.   He was referred to in the contemporary press as "one of Montreal's most upright,
honourable and useful citizens"; and speaking a few
days after his death, on his connection with McGill,

Lord Landsdowne said, "In this University he leaves an irreparable void and an enduring memory."

With the approval of the amended Charter in the autumn of 1852, efforts were made to reorganise the University, and to commence a forward movement. The new Board of Governors authorised and established under the amended Charter found the University in an unsatisfactory and almost hopeless predicament. It was struggling under lamentable deficiencies in its educational arrangements; it was faced by heavy pecuniary embarrassments and altogether inadequate resources. It was, in short, destitute of funds. Even its buildings had been abandoned, but it was hoped only temporarily. Conditions in the Faculty of Arts were particularly bad. Yet there was hope. It was evident to the Governors that an attempt at resuscitation must immediately be undertaken. An agreement was entered into with creditors for the making of small periodical payments with interest. Arrangements were made for the appointment of a competent Treasurer, and for the holding of regular meetings of Governors and of Corporation. A Committee on Ways and Means was selected, consisting of the President, Judge Day, and Messrs. Davidson, Ramsay and Dunkin. The Provincial Government was appealed to, and in December, 1852, the Legislature gave the College a grant of £1000 "to help liquidate the debts." It was clear that a new era in the University's life was about to begin, but that persistent energy and determination would be required to guide the University through the night that still covered it.

In February, 1853, a Finance and Building Committee of the Board was appointed, consisting of

James Ferrier, Benjamin Holmes, and T. B. Anderson. One of the first acts of this Committee was to take legal proceedings against the purchasers of lots, for the most part "persons of ample means" who had failed to make payments long overdue. In June, 1853, a sum of £75 was voted by the Governors to complete the portico of the Arts Building, "the Board being very desirous of correcting as soon as possible the present unsightly aspect of the Centre building." They also called for estimates for "the putting up in front of the College on Sherbrooke Street of a fence of the same description as that of the new Cemetery." To effect greater efficiency the office of the Secretary of the Royal Institution was moved to one of the rooms of the McGill buildings —the East wing—in July, 1853, and the Secretary became also Secretary of the Governors. The two offices became identical. Later, because of the cold and the general discomfort, the office was transferred for some time to a building at the corner of Dorchester and University Streets, known as Burnside Hall. But that conditions there were not ideal is evident from an appeal made in December, 1854, to the firm that had previously repaired the antiquated furnaces. The Secretary wrote: "Instead of imparting to us an equable and cheering warmth such as might reasonably be expected from their matronly development . . . to me they are painfully and consistently cold. Do, then, come to our relief and save us from the horrors of frozen limbs, hospitals and amputations; or first, if you prefer it, pass a morning without overcoat, cap and comforter in my office with the thermometer at zero."

In the summer of 1853 repairs were made to the

College buildings in the hope of making them again habitable. The blasting in connection with the reservoir had caused much damage. Windows were wholly shattered and there were wide cracks and breaks in roof and walls. The contractor failed to make restitution, and the City Corporation was then urged to make the necessary repairs and to guarantee that there would be no further wreckage. The City authorities were slow to respond, but in the end they made reparation. Fences were also restored or newly built, and an effort was made to lay out the College grounds in some semblance of order. In September the lower part of the grounds was granted free for the holding of the annual Agricultural and Industrial Exhibition. In the spring of 1854 the City threatened to enter suit against the College for unpaid taxes, but the dispute was amicably settled. The total income from rents on which the taxes were based amounted to £182, of which the sum of £102 was derived from the rent of Burnside House and gardens, £60 from the Professor and £20 from two students who still occupied rooms in the College buildings. This income was exclusive of the rents of lots, which amounted to about £400. In the summer of 1854 the Governors gave to the city free of charge land for the opening of streets "on condition that all the College property shall be entirely exempt from every sort of assessment until it shall have been sold." Land for the opening up of University Street had been given in 1851. The Streets now provided for were Union Avenue, between Dorchester and St. Catherine Streets; McGill College Avenue; Burnside Place; Victoria, Mansfield, St. Catherine, Cathcart, Dorchester, and

Monique Streets.   It was stipulated that Victoria
Street and McGill College Avenue "should not be
opened, for the present, higher than Burnside Place."

But notwithstanding the Governors' efforts, the
University was still far from adequate prosperity.
It was not yet in a flourishing condition and its outlook while hopeful was not wholly auspicious.
Greater co-operation on the part of the public was
obviously needed, and the contemporary press frequently deplored the lack of public encouragement.
There was peace and concord in its administration,
but there was little advancement in its academic
activities.   It was clear that it had either to go forward or to cease to function.   It was plain, too, that
in addition to funds a new Principal and several
instructors should be appointed as expeditiously as
possible.   The Governors, it was rumoured, were
looking abroad for a Principal; they were also, it
was said, considering the reorganising of the College
on the plan of English Universities.   Neither of
these suggested procedures was popular, and neither
was in the end followed.   In August, 1854, one of
the contemporary newspapers, the *Sun,* which has
long since disappeared, in referring to the needs of
the University voiced editorially the opinions of
the people:

"All we need," it said, "are persons at the helm
who will take an *active interest* in the progress and
advancement of the institution. . . . It won't do to
sit idly down—to follow the dignified and majestic
example of Cambridge and Oxford.   Montreal is
not in England—it is in Canada.   We have a way of
doing things for ourselves.   It is not necessary in
order rightly to accomplish an end to ask how they

do it 'at home'; we can find out a mode ourselves.
McGill College will never be anything until some
exertion is made by those who have control of it. A
languid indifference or a sickly half-dead interest will
never secure to it a permanency among the institutions of the day"; and the writer added that "unless
measures for its improvement are speedily undertaken there is a danger that McGill College will soon
be numbered among the things that were."

The Governors in the end decided to look nearer
home for a Principal—a man of strong personality
to take the helm in this critical period. They determined, if possible, to appoint a Canadian who
was familiar with the country, its spirit, its temper
and its educational needs. Down in Pictou County,
Nova Scotia, they found him in the person of William Dawson, a native Canadian and a graduate of
Edinburgh University. In 1855 they offered him
the Principalship. He accepted the position and
began his duties in the autumn of that year. In
the thirty-four years that had gone since its establishment and the twenty-six years since its opening,
the College had struggled through many vicissitudes
and trials. It had frequently been on the border of
extinction. But the crisis in its troubled history had
at last been passed. A new era, more wonderful
and more successful than even its most optimistic
friends dared look for, was about to begin. The
foundations had been laid, perhaps not always wisely,
but at least firmly and hopefully. The College was
now to go forward—for again, as in the past, its
sign-posts pointed onward. The faith of its founder
was at last to be justified. It remained for the new

Principal, William Dawson, to guide it on its un-wavering march to usefulness and to power, and by his tact, his judgment, his wisdom and his strength to impress his name upon its century story as the man who was greatest among "the makers of McGill" in the first hundred years of its existence.

CHAPTER VIII

College Life in Mid-Century

COLLEGE life in mid-century, or rather in the "forties and fifties," during the early dark days of struggle and ten years thereafter, differed greatly from College life in our day. It is difficult perhaps fully to realise the changes since that time in other ways than growth. The McGill of our day is not the McGill of seventy years ago, not merely in its accommodation and its advantages, but in its internal activities.

Under the original Statutes of the College the administration was under the control of four distinct bodies: (1) The Corporation, which met annually on the day after commencement day "to inspect the Books and Accounts of the Registrar, Bursar and Secretary and to transact all such business relative to the property of the University as might be necessary." This body seems to have taken no part in strictly Academic discussions. (2) The Board of Governors, which met quarterly in March, June, September and December, and which was in supreme control; two constituted a quorum and the Principal had a double or casting vote. (3) The Caput, which met weekly and consisted of the Principal, Vice-Principal and Professors, three forming a quorum. The duty of this body was "to frame Rules and Regulations for the discipline, lectures, studies and

McGill College in 1855

internal government of the Lecturers, Scholars, Students, Inferior Officers and other members of the College and to make regulations regarding the expenses and system of living within the College." They had no control at first, however, over studies or lecturers in the Faculty of Medicine. (4) The Convocation, which met "four times in every Term for the purposes of conferring Degrees, such meetings being regulated by the Caput." Every Professor, Lecturer and Tutor had to take the oath of allegiance and of office.

Discipline was severe and was rigidly enforced. Every Professor was given power to punish students by confinement and fine, the fine not to exceed five shillings and the confinement not to exceed twelve hours. Many of the early regulations are of interest. The duties of the Vice-Principal seem to have been responsible and arduous. All disciplinary measures as well as the general conduct of the University were under his direct supervision. He was compelled to reside in the College, and during the non-residence of the Principal he was to be "the parent and guardian of the College Household." It was his duty "to examine students for matriculation, maintain the observance of the Statutes by Professors, Students, Inferior Officers and all other resident members of the College, enforcing such observance by admonitions and punishments; to direct the students in their studies, promoting by all the means in his power their progress in Religion, and Learning; to preside over the Collegiate Exercises and regulate the Inferior Officers and Servants of the College." At meals served in the College distinctive tables were provided, one for "Members of

Convocation and Bachelors of Civil Law, Lecturers, Fellows and Tutors"; one for Bachelors of Arts and Students in Law and Medicine who had graduated in Arts; and one or more for undergraduates. The academical year consisted of three terms, the Michaelmas Term, the Lent Term and the Easter Term, and it extended from the first Wednesday in September until the third Wednesday in June. The Arts course extended over three years. Until a Chapel should be built it was imperative that Divine Service should be held in some convenient room, and on the first and last days of every term the Principal or one of the Professors, Lecturers or Tutors selected by the Principal for the purpose, preached a sermon in the College or in one of the Protestant churches of Montreal; attendance in full academic dress of all the members of the University excepting those who had obtained a dispensation was compulsory. The prayers in the College Chapel were said morning and evening; the service was conducted in rotation by Officers of the College.

It was required that "the dress of all members of the University should be plain, decent and comely without superfluous ornament." No member of the Arts Faculty was allowed to appear in Church, Chapel, Lecture or Dining-hall without his gown and only by special permission from the Vice-Principal was a student permitted to go outside of the College grounds without his academic dress. Students were not allowed to resort to any inn or tavern or place of public amusement without special permission from the Vice-Principal. They were not allowed to remain out of College nor to entertain visitors in their rooms after 10 o'clock at night, and the Vice-Principal, Professors, Lecturers and Tutors had authority to enter at all hours the rooms of undergraduates. Junior students were required "to pay the respect due to their Seniors both in public and in private by taking off their caps, giving place to them and by other useful modes of attention and civility."

The course of study leading to a degree in the Faculty of Arts was of three years' duration. Courses were of two kinds, from which students could make a choice. One consisted of Mathematics, Logic, and Ethics; the other of Classics. In the former the First Year was devoted to the study of six books of Euclid, Algebra to the end of Quadratic Equations, and Trigonometry to the end of the solution of Plain Triangles. In the second year the course included a repetition of all the first year work, Analytic Geometry, Differential and Integral Calculus, and Logic, consisting of Fallacies, Induction and "a sketch of a system of Philosophy of the Human Mind." The work of the third or final year was in Physics, Astronomy, and Ethics, principally "Butler's Analogy." In the Classics course selections from Homer, Virgil, Euripides and Horace were read in the first year; selections from Cicero, Horace, Demosthenes and Sophocles in the second year; and selections from Herodotus, Æschylus, Thucydides, and Tacitus in the third year. In the first and second years the students were "exercised in Greek and Latin Composition, and they were also given a few lectures in Ancient History and Geography." In the third or final year they were exercised in English Composition.

Conditions in the Medical School at that period

have been described by a contemporary, Dr.
D. C. Maccallum, who graduated in 1850, when
the Medical Classes were held in two rooms of the
Arts building:

"A large proportion of the students," he said,
"were men verging on, or who had passed, middle
age.   Indeed, several of them were married men
and the heads of families.   There was sufficient of
the youthful, however, to keep things lively.   'Footing Suppers,' practical jokes, and special country
excursions to secure material for practical anatomy,
were of frequent occurrence.   The last, involving
as it did a certain amount of danger, commended
itself particularly to the daring spirits of the class,
who were always ready to organise and lead an ex-
cursion having that object in view.   These excursions
were not at all times successful, and the participators
in them were sometimes thwarted in their attempts
and had to beat a precipitate retreat to save themselves from serious threatened injury.   They contributed, moreover, to the unpopularity of the medical
student.   'Footing Suppers' were functions of the
simplest and most unpretentious character.   Each
new matriculant was expected, although many failed
to conform to the arrangement, to select an evening
on which to entertain his fellow students, the entertainment consisting generally in furnishing biscuits
and beer—the old, time-endorsed 'cakes and ale.'   In
partaking of these, smoking, relating humorous
stories, chaffing each other and singing rousing songs,
the evening usually passed with much *bonhommie*.
But sometimes they were rather boisterous, or, at
least, noisy and exciting. . . .

"Dissections and demonstrations were made only

at stated times during the morning and afternoon of the day. There evidently existed a marked disinclination on the part of both demonstrator and student to work at night in the highest story of a lonely building, far removed from other dwellings, imperfectly heated, and lighted by candles, the light being barely sufficient to render the surrounding darkness visible. Having occupied for two seasons the position of Prosector to the Professor of Anatomy, I had to prepare, during the greater part of the session, the dissections of the parts which were to be the subject of the Professor's lecture on the following day. This necessitated my passing several hours, usually from nine to twelve o'clock at night, in the dismal, foul-smelling dissecting room, my only company being several partially dissected subjects, and numerous rats which kept up a lively racket coursing over and below the floor and within the walls of the room. Their piercing and vicious shrieks as they fought together, the thumping caused by their bodies coming into forcible contact with the floor and walls, and the rattling produced by their rush over loose bones, furnished a variety of sounds that would have been highly creditable to any old-fashioned haunted house. I must acknowledge that the eeriness of my surroundings was such that I sometimes contemplated a retreat, and was prevented from carrying it into effect only by a sense of duty and a keen dislike to being chaffed by my fellow-students for having cowardly deserted my work. . . .

"The examinations for the degree of the University were conducted orally, ten minutes being allowed to each examiner. The janitor, supplied with a

watch and a large bell, was placed in the hall outside
the door of the library, the room in which the examinations took place. At the expiration of each
ten minutes he rang the bell, and the candidates
went from one examiner to another. This was repeated until the student had completed the round of
examining professors. Immediately on the termina-
tion of the examinations, the professors met and decided then and there the fate of the candidates. The
latter, in the meantime, waited in the College in a
rather painful state of suspense. They were sum-
moned separately before the Professors, and the
result, favourable or unfavourable, was in each case
made known to the individual. . . .

"It was customary at this time for the student to
be indentured to a practicing physician, or, if not so
bound notarially, to make a private arrangement
with him to be allowed to study in his office and to be
considered as his pupil. For this privilege a fee of
£20 was usually demanded. Apart from the éclat
which was supposed to be attached to the position of
a student under a popular physician, and the belief
of the possibility of the patron being able to forward
the interests of his pupils, there were, as a rule,
few advantages derived from this association. It
is true that in exceptional cases, if the physician had
a large clientele and took a warm interest in his
students, he could, by arranging their studies, occasionally examining them on the work done, and
directing them in the routine of office work, be of
material assistance to them. The office work of a
physician in large practice, however, offered an excellent opportunity to acquire much practical knowledge. As, with few exceptions, physicians prescribed

and dispensed their own medicines, the articled student had the opportunity of making up all the prescriptions. He compounded pills, a variety of which were always kept prepared for use, and he made the different tinctures and ointments. He had the privilege, also, of assisting at minor surgical operations, such as were performed in the office, of making physical examinations, of applying tests; in short, office practice offered the same facilities for acquiring practical knowledge, although in a minor degree, that the outdoor practice of a hospital or the practice of a dispensary affords. . . ."

The recreations of students who dwelt in the College or its vicinity were few and simple. There were no athletic teams or athletic games. Indeed, the number of students in Arts and Law was scarcely sufficient to permit the forming of athletic teams, and the medical students were too busy all day and were too far from the College grounds to take an active part in college sports. There was no gymnasium and no physical instruction. There were no fraternities other than the fraternity of McGill itself. There was no Union, no Y. M. C. A. On evenings in spring and summer a military band usually played near the "ornamental bridge" over the stream in "the hollow" near the present Physics building. Citizens came up from the City to listen to the band, and before the Easter term ended students, too, enjoyed the music. The College grounds were long used by citizens as a park. The students seemed to have had an occasional dance during the spring term, and at times there were receptions in Professors' rooms to which students were invited. Later in the "fifties," after the coming of Principal Dawson, other forms of entertainment were added. Of these Dr. Dawson wrote: "Evening gatherings at regular intervals during the session were arranged, and cards of invitation for these were sent to the different classes or years in rotation. At such gatherings there was usually music, sometimes a short recitation or address on some topic of interest, and scientific instruments, specimens and photographs were shown, simple refreshments provided, and every effort made to cause those who attended to feel thoroughly at home." Sometimes there were gatherings which took the form of what were known as "conversaziones," during which conversation, supposedly on literary or scientific subjects, but more frequently on less dignified topics, took the place of the dances of to-day.

On the whole, college life in the mid-century was characterised by a Spartan simplicity. The students of that period seemingly enjoyed its somewhat humble joys and its unostentatious and frugal amusements. Life in that time was, at least, not artificial or luxurious or competitive or sectional; but whether the plain living of the period was more conducive to high thinking than the multifarious student activities of a later day cannot here be answered.

CHAPTER IX

Sir William Dawson and the Making of McGill

JAMES McGILL made his will, providing for the founding of McGill College, on January 8th, 1811, two years before his death. He was dreaming of a great University which would rise at some distant but certain day in the new land of his adoption. He was doubtless dreaming, too, of a strong personality who would guide the University to its destined place in the country in which he had made his fortune and in which he had unbounded faith. At that very time another Scotchman, twenty-two years of age, was dreaming in his home in Banff-shire—also, by a strange coincidence, the home of James McGill's ancestors—of the land beyond the horizon from which tales of fortune and happiness came drifting across the ocean. He was a Liberal in politics and a dissenter in religion. His independent spirit was revolting against conditions in his own land. It was not easy to sever the ties which bound him to the old home and to venture alone into an unknown and far-off country. But the new land was calling, and its lure was upon him. He resolved to go to Canada where he had heard that all things were possible to the courageous and the industrious, and where men lived a man's life based on merit and achievement, and unhampered by the fetters of worn-out fetishes and conventions. And so it happened that on the 8th of March, 1811, exactly two months after James McGill had made his will, this young Scotchman set out for the new world. The ship in which he was to take passage—a square-rigged, clipper sailing vessel in those steamless days—was to clear from Greenock, one hundred and eighty miles from Keith, his Banffshire home. He had no money to spare to pay for a conveyance. He must cover the distance on foot. He sent his heavy luggage by carrier, and with a pack of necessary clothes and provisions on his back, he set out with three adventurous but hopeful comrades on his journey. He walked through the Grampians, by Kildrummy Castle, on through the town of Perth, along the base of Cairngorm in the Highlands, through the long valley of Glenavon, and thence to the sea-port town of Greenock from which the packet ships went weekly out into the mists, heading for the land of promise somewhere beyond the sky-line. He slept with his companions on heather beds in front of peat fires in the homes of the Highlanders through whose villages they passed, and the Gaelic tongue of one of their number was always a charm sufficient to secure them food. He reached Greenock on the 20th of March, but because of unforeseen delay it was not until April 11th that he embarked for Canada. After a voyage of five tempestuous weeks he landed in Pictou, Nova Scotia, on May 19th, 1811, and there he determined to make his home. The young Scotchman was James Dawson, whose son was destined in 1855 to become Principal of McGill.

In his new home James Dawson soon prospered as a merchant and ship-owner, and later as a pub-

Sir William Dawson,
C. M. G., M.A., L.L.D., F.R.S.,
Principal of McGill University
1855-1893

lisher, and in a few years he was head of one of the most successful business firms in Eastern Nova Scotia. In 1818 he married Mary Rankine, a Scotch girl from Lonerig, in the parish of Salamannan, who had emigrated to Nova Scotia after her parents' death with her brother William, the only other member of her family. Like the other pioneers of that time, they, too, were resolved to make a new home and to restore their shattered fortunes in the new world. To James Dawson and Mary Rankine two children were born, William and James, the latter of whom died while still a boy.

William Dawson was born in the town of Pictou, Pictou County, Nova Scotia, on October 13th, 1820, and there he received his early schooling. His parents believed in the value of education. Early in his career they determined that he should have whatever school privileges the country provided, and that he should later receive a college training. Many years afterwards he wrote: "To this day I cannot recall without deep emotion the remembrance of the sacrifices they made, and of the anxieties they incurred to secure for me opportunities of improvement. . . . I would specially record with gratitude that, at a time when he was in straitened circumstances, my father contributed liberally in aid of educational institutions then being established in Pictou, with the view of securing their benefits for his sons, and that he and my mother aided and stimulated our early tastes for literature and science."

The childhood influences that moulded William Dawson were typical of the homes of the early Scottish pioneers in the Maritime Provinces of Canada at the beginning of the last century. They were

characterised by simplicity, by frugality and by reverence.   They were founded on an unwavering belief
in religion and education and honest labour as necessary to the development of the individual and the
nation.   They were based on principles inculcated
in the youth of these early Canadian days long before
Carlyle with rugged pen and organ tone declared
them.   Later, when Principal of McGill, Dr. Dawson used to speak with affectionate remembrance
of the agencies which fashioned him in the little
seacoast town of black wharves, and tossing tides,
and far-come sailing ships bearing mysterious car-
goes from unknown and romantic lands, and manned
by strangely-garbed and bearded seamen speaking
a foreign tongue.   "Our home," he said, "was a very
quiet one except when strangers, especially men engaged in missionary and benevolent enterprises, were
occasionally invited as guests.   To some of these I
was indebted for much information and guidance.
. . . There was always much work and study in the
winter evenings, and I remember with what pleasure
I used to listen to my father's reading, chiefly in
history and biography, for the benefit of my mother
when busy with her needle, as well as of my brother
and myself, after our lessons were finished. . . .
My early home had much in it to foster studies of
nature, and both my parents encouraged such pursuits.   A somewhat wild garden, with many trees
and shrubs, was full of objects of interest; within
easy walking distance were rough pastures, with
second-growth woods, bogs, and swamps, rich in
berries and flowers in their season, and inhabited
by a great variety of birds and insects.   Nothing
pleased my father more than to take an early morn-

ing hour, or rare holiday, and wander through such places with his boys, studying and collecting their treasures. The harbour of Pictou, too, with its narrow entrance from the sea, affords ample opportunities for such investigations, and its waters teem with fish: from the gay striped bass and lordly salmon to the ever-hungry smelt—the delight of juvenile anglers. In such a basin, visited every day by the ocean tides, there is an endless variety of the humbler forms of aquatic life, and along the streams entering it a wealth of curious animals and plants with which an inquisitive boy could easily make himself familiar in his rambles and occasional angling expeditions." It was here that the interest of the future scientist was first aroused in natural history. Of his mother he wrote: "She was a woman of deep affections and many sorrows . . . her girlish years had been saddened by the death of her parents, and by the mournful breaking up of her old home. . . . She had a few warm and attached friends, and was very kind to such of the needy as she could help."

The first scholastic training of William Dawson was received in a small private school in Pictou. From there he went to the recently founded Grammar School conducted on "the good old-fashioned plan of long hours, hard lessons, no prizes, but some punishments." His parents desired that he should study for the Church; he began his college career with that object in view, but it was changed by circumstances. He entered Pictou Academy, which had just been established primarily for the training of young men for the Christian ministry; it was presided over by the Rev. Dr. Thomas MacCulloch, a Scottish teacher and preacher who exercised a large

influence on the intellectual life of Nova Scotia. It
was during his course at the Academy that William
Dawson first became interested scientifically in
geology and natural history, subjects which were
later to form so large a part of his life work. As a
result he took long excursions during vacations for
the purpose of obtaining specimens and studying the
minerals of his native province. In 1840, he entered Edinburgh University, where he completed his
course in 1847. It was in one of his summer vacations in the Maritime Provinces that he first met
Sir Charles Lyell, the distinguished geologist, and
Sir William Logan, who later originated the Geological Survey of Canada. In 1847 he married Mar-
garet Mercer of Edinburgh and with his wife he
returned to Pictou. For a time he gave a special
course of extension lectures at Dalhousie College,
Halifax. In 1850, Joseph Howe, for whom he had
a deep admiration, and with whom he had formed a
friendship early in life, offered him the Superin-
tendency of Education in Nova Scotia,—a newly established office. He accepted the post with many
misgivings; and for the next few years he devoted
all his efforts to bettering the educational conditions
of the Province, addressing school meetings throughout the country and stimulating improvements.

In 1853 while he was still Superintendent of Education, his old friend, Sir Charles Lyell, revisited
Nova Scotia and the friendship formed a few years
before was renewed. On the same ship with him was
Sir Edmund Head, then Governor of New Brunswick, who, on this first meeting, was deeply impressed
by Mr. Dawson's views on educational reforms. As
a result he appointed him the following year to the

commission formed to report on the re-organisation
of the University of New Brunswick, which was then
in a precarious state.

In 1854, the Governors of McGill, on the advice
of Sir Edmund Head who was about to become Governor-General of Canada in succession to Lord Elgin,
offered the Principalship to William Dawson. He
accepted the post and began his duties in the autumn
of 1855. The outlook of the University when he
arrived was not encouraging. The College buildings
were not used for classes, but part of them was occupied by professors and students; Medical classes
were held in the Coté Street building; classes in Arts
and Law were held in part of the High School building. The conditions of James McGill's will were
not being carried out; there was a College building
on the Burnside Estate, it was true, but it was not in
operation.

But nevertheless the call for educational opportunities was urgent. One hundred and ten students
registered at the commencement of the session in all
departments of the University, of whom fifteen were
in Law, thirty-eight in Arts and fifty-seven in Medicine. The Faculty of Arts consisted of five professors and one lecturer; the Faculty of Law had
one professor and two lecturers; and the Faculty
of Medicine had nine professors. The annual calen-
dar for the previous session, 1854-55, announced
that "the board and lodging of students is a matter
of much practical importance. From fifteen to
twenty [Arts and Law students] may be received by
the Professors resident in the College buildings and
provision will be made when necessary for the reception of others into boarding houses, licensed by

the Governors, upon settled economical terms and
subject to proper rules of discipline and conduct."
Medical students, it was pointed out, "could obtain
board and lodging in the town for from eight to
sixteen dollars a month." It was clear that the attendance would rapidly increase in succeeding years,
and that provision must at once be made for their
accommodation and instruction. The greatest hin-
drance to advancement was of course lack of funds.

The actual condition of the University at that
time and the obstacles to be overcome were afterwards frequently described by Sir William Dawson,
whose reminiscences of the period were always vivid:

"When I accepted the principalship of McGill,"
he said, "I had not been in Montreal, and knew the
college and the men connected with it only by reputation. I first saw it, in October, 1855. Materially,
it was represented by two blocks of unfinished and
partly ruinous buildings, standing amid a wilderness
of excavators' and masons' rubbish, overgrown with
weeds and bushes. The grounds were unfenced and
were pastured at will by herds of cattle, which not
only cropped the grass, but browsed on the shrubs,
leaving unhurt only one great elm, which still stands
as the 'founder's tree,' and a few old oaks and butter-
nut trees, most of which have had to give place to
our new buildings. The only access from the town
was by a circuitous and ungraded cart track, almost
impassable at night. The buildings had been abandoned by the new Board, and the classes of the Faculty of Arts were held in the upper story of a brick
building in the town, the lower part of which was
occupied by the High School. I had been promised
a residence, and this, I found, was to be a portion of

one of the detached buildings aforesaid, the present east wing. It had been very imperfectly finished, was destitute of nearly every requisite of civilised life, and in front of it was a bank of rubbish and loose stones, with a swamp below, while the interior was in an indescribable state of dust and disrepair. Still, we felt that the Governors had done the best they could in the circumstances, and we took possession as early as possible. As it was, however, we received many of the citizens, who were so kind as to call on us, in the midst of all the confusion of plastering, papering, painting, and cleaning. The residence was only a type of our difficulties and discouragements, and a not very favourable introduction to the work I had undertaken in Montreal. . . .

"On the other hand, I found in the Board of Governors a body of able and earnest men, aware of the difficulties they had to encounter, fully impressed with the importance of the ends to be attained, and having sufficient culture and knowledge of the world to appreciate the best means for achieving their aims. They were greatly hampered by lack of means, but had that courage which enables risks to be run to secure important objects. . . .

"Our great difficulty was lack of the sinews of war, and the seat of Government being, at the time, in Toronto, I was asked by the Governors to spend my first Christmas vacation in that city, with a view of securing some legislative aid. There was as yet no direct railway communication between Montreal and Toronto, and of course no Victoria Bridge. I crossed the river in a canoe, amidst floating ice, and had to travel by way of Albany, Niagara, and Hamilton. The weather was stormy, and the roads blocked with snow, so that the journey to Toronto occupied five days, giving me a shorter time there than I had anticipated. I received, however, a warm welcome from Sir Edmund Head, saw most of the members of the Government, and obtained some information as to the Hon. Mr. Cartier's contemplated Superior Education Act—passed in the following year—which secured for the first time the status of the preparatory schools, whilst giving aid to the universities. I was also encouraged by Sir Edmund and Cartier to confer with the Superintendent of Education and with the Governors of McGill on my return to Montreal, with reference to the establishment of a Normal School in connection with the University. This was successfully carried through in the following year."

With the loyal aid of the Board of Governors the Principal at once undertook to arouse the interest of the general public in the University. He realised the necessity of securing their speedy co-operation and assistance. His belief was that the University should not be isolated nor removed from the stream of national life; his hope was that it should minister in a practical and tangible way to the community in which it was situated. On November 5th, 1855, he was inaugurated as Principal. A few days later he established the first real link between University and citizens, on the purely instructional side, by the commencement of a course of thirty popular lectures in Zoology, Natural Philosophy, Civil Engineering, Palæography and the Chemistry of Life. The fee for the course was £1. The course in Engineering was the origin of the department of Applied Science, which later expanded into a Faculty. Soon afterwards a course of lectures in Agriculture was given by the Principal, who, while Superintendent of Education in Nova Scotia, had given several lectures on that subject throughout the province. The fee for this course was £1 5s.

A direct appeal for financial assistance was then made to the citizens of Montreal. It met with an encouraging response, which greatly relieved the situation and was what Dr. Dawson, forty years later, called "the beginning of a stream of liberality which has floated our University barque up to the present date." But other anxieties were soon to be felt. Early in 1856 the building occupied by the High School and the Faculty of Arts was destroyed by fire, together with the few books and the scanty apparatus that had been collected or had been given by Dr. Skakel many years before, as well as many of the Principal's natural history specimens. Teaching was not interrupted, however, and during the remainder of the session, the classes in Arts were held again, in part, in the original College buildings, then undergoing repairs, and, in part, in the Medical Faculty's building on Coté Street, in which rooms were generously placed at the disposal of the Faculty of Arts. Because of the occupation of part of the College buildings, and the expectation of soon again putting them to permanent use, improvements were commenced on the College grounds, by the planting of trees and the making of roads and walks, the cost of which was borne largely by the Principal. In 1856, general courses in Applied Science were established in connection with the Faculty of Arts, and degrees were first conferred in that department in 1859. The courses in the Law School, which had been formed into a separate Faculty in 1853, were extended to suit the conditions and needs of the country. But funds were necessary to meet the heavy extra expenses incurred, and in order to provide sufficient money for the payment of debts and contingencies, it was thought prudent to sell a portion of the College lands. From 1858 to 1860, therefore, forty-four lots, averaging in size one hundred by one hundred and twenty feet, were offered for sale by the University. Some of these were sold at auction. They were situated on Sherbrooke, Victoria, Mansfield and University Streets. Money was also loaned by the College authorities to purchasers of lots to enable them to erect buildings. The temporary revenue of the College was thus increased and expansion was consequently made possible.

In 1860, the number of students in Arts, Law and Science had increased to one hundred and five, of whom sixty were in Arts. It had been previously decided that when the students in Arts should exceed fifty, the original College buildings should again be wholly occupied. They had meanwhile undergone extensive repairs. The College grounds were now taking on some semblance of order as a result of trees and walks and clearings. Accordingly, in the autumn of 1860 the classes in Arts, Science and Law were moved back to the buildings which had been practically abandoned eight years before. The centre building was used for classes; the east wing was given up to rooms for the Principal and some of the professors and students. The erection of a third building, corresponding with the east wing, was then undertaken through the generosity of William Molson. It provided for a convocation hall

William Molson, Esq,
1793-1875
Founder of Molson Hall

above, and a library below. It was formally opened
in 1862, and is known as the William Molson Hall.
Through the efforts of Mrs. Molson the three buildings were soon afterwards connected into one, by
intervening structures, and the Arts building as we
know it was completed. One of the connecting structures was used first as a museum; the other as a
Chemical and Natural Science room and laboratory.
The museum received at once a portion of the Principal's own collection of specimens, and others purchased by the Principal from his own resources.
Later Dr. Carpenter's valuable collection of shells
was added, and the whole furnished the nucleus for
the present Peter Redpath Museum. The Science
room and laboratory were used for chemistry and
assaying. It was there, in small rooms and with but
scanty equipment, that Dr. Harrington later laid the
foundations for the departments of Chemistry and
Mining which were subsequently to contribute so
largely to the industrial development of Canada.
The Library in Molson Hall had room for twenty
thousand volumes, but when it was opened the College possessed only two thousand books. These,
however, formed the nucleus for the Peter Redpath
Library.

During the following years the expansion of the
University was steady. It is unnecessary here to
describe its growth in detail and only outstanding
additions to its equipment can be mentioned. The
deeper interest of graduates in their University was
manifested in the formation of a Graduates' Society
by a small number of McGill men resident in Montreal. Greater co-operation with the smaller colleges in the Province was effected, and St. Fran-

cis College, Richmond, and Morrin College, Quebec, were affiliated with the University. Theological schools established by the various Protestant denominations were erected in the shadow of the University and were granted affiliation. The Congregational College was affiliated in 1865; it was followed by the Presbyterian College in 1873, the Wesleyan College in 1876, and the Diocesan College in 1880. Speaking of the connection of the Theological Colleges with McGill, Principal Dawson said: "The value of these to the University no one can doubt. They not only add to the number of our students in Arts, but to their character and standing, and they enable the University to offer a high academical training to the candidates for the Christian ministry in four leading denominations."

The growth and development of the University was made possible only by the generosity of its graduates and friends. In 1871 a second appeal was made for funds, and the result was a large increase in endowments, and in revenue. Several chairs were established and scholarships and exhibitions were provided. It was in this year that the first attempt was made to offer facilities for the higher education of women, not yet, however, within the University, but unofficially connected with it. But this movement must be left to another chapter.

At this period the Medical Faculty which had carried on its work for twenty years in the Coté Street building required more accommodation and a closer connection with the University. Funds for its adequate equipment were not available. Indeed, ten years later Principal Dawson wrote: "It is somewhat singular that this school so ably conducted and so useful, has drawn to itself so little of the munificence of benefactors. Perhaps the fact of its self-supporting and independent character has led to this." It was decided, however, to undertake the construction of a Medical Building on the College property. In 1872 the front block of what was afterwards known as "the old Medical Building" was erected for the Medical School, and the Medical Faculty returned, this time permanently, to the College grounds. Funds for its endowment were afterwards given by its friends. The year 1872 is a notable one in the history of the McGill Medical School, for another reason than the erection of its first McGill building,—it was also the year of the graduation of William Osler, destined later to exercise so great an influence on medical education in Canada, America, and Europe. The department of Applied Science which had been connected with the Faculty of Arts since 1856 was expanded into a separate Faculty in 1878. It had been temporarily suspended because of a lack of funds in 1870; it was now re-created, greater than before. But it had yet no building and no adequate equipment. These, however, were to come in due course.

Speaking later of the decade between 1870 and 1880, Principal Dawson referred to it as the middle period in his connection with McGill, "a period of routine and uniformity, succeeding the period of preparation and active exertion and preceding the period of culmination. During these ten years," he said, "the University outlived for the most part its earlier trials and struggles. Its revenues expanded considerably. . . . The number of its students greatly increased, as did also its staff of instructors.

Gold medals and scholarships were founded. The beginning of a museum was formed, and the library, although still small, was growing rapidly, by donations and occasional purchases. A suitable building on the College grounds was provided for the Medical Faculty. A new Faculty of Applied Science was active and prosperous, though as yet without any building of its own. The statutes and regulations had become fixed and settled, and the whole machinery of the institution was moving smoothly and regularly. It had, in short, reached a position in which it could challenge comparison with its sister institutions and rivals and which to many seemed adequate to all the requirements of the time. Still, there were many wants unsupplied, and constant difficulty was experienced in meeting the demands made upon us, from our limited resources, whilst many promising fields of usefulness had to remain uncultivated. . . . On the whole, the ten years had been characterised by steady, if slow, advance, achieved by much toil and many sacrifices."

But the Principal was not yet satisfied with the University's service to the community. "It has been a matter of sorrow to me," he said, "that we have been able to do so little, directly, for the education of the working class and of the citizens generally, more especially in science."

The final period of Principal Dawson's connection with McGill, from 1880 to his retirement in 1893, saw a further growth in the University. Into the details of that growth we cannot here enter. The University was now becoming a national rather than a local institution; it was contributing more and more to national development. The Principal wrote, "we

Peter Redpath
Founder of the Redpath Library
and the Redpath Museum

should not regard McGill merely as an institution for
Montreal or for the Province of Quebec but for the
whole of Canada." Its expansion was fortunately
in keeping with this ideal. In 1881 the erection of a
museum was undertaken through the generosity of
Peter Redpath, and in 1882 the Peter Redpath
Museum was formally opened. In the former year,
too, another appeal was made to the citizens of Montreal for funds to relieve its now straitened circumstances, and again the response was generous and encouraging. In 1882 Principal Dawson said in his
annual University Lecture: "In these thirty years,
[since 1852 when the amended Charter was ob-
tained] the College revenues have grown from a few
hundred dollars to about $40,000 per annum, with-
out reckoning the fees in professional Faculties and
the income of the more recent benefactions. Its staff
has increased from the original eight instructing officers to thirty-nine. The number of students has increased to 415 actually attending college classes, or
reckoning those of the Normal School and of affiliated colleges in Arts, to nearly 600. Its Faculties of
Law and Applied Science have been added to those
of Arts and Medicine. It has two affiliated Colleges
in Arts and four in Theology, and has under its
management the Provincial Protestant Normal
School. Its buildings, like itself, have been growing
by a process of accretion, and the latest, that in which
we are now assembled, [the Peter Redpath Mu-
seum], is far in advance of all the others, and a
presage of the college buildings of the future. We
have five chairs endowed by private benefactors, fourteen endowed scholarships and exhibitions, besides
others of a temporary nature, and eight endowed

gold medals. More than this, we have sent out about
1,200 graduates, of whom more than a thousand
are occupying positions of usefulness and honour in
this country."

This final period of Principal Dawson's work saw
a sure and steady advancement and many changes in
the University. Among the evidences of growth
were the establishment of courses for women in 1884,
with their extension in 1886; the addition of the Medical Building in 1886, and its still further enlargement in 1893; the endowment of several chairs; the
increase in the teaching staff; the establishment of
scholarships and exhibitions; the creation of new
courses, and the plans for new and much-needed
buildings. In 1886 the Vice-Principal, the Rev. Dr.
Leach, retired after over forty years of service. He
was succeeded as Vice-Principal by Dr. Alexander
Johnson, Professor of Mathematics. Towards the
close of this period the Faculty of Applied Science,
which had been established as a separate school in
1878, was placed, at last, on an independent foundation—after its many trials and struggles—by the
munificent gifts of Thomas Workman and William
C. Macdonald, afterwards Sir William Macdonald,
a native of Prince Edward Island. Preparations
were made for the erection of Science buildings with
adequate equipment and endowment. In February,
1893, a few months before Sir William Dawson's
resignation of the Principalship, two buildings for
the Faculty of Applied Science were opened—the
Macdonald Engineering Building, including the
Workman wing, and the Macdonald Physics Building, the equipment and facilities of which soon afterwards enabled Professor Ernest Rutherford to

Sir William Macdonald

carry on his experiments in radioactivity. Meanwhile the Library in Molson Hall had become totally inadequate for the volumes and documents that had been gathered by the University. Peter Redpath, who had already given the Museum, was now the Senior Governor of the University. On November 12, he wrote to the Chancellor enclosing plans of a projected library and proposing to commence building operations early in the following spring. The building was practically completed before Sir William Dawson's retirement, but it was not formally opened until October, 1893. In the last four years of the Principalship of Dr. Dawson the University was given more than a million and a half of dollars for endowment and equipment. What gratified him most in receiving this amount was the fact that it included many minor gifts which testified, at the close of his long career, to the good will and confidence and co-operation of the general public.

As a result of Sir William Dawson's constant anxieties and strenuous labours, his health had been for some time in a precarious state. In his annual University Lecture ten years before, he had said, "My connection with this University for the past twenty-eight years has been fraught with that happiness which results from the consciousness of effort in a worthy cause, and from association with such noble and self-sacrificing men as those who have built up McGill College. But it has been filled with anxieties and cares and with continuous and almost unremitting labour on the details of which I need not now dwell." Ten years had passed since then, and the "anxieties and cares and unremitting labour" to which he referred had not grown less. They had finally broken

his already weakened strength. On the 26th of
May, 1893, after thirty-eight years of arduous service, he tendered his resignation of the Principalship
of McGill to the Board of Governors, and reluctantly
it was accepted. After his retirement his interest in
the University did not diminish. He continued his
researches and his writings. There was a last visit
to England in the summer of 1896, to attend meetings of the Evangelical Alliance, the Royal Society,
the Victoria Institute, the Geological Society, and the
British Association, at the latter of which he illus-
trated to a large meeting of eminent geologists the
structure of *Eozoon*. In the summer of 1897 he was
stricken with partial paralysis from which he recovered somewhat, but which left him an invalid. Two
years later, in the autumn of 1899, his illness became
acute. He lapsed into partial unconsciousness. For
several days he lingered. Then on November 19th,
a gray Sunday morning, very quietly at the last, he
slipped away. The next day, the Governors, Principal, members of the teaching staff, and students
gathered in the Molson Hall to do honour in a Memorial Service, to the memory of the teacher, the
administrator and the man they admired and loved.
The Memorial Address, here included in the Appendix, was given by his successor, Principal Peterson.

Sir William Dawson was Principal of McGill for
thirty-eight years, more than a third of the century
that has passed since the establishment of the University, and almost half of the period since its actual
opening. It has not been possible here to speak of
his researches, his writings, his connection with
learned societies. Many honours came to him from
Britain, from America, and from Canada. He was

Sir William Peterson
Principal of McGill University
1895-1919

the first President of the Royal Society of Canada;
he was President at various times of the American
Association for the Advancement of Science, of the
American Geological Association, and of the British
Association.   In 1884 he was knighted.   He was
elected a Fellow of the Royal Society, and he received honorary degrees from Edinburgh,—his old
University, from McGill and from Columbia.   But
all his activities were incidental and subservient to
his work as Principal of McGill and to his efforts for
the advancement of the University.   He saw the
institution grow slowly but surely under his guidance, in the face of many discouragements, from very
small beginnings to a foremost place among the great
seats of learning of America and Europe.   He found
in 1855 a college struggling under debt, with inadequate revenue, with abandoned buildings, with few
professors and with only one hundred students.   In
the last session of his Principalship more than a thousand students were in attendance, of whom three
hundred and fifty were in the Faculty of Arts, and
one hundred and thirty-five degrees were conferred;
more than half a dozen spacious college buildings
had been added to the original structure; the lower
campus or yard was practically what it is to-day
except for the new Medical Building; the endowments
had increased to over a million and a half of dollars,
the yearly income to nearly a quarter of a million and
the disbursements to nearly two hundred thousand
dollars.   The growth of the University in equipment,
in instructors, in courses and in general educational
opportunities has already been indicated.   In bringing about this marvellous growth, the Principal had
the generous assistance and sympathetic encourage-

ment of a loyal band of friends, among whom his
greatest gratitude was recorded to William Molson,
John H. R. Molson, Peter Redpath, Sir Donald
Smith, afterwards Lord Strathcona; Thomas Workman, and William C. Macdonald. Without their
aid and their generous gifts the expansion of the
University, needless to say, would not have been
possible.

But greater perhaps than the material and numeri-
cal growth which he accomplished, was the spirit of
service William Dawson brought to McGill, and the
influence of that spirit on the men and women who
went out from the University to help in the development of Canada. It is difficult briefly and adequately
here to outline the ideals which shaped his policy in
guiding the University and the students over whose
instruction he presided. They are found in his
addresses on various occasions. Perhaps they are
best summed up in his farewell message to the students in December, 1893, when he was leaving the
University to pass a few months in the South in a vain
effort to restore his already shattered health:

"I had hoped, in the present session," he said,
"to be among you as usual, doing what I could, officially and personally for your welfare, but was sud-
denly stricken down by a dangerous illness. In this,
I recognised the hand of my Heavenly Father, doing
all things for the best, and warning me that my years
of active usefulness are approaching their close, and
that it is time to put off my armour and assume the
peaceful garb of age, in which perhaps I may yet be
spared to be of some service in the world.

"For the time being, I must be separated from the
work that has always been to me a pleasure, and you

will excuse me for addressing to you a few words, on topics which seem to me of highest moment to you as students. I may group these under the word 'Loyalty,' a word which we borrow, with many others, from the French, though we have the synonym 'leal,' which if not indigenous, has at least been fully naturalised both in English and Scottish. These words are directly associated with the idea of law and obligation, and with the trite, though true, adage, that we who would command must first learn to obey.

"I need scarcely remind you of that loyalty which we owe to the sovereign lady the Queen, and to the great Empire over which she rules. I have had frequent occasion to note the fact, that this sentiment is strong in the rising generation of Canadians, and nowhere more so than in McGill. It is indeed not merely a sentiment, though, even in a time which boasts of being practical and utilitarian, the feelings of the heart count for something: it is based also on the rational appreciation of the benefits of a rule, which, while allowing the greatest freedom of individual action, secures equal rights and protection for all.

"We are, every one of us I hope, loyal to our University, and *to the University as a whole,* not merely to any particular faculty of it. McGill has endeavoured, more than most universities, carefully to adapt its teaching to the actual wants and needs of the student, whether in the matter of that general academical learning which makes the educated man, or of that special training which fits the graduate for taking his place, creditably, in the highest walks of professional life. To this, I think, its success has been largely due. Yet, with all the breadth and the elasticity of our system, we cannot perfectly meet every case, and there are still desiderata, the want of which is most deeply felt by those engaged in the management of the University. Our course, however, has been onward and upward, and it may be truly said that no session has passed in which something has not been added to our means of usefulness. The future, indeed, has endless possibilities, and there will be ample scope for improvement—and perhaps also for occasional complaints—when the youngest students of to-day have grown to be grey-haired seniors. You have good cause, notwithstanding, to be proud of your University, and to cherish feelings of affection and gratitude to the wise and good men, who, amid many difficulties, have brought it to its present position, and are still urging it onward.

"You should be loyal to the ideal of the student. You are a chosen and special band of men and women, selected out of the mass, to attain to a higher standing than your fellows, in those acquirements which make life noble and useful. It is not for you to join in the follies of frivolous pleasure-seekers, or to sacrifice the true culture of your minds and hearts to the mere pursuit of gain. Your aims are higher, and require isolation from the outer world, and self-denial, in the hope that what you are now sowing and planting, will bear good fruit in all your future lives. Live up to this ideal, and bear in mind that self-control, and the habits of mind which it implies, are of themselves worth more than all the sacrifices you make.

"Be loyal to the memories of home. I regret very much that McGill cannot at present offer to its stu-

J. H. R. Molson

dents such temporary homes as college halls could supply. The time for this is coming, I hope soon. But most of you have those at home who look on your residence here with solicitude and longing, who will rejoice in your successes, and perhaps be heart-broken should any evil befall you. It is customary to say that young people at college are removed from the restraints of home and its influences for good. But this need not be. To the truly loyal, absence should make these influences more powerful, and the thought of those who are watching you with loving hearts, in distant homes, should be a strong impell-ing motive in the students' life.

"Next to home is heaven, and let me now add, loy-alty to Him who reigns there, and to the Captain of our salvation made perfect through suffering for us. Many of you, I know, are earnest Christians and growing in spiritual life, as you advance in learning. To those who are not, let me say,—read, as a serious study, the life of Jesus Christ as given in the Gospels. Read it in the light of His own sayings, that 'He came not to be served, but to serve, and to give His life a ransom for many,' and that 'God so loved the world that He gave His only begotten Son, that who-soever believeth in Him should not perish, but have eternal life.' Read of His life as the Man of Sor-rows, of His agony in Gethsemane, of His death on the Cross, crushed not merely by physical agony, but by the weight of our iniquities—and you may then judge, if there is any obligations so great as that under which we lie to Him, any loyal service so blessed as that of the Saviour. The gate may be strait, and we may have to leave some things out-side, but it is held open lovingly by the pierced hand

of our Redeemer, and it leads through a happy and
fruitful life to eternal joys—to that land which the
Scottish poet, whose religious ideal was so much
higher than his own life, or the current theology of
his time, calls the 'land o' the leal.' That happy
country is near to me, but I hope separated from you
by a long, useful and happy life; but let us all alike
look forward to meeting beyond the River of Death,
in that promised land where He reigns who said
'Him that confesseth Me before men will I confess
before My Father that is in Heaven.'

"In the meantime you remain here to pursue useful
work; I go to seek restored health elsewhere, and
can only remember you in my prayers. Let us hope
that when the winter is passed we may meet once
more, and that I may be able to congratulate you on
well merited success, not merely in regard to the
prizes and honours which few can obtain, but in that
abiding education of the mind and heart, which
McGill offers to all her studious children without
exception."

On his last convocation as Principal, on April 29,
1893, he said to the graduating class: "I may say,
we have full confidence that you will sustain the
honour of the University, and will regard the education you have received as a sacred trust, of which you
are the stewards, and which is to be used for the
good of all, for the advancement of your country,
and for the glory of God."

Those who worked with him or who studied under
him and who are best qualified to speak, tell that it
was, after all, the noble humanity with which Dawson
invested his teaching and his administration that gave
greatness to his occupancy of the Principalship. It

was his personality, his energy, his deep and vivid sympathy with student interests, even more than his learning and his contemporary influence in other spheres, that helped to re-create McGill. Under his spell there were many undergraduates who had thoughts and aspirations beyond the McGill of their day, thoughts of sacrifice, and of future service to the world.

In forwarding his resignation to the Governors, he wrote: "Much has been attained, but much still remains to be accomplished, especially with reference to the purely educational or academical faculty, which, in the present stage of Canadian society, demands more than any other, generous support. Means for this have hitherto been deficient, and much precious time and energy have been wasted in the inevitable struggle to maintain the ground already gained. It has been my earnest prayer that I might be permitted to carry out in the case of McGill my ideal of a complete and symmetrical university suited to this country, and particularly to the English population of this Province. It has pleased God to deny me this satisfaction; but I entertain the firm belief that good foundations have been laid, which will not be disturbed, but will be built on and carried to full completion, by the energy, care, and judgment of my immediate successors." These hopes were destined to be fulfilled in the larger McGill of our day.

CHAPTER X

HIGHER EDUCATION FOR WOMEN

WHEN Sir William Dawson became Principal of McGill in 1855, there was no provision in the University for the instruction of women. They were not permitted to attend the classes available to men. Indeed, women's education was then under discussion and debate in Great Britain and the United States. It had many supporters but it had also many opponents. The agitation for the higher education of women on equal terms with men, particularly in the liberal arts, went back to the days of Defoe's "Essay on Projects" in which he included a section on "an Academy for Women." It had echoed from his time down through the eighteenth century until 1791 when Mary Wollstonecraft published her systematic treatise, "A Vindication of the Rights of Women." Thereafter the original plea merely for education became but a minor part of a larger demand for the franchise and for general equality; and instead of a sober emphasis on the necessity for learning, there was a somewhat hysterical clamour that women "should be admitted side by side with men into all the offices of public life with respect both to kind and degree." This agitation soon gathered abundant ridicule by the advocacy, led by Amelia Jenks Bloomer, of reform in women's dress, which would make it, as far as possible, the

Dr. Alexander Johnston
Vice-Principal of McGill University
1886-1903

same as that of man, and would consequently be an outward and visible sign of the equality of the sexes.

The derision and scorn incurred by the movement because of the unwise zeal of some of its advocates had not yet passed in the fifties. In Canada, the question of higher education for women was avoided, or regarded with doubt or indifference. But Principal Dawson was an earnest and enthusiastic believer in women's education, and early in his connection with McGill he formed plans for the providing of facilities to make such education possible in the University. Because of the indifference and the opposition to what was looked upon as a useless innovation, these plans were slow in maturing and in actual accomplishment. The Principal, however, persevered; circumstances were favourable, and in the end his hopes were fulfilled.

In Montreal at that time there was a girls' school, presided over by Hannah Willard Lyman, who later received an appointment to Vassar College. In this school no adequate course of instruction was given in Natural Science. Miss Lyman was desirous that her students should receive some knowledge of that subject, and she asked permission to have her pupils listen to Dr. Dawson's lectures, which were given in the afternoons. Her request was granted and the school girls attended the lectures for one session. But the experiment, for some unexplained reason, was not satisfactory and it was not repeated.

In his annual University Lecture in the autumn of 1869, the Principal expressed his belief in the benefits that might be conferred by the University in providing means for women's education. "I think," he said, "it would be quite possible for the

University to provide lectures on scientific and literary subjects, which would be open to all the ladies' schools in the city, and that certificates of attendance and examination might be given to such pupils. I do not propose either that young women should attend the ordinary College classes, or that except in special cases the ordinary professors should lecture to them. I should have special classrooms, and in many instances at least special lecturers appointed by the University. Of course, this is a purpose for which the constitution of the University does not permit its funds to be used, even if they were sufficient for it—which they are not. I only wish to intimate my conviction that an opening for usefulness lies in this direction—one which I have often wished to have the means of cultivating, knowing that in this country very few young women enjoy, to a sufficient extent, the advantages of the higher kind of education; and that the true civilisation of any people is quite as much to be measured by the culture of its women as by that of its men."

A few months later, at a meeting of Governors and friends of the University, held in February, 1870, preparatory to making an appeal for funds to the citizens of Montreal, the following resolution was unanimously passed:

"That this meeting rejoices in the arrangements made in the mother country, and on this continent, to afford to young women the opportunity of a regular college course; and being persuaded of the vital importance of this matter to the cause of higher education, and to the well-being of the community, respectfully commends the subject to the consideration of the Corporation of the University, for such action as the expected addition to the endowment may enable them to take."

But no part of the funds which were contributed as a result of the appeal were specially assigned to the education of women. In December following a reception was given in Molson Hall to the benefactors of the University who had recently subscribed so generously to its revenue. At this gathering, Chancellor Day referred to the necessity for providing the means of furnishing a higher education for women, "a matter," he said, "in which we are wofully behind the age. . . . I trust the time is not far distant when McGill College may become the privileged instrument of ministering to this urgent need. In this whole matter of education for either sex, women are directly and deeply interested."

A few months later, in 1871, Hannah Willard Lyman, the former Principal of the school for girls, died. Her former pupils in Montreal determined in some way to perpetuate her memory. They collected the "Hannah Willard Lyman Memorial Fund" for the establishment of a scholarship or a prize for women to be awarded in McGill when women would be admitted to its classes, "in a College for women affiliated to the University or in classes approved by the University." But no way existed for the carrying out of this desire. The Governors showed little sympathy with the idea of admitting women students to men's classes; they had no objection to a distinct women's College, but no funds for such an undertaking were available. Dr. Dawson then appealed for help to the women friends of McGill, and his appeal at once met with a ready response. In the autumn of 1871 a number of women interested in the higher education of their sex met at the residence of Mrs. John Molson, and formed the "Ladies' Educational Association of Montreal," for the purpose of obtaining, in the absence of University opportunities, instruction for its members. This Association carried on its work for thirteen years, until women were at last admitted to McGill. It was self-supporting, although it asked only very moderate fees from its students and paid its lecturers generously. Principal Dawson gave the introductory lecture of the first session in October, 1871. The students who took the full course of lectures and passed an examination on the work received a certificate of "Associate in Arts."

But the hope of admitting women to the classes in Arts had not been abandoned. On October 25th, 1882, Professor Clark Murray moved at a meeting of the Arts Faculty a resolution, which was carried, to the effect "that the educational advantages of the Faculty of Arts should be thrown open to all persons without distinction of sex." In the summer of 1884 a deputation of women who had already passed the examinations for Associate in Arts waited on Principal Dawson and asked that opportunities be provided in the College to enable them to proceed to the degree of Bachelor of Arts. The obstacle in the way of granting this request was the lack of funds. But a few weeks after the request was made, Sir Donald Smith agreed to give a sum of $50,000 for the purpose, on conditions to be settled by him. These conditions stipulated that the classes for women were to be wholly separate and distinct from those for men, and that no expenditure was to be incurred beyond the income of the endowment. The

Percy Molson
Founder of the Molson Stadium
Killed in action July, 1917

offer was accepted by the Board of Governors. The sum given was sufficient to provide the necessary duplicate courses for the first and second years in the Arts Faculty, and in the autumn of 1884 the first session for women in McGill commenced with fourteen regular and thirteen partial students. The women's classes were given in the lecture rooms of the east wing of the Arts Building. The students were known as "Donaldas," after the name of their generous benefactor, and the course was known as the "Donalda" course.

After two years had passed, in October, 1886, Sir Donald Smith increased his endowment to $120,000 in order to provide sufficient income for courses in all four years, and thereby to enable women students to proceed to the B.A. degree. In the session of 1886-87 there were twenty regular and fifty-eight partial students enrolled in women's courses, and in 1887-88 the number increased to twenty-six regular and eighty-two partial students. At the end of that session eight women received for the first time the degree of Bachelor of Arts. Higher education for women in McGill was now an assured fact. The Principal's dream had at last been realised.

But Dr. Dawson had hope of a still greater development of women's education. He said: "This great work is not yet complete. We look forward to a College for women, either a College of the University co-ordinate with McGill College, or affiliated to the University. Such College while taking advantage of the Museum, Laboratories, Library, and other appliances of McGill College, and to a certain extent of its staff, will have its own building, provided with all modern improvements and refinements for educational work. . . . I desire to express, as a matter of personal experience, my entire sympathy with those who hold that the education of women should be conducted, as far as possible, in separate classes." The hope here expressed was again to be realised—and Principal Dawson lived to see the accomplishment of his plans. Sir Donald Smith, then Lord Strathcona, was again appealed to. He increased his endowment fund for the erection and equipment of a building such as the Principal had in view, and the building of the Royal Victoria College was begun in 1895. On September 4th, 1899, two months before Sir William Dawson's death, the Royal Victoria College for women was opened, and the women students of McGill had at last a home and lecture-rooms of their own, "provided," as Sir William had dreamed, "with all modern improvements and refinements for educational work."

Since the opening of the Royal Victoria College the opportunities for the education of women in the University have been greatly enlarged and developed. To-day women students are enrolled on equal terms with men, not only in the Faculty of Arts, but in the Faculties of Law and Medicine, and in the Departments of Commerce and Physical Education. Indeed, women students are admitted to all Faculties and Departments of the University with the exception of the Faculty of Applied Science. Women graduates of McGill have continued to go out for thirty-three years to fill important posts and to take a prominent place in the building up of Canada and in service to humanity. In the half-century that has passed since the formation of the

Lord Strathcona

"Women's Educational Association of Montreal," with its humble beginnings and its scanty courses for "Associates in Arts," the higher education of women has made undreamed of progress. In McGill it owes its guidance and its growth to the tolerance in a time of prejudice, the determination in a period of opposition, and the patient faith in a day of discouragement, of Sir William Dawson, who believed in the greatness of women's sphere and influence in his country and in the world.

CHAPTER XI

THE LARGER McGILL OF OUR DAY

IN writing of the final epoch in McGill's first century, and the larger McGill of our day, we must of necessity be brief. We are too close to that epoch justly to judge its significance, or to give to the events and the incidents of which it is made up the fair and adequate reference which they doubtless deserve. Only the passing of the years can place them in their true perspective. Any estimate of them in our day would perhaps be proved false by time. Matthew Arnold said: "No man can trust himself to speak of his own time and his own contemporaries with the same sureness of judgment and the same proportion as of times and men gone by." The growth and development of McGill, then, during the last quarter of a century will be here given in bare outline only. The details of that growth are vivid in the memory of living men.

In May, 1895, Dr. William Peterson, Principal of University College, Dundee, Scotland, was appointed to succeed Sir William Dawson as Principal of McGill University, and at the opening of the session in the following September he arrived in Montreal to begin his work. The new Principal was born in Edinburgh in May, 1856. He received his education at the Edinburgh High School and at Edinburgh University, where he graduated in 1875 with

Honours in Classics. On his graduation he was awarded the Greek Travelling Fellowship, and after a period of study on the continent he entered Oxford University for further post-graduate courses in Classics. On leaving Oxford he was appointed Assistant to the Professor of the Humanities in Edinburgh University. Two years later, in 1882, he was appointed to the Principalship of University College, Dundee, which included among its other duties the Professorship of Classics and Ancient History. Thirteen years later he became Principal of McGill.

The twenty-four years during which Principal Peterson guided the destinies of McGill were years of steady growth and development. They were years, too, of notable and generous gifts from men of wealth and vision who believed in the value of education and of the beneficent influence of McGill in Canada and the world. Soon after Principal Peterson's appointment two projects for which his predecessor, Sir William Dawson, had planned were carried to completion. Both of these were made possible by the loyal aid of two benefactors who had already contributed greatly to the expansion of the University. William C. Macdonald had already given the Macdonald Engineering Building and the Macdonald Physics Building for the advancement of Applied Science. He now added to these the Macdonald Chemistry and Mining Building with full equipment for the carrying on of courses which, we have seen, Dr. Harrington had originated years before in the cramped and poorly furnished rooms in the narrow corridor of the Arts Building. The building was opened on December 20, 1898. The Faculty of Applied Science had now passed from small beginnings and inadequate accommodation to a complete organization and a modern home. On September 4th, 1899, the Royal Victoria College for women was formally opened. It was the gift of Lord Strathcona, formerly Sir Donald Smith, who, in 1884, had made possible the establishment of the first courses for women given in McGill, and who, in 1886, had made provision for the complete four years' courses in Arts, the Donalda courses leading to the B.A. degree. The former Principal, Sir William Dawson, lived to see realised the two dreams for the fulfilment of which he had worked so arduously—the completion of the Science Buildings and the erection of a women's College as part of the University.

Over the period that followed since the turn of the century we may pass briefly. It was a period of continued development, not always, however, without its discouragements and problems which need not be here recorded. But disappointments and obstacles were met by Dr. Peterson with courage and energy and hope. The result was progress. The Medical Faculty, which had grown beyond its quarters, needed more room if it was to keep pace with modern research and with the increased number of its students. Lord Strathcona, who had given the first Medical endowment fund in 1882, again came to the rescue, and in September, 1901, a new wing to the Medical Building was opened. In October, 1904, the Conservatorium of Music was established. Later, by the will of Sir William Macdonald, it was left an endowment fund which placed it on an independent basis and enabled it to be expanded into a Faculty of the University. In 1903 Dr. Alexander

Dr. Charles E. Moyse
Vice-Principal of McGill University
1903-1920

Johnson, who had been Vice-Principal for seventeen years, retired and was succeeded by Charles E. Moyse, Professor of English. In the spring of 1907 two disastrous fires occurred; in April, within eleven days of each other, the Macdonald Engineering Building and the largest part of the Medical Building were destroyed. Again the University's two great benefactors came to its assistance. Sir William Macdonald replaced the Engineering Building with a new building which was opened on April 27th, 1909, and Lord Strathcona provided for the erection of the new Medical Building, which was opened on June 5th, 1911.

Meanwhile Sir William Macdonald had undertaken to provide in connection with the University an institution intended to meet the needs of the country at large, particularly the rural districts, and to afford better facilities for the training of teachers. With this object in view he founded, in 1907, Macdonald College, at St. Anne de Bellevue, twenty miles from Montreal. It was designed to include three schools, one for Agriculture, one for Household Science and one for Normal Training. The gift for buildings, grounds, consisting of nearly eight hundred acres, equipment and endowment amounted to over six million dollars. The College was incorporated in the University as the Faculty of Agriculture.

There were many other gifts from Sir William Macdonald during this period. In 1909 an attempt was made by a syndicate to purchase the block known as the Joseph property at the southwest corner of the College yard or campus, for the purpose of building an hotel. The Principal was alarmed. He appealed to Sir William, whose pride was great in

McGill and in the buildings he had erected. Sir
William had no desire that the grounds of McGill
should become the backyard of an hotel, however
exclusive. He at once purchased the corner, and
presented it to the University, thus completing the
McGill square and providing a home for the Mc-
Cord National Museum. Two years later he purchased, as he said, "for a playground for McGill
students, the grown-up children of all Canada," the
Frothingham, Molson and Law properties, consisting of twenty-five acres, just east of the Royal Victoria Hospital and the Medical Building. This
property, known as Macdonald Park, is the athletic
centre of the University. In October, 1920, the
Stadium in this park was formally opened. It was
the gift of Percival Molson, B.A., who graduated
in Arts in 1901, and who was killed in action in
front of Avion, near Lens, on July 3rd, 1917, while
serving as a Captain in the Princess Patricia's Canadian Light Infantry. The McGill Union, erected
on Sherbrooke Street, as a centre of student activities, was also the gift of Sir William Macdonald,
McGill's greatest benefactor, whose donations to
the University during the Principalships of Sir William Dawson and Sir William Peterson amounted to
over twelve million and a half of dollars. In 1912
the four affiliated Theological Colleges formed a co-
operating Divinity School in affiliation with the University for the instruction of joint classes, and Divinity Hall on University Street was opened.

The last five years of Sir William Peterson's Principalship were the years of war tragedy. When the
war came in 1914 the University gave all its energy
to the allied cause. When the trumpet blew for

freedom, the Principal, although he could not actually enter the combatant lists, gave all his strength unstintingly. The part taken by McGill in the war cannot be here detailed; it must be left for another story. Only the bare outline need be mentioned. When the war cloud broke, the Canadian Officers Training Corps already in connection with the University was reorganised, and grounds and buildings became centres of military activity. In the spring of 1915 the McGill General Hospital, known later as No. 3 (McGill) went overseas. It was a distinctively McGill unit. It was organised within the Medical Faculty. All its officers were members of the teaching staff or graduates of the Medical School. The nurses were graduates of either the Royal Victoria Hospital or the Montreal General Hospital, and practically all the men in the unit were drawn from the student body. Early in the following year a heavy artillery unit was organised within the University, and was permitted by the Militia department to use the name McGill until its arrival in France. It was also allowed to embody the McGill crest with the artillery badge. It was organised as No. 6 (McGill) Siege Battery, but after its arrival at the front it was known as No. 7 Battery, Canadian Siege Artillery. The Commanding Officer and the second in command were members of the teaching staff of the University; the other officers and non-commissioned officers were largely graduates, and more than half the gunners were McGill students. Because of rapid promotions and consequent transfers of officers and men, as well as of the usual circumstances and changes of war, this unit lost before the end of hostilities its distinctively McGill character. The majority of McGill men in the original unit received commissions. Five full companies of infantry and part of a sixth were recruited in the University. They were known as "The University Companies," and were sent to the front as reinforcements for the Princess Patricia's Canadian Light Infantry. The majority of the officers of these companies and a large number of the men were graduates or students of McGill. The 148th Battalion, Canadian Infantry, recruited in Montreal, although not under the authority of the University, was affiliated with the McGill Canadian Officers Training Corps, and a large number of its officers and men were members of that organization. Later, two reinforcement drafts were organized in the University and each contained a large proportion of students. One was a heavy artillery draft, which on arrival in England in the autumn of 1917 was absorbed into the artillery pool and was used to supply new siege artillery batteries about to be organised or to reinforce field and heavy batteries already at the front. The other draft was recruited for the Tank Battalion raised in the universities of Canada. But apart from the men in the units and drafts organized in the University, McGill men, students, graduates and professors, were found in practically every branch of the service, whether army or navy. The attendance of students in the University was reduced to a minimum; the teaching staff was depleted. In all, over twenty-five hundred McGill men enlisted. Three hundred and forty-one were killed in action, or died of wounds or disease; five hundred and twenty-two were wounded; three hundred and eighty-two received decorations or honours, two of which were the

Victoria Cross.   In recognition of its services in the allied cause the University received a grant of one million dollars from the Carnegie Foundation for the Advancement of Teaching.   McGill's war record, tragic but glorious, is one of her proudest possessions.

Principal Peterson's health had been impaired even before the war by the cares of an active and busy life spent unsparingly in the interests and the advancement of the University.   Like his predecessor, his life at McGill was one of unremitting labour and ceaseless, strenuous tasks which drew in the end a heavy toll from his strength.   Then the war came. With its activities and the continuous demands it made upon his time and energy, it severely taxed his already weakened constitution.   During the summer of 1918 he had been urged by his physicians and friends to rest because of his failing health.   He did not heed the advice; he felt, indeed, that he could not in that troubled and anxious time obey it.   He refused to curtail his exertions, and he continued to give his great ability and his unstinted service in every way to help the allied cause.   On Sunday, the 12th of January, 1919, although he was not then in good health, he presided at a meeting on behalf of a fund for the benefit of the dependents of Scottish soldiers and sailors killed or disabled in the war. While the meeting was in progress he was stricken with apoplexy and partial paralysis.   In the course of a few weeks he recovered his speech almost entirely, and later he regained the partial use of his right leg.   When it became evident that he could not recover sufficiently to resume his place at the head of the University he resigned, and after May

1st he ceased to be Principal of McGill.   On July
the 24th he sailed from Montreal for England,
where he resided until his death in February, 1921.

Sir William Peterson was Principal of McGill
University for a period of twenty-four years, one
quarter of its century of life.   During that time
many honours came to him.   He occupied the presi-
dency of many learned societies; he was knighted
in 1915; he received honorary degrees from the
leading universities of Britain, America and Canada; he was Chairman of the Board of Trustees of
the Carnegie Foundation for the Advancement of
Teaching; he won great distinction as a scholar and
a writer.   It would be unwise here to attempt to
estimate the significance of his work as Principal of
the University.   We are perhaps too close to judge
it with correctness or with justice.   The McGill he
left in 1919 was not the McGill he found in 1895.
In the intervening years its development on the sure
foundations that had already been laid was extraordinary and unprecedented for a university.   Among
the external evidences of growth during that time
are the McGill Union, the centre of student activities; the Conservatorium of Music, with courses
leading to the degree of Bachelor and Doctor of
Music; the establishment of a Department of Den-
tistry, now grown to the stature of a Faculty; the
acquisition of the Joseph property at the southwest
corner of the Yard, and the new Molson and Law
properties, consisting of 25 acres, the site of the
Molson Stadium, and of the gymnasium and student
residences of the future; the new Medical building;
the establishment and development of the Graduate

School, and of the Departments of Commerce, Social Service and Physical Education, and above all,
the addition of Macdonald College with its vast
acres at Ste. Anne de Bellevue, where the work of
the Faculty of Agriculture, Household Science and
the training of teachers is carried on. In these
twenty-five years the number of students more than
doubled. Financially, too, there was a change. In
1895 endowments amounted to over a million and
a half of dollars, in 1919 they were over twelve
millions, a sum to which the citizens' response to the
appeal for funds in 1911 largely contributed; the
income in 1895 was two hundred thousand dollars
and the disbursements one hundred and eighty thousand; in 1919 the income and disbursements each
amounted to approximately one million dollars. In
addition to these visible evidences of progress many
new and improved courses were established; the
teaching staff was greatly increased, and the reputation of the University was enhanced at home and
abroad. Externally and internally the newer and
greater McGill bears testimony to the energy and
determination of Sir William Peterson during his
twenty-four years' occupancy of the Principalship.
With the criticisms of his administration—that as
Principal Sir William was an Imperialist first and
afterwards a Canadian, and that in making profes-
sorial appointments he did not often consider Canadian scholars, with at least equal qualifications—we
are not here concerned.

In the spring of 1919 Sir Auckland Geddes, Minister of National Service in the British Cabinet, and
formerly Professor of Anatomy in McGill, was ap-

pointed Principal. He never assumed the duties of his office and a year later he resigned to become British Ambassador at Washington, U. S. A.

In May, 1920, Sir Arthur Currie, formerly Commander of the Canadian Corps in France, was appointed Principal, and in the following August he took up his new duties. In June of that year Vice-Principal Moyse resigned after forty-one years of service as Professor of English. He was succeeded as Vice-Principal by Dr. Frank D. Adams, Dean of the Faculty of Applied Science.

One of the first acts of the new Principal was the making of a general appeal, with the Governors, in the autumn of 1920, for public subscriptions to increase the endowment fund and revenues for the purpose of increasing professors' salaries and for the erection of new buildings or extensions. The response to this appeal was generous; a sum of over six million dollars was subscribed, of which one million was from the Province of Quebec. The renewed interest of graduates in their University was evidenced by the fact that they subscribed over half the amount raised. As a result of the increased endowment, two structures were at once undertaken, one an extension to the Library, and the other a new building for the Medical Faculty.

With an encouraging interest in its welfare by graduates and by citizens, with a large increase in students who last year numbered over three thousand, with forward face looking hopefully to the future, McGill University has rounded out its first century of life. The road over which it has passed, as we look back from the hilltop of to-day, has been long and arduous. It has been beset with many trials

Sir Arthur Currie
Principal McGill University 1920

and difficulties.   But the obstacles in the way of its advance were not unsurmountable; they were perhaps objects of discouragement, but never objects of total despair to the men of stout heart and firm faith and far-off vision who made McGill.

Dr. Frank D. Adams
Vice-Principal of McGill University
1920

EPILOGUE

EPILOGUE

WHAT has been written in these pages is based on authentic documents and sources rather than on tradition—on fact rather than on rumour. Necessity required that it should be the story of epochs rather than of individuals. It is sometimes said unwisely that "epochs are but resting-places or halts in history." But that is not a truthful definition when applied to the epochs of McGill, for they have all been times of progress. With steps sometimes accelerated, sometimes slow, sometimes even faltering, its movement has been always onward. There have been no stopping-places in its life. It has not been possible here to give adequate notice or even reference to all its benefactors and to all the noble and unselfish men and women who helped in its advancement, to the distinguished graduates and sacrificing professors who brought honour to its name, to the discoveries, the theories and doctrines for improvement, whether intellectual or social or political, first fashioned in its shadow. Through the medium of these men and women, and their theories and doctrines carried into practice, it has won undying glory. Their names are safe in our University's past; we can leave their memories in its keeping.

When James McGill made his bequest he was dreaming of a University that would first serve Canada and assist in its development. He himself had set his face westward. When he made his will he knew that he was of the past, but he had faith in the coming youth and manhood of his adopted land. He saw the possibilities of the vast new country in which he had prospered but which he was so soon to leave, and he had a firm belief in its future greatness. The Founder's dream has been realised even to a greater extent than perhaps he hoped. The men who in its hundred years of life brought to McGill the largest portion of its fame, whether graduates or professors, were products of the new country in the young manhood of which he had such unbounded faith. They were, for the most part, native Canadians whose feet were rooted in the soil. They were men whose ancestors, like the Founder himself, had crossed the ocean in comfortless craft to face unknown hardships in forest and on plain, to build homes from the wilderness in which they might find happiness and fortune. Dawson in Education, Osler in Medicine, Laurier in Statesmanship, and a host of others, these are gone; they are behind us; their achievements are part of our century story. Elsewhere than in McGill their services, their doctrines, and their theories have been assimilated; they have ministered to the nation's and the world's life. And the men and boys who went out from McGill to die for their principles during the world's five years of tragedy were similar to them in sacrifice and spirit; they contributed in another form to the advancement of civilization. In their ideals they were typical of the Canadian youth of James McGill's vision. They justified the Founder's faith.

McGill College in 1921

With this reference to our great dead we bring these chapters to a close. The next, unwritten, chapter in McGill University's history is one of which we do not see the end. It must be left to other hands and other pens. When it is written it may or may not revolve about individuals. Like its preceding chapters it, too, will more probably be the story of an epoch. For while the individual must always vanish in his due time, the College must survive. One fact is certain—after one hundred years of struggle and of ultimate triumph, life still beats strongly in the veins of the University—more actively than in the days of its youth, and more hopefully than at any period in its history. There is a new spirit in McGill. To-day its pulsing life, under the guidance of its great Canadian leader, reaches through all grades and faculties and departments of its students as it has never done before. There is a general forward movement, unhampered and undivided by considerations or competitions of sections or of faculties. The University is closer, too, than it once was to the current of national feeling. It is seeking to minister to Canada, the land which gave it birth and from which its greatness sprang. But while it will serve Canada, it will continue to draw its students, like the true *Studium Generale,* from every country on the globe, and to send them back to serve their individual countries to advance the enlightenment of the world. McGill's first century has been a century of trial, but a century of great accomplishment. Its struggles and its triumphs are an inspiration for the coming days. If we but follow the ideals of the men who made our University, with their noble sacrifice, their splendid achievement and their unwavering faith as our heritage, the unwritten story of McGill's future will be more glorious even than the record of its past.

APPENDICES

APPENDIX A

"I give and devise all that tract or parcel of land, commonly called Burnside, situated near the city of Montreal aforesaid, containing about forty-six acres, including an acre of land purchased by me from one Sanscrainte, together with the dwelling-house and other buildings thereon erected, with their appurtenances, unto the Honourable John Richardson and James Reid, of the City of Montreal aforesaid, Esquires, the Rev. John Strachan, Rector of Cornwall, in Upper Canada, and James Dunlop, of the said City of Montreal, Esquire, and to their heirs, to, upon, and for the uses, trusts, intents, and purposes, and with, and subject to, the provisions, conditions, and limitations, hereinafter mentioned and expressed, of and concerning the same, that is to say, upon trust that they the said John Richardson, James Reid, John Strachan, and James Dunlop, or the survivors or survivor of them, or the heirs, executors, or curators of such survivors or survivor, do and shall, as soon as it conveniently can be done after my decease, by a good and sufficient conveyance and assurance, convey and assure the said last-mentioned tract or parcel of land, dwelling-house, buildings, and premises, to the Royal Institution for the Advancement of Learning, constituted and established, or to be constituted and established, under and by virtue of an Act of the Parliament of the Province of Lower Canada, made and passed in the forty-first year of His Majesty's Reign, intituled 'An Act for the Establishment of Free Schools and the Advancement of Learning in this Province'—upon and under the conditions, restrictions, and limitations, and to and for the ends, intents, and purposes following, that is to say, upon condition that the said 'Royal Institution for the Advancement of Learning' do and shall, within the space of ten years, to be accounted from the time of my decease, erect and establish, or cause to be erected and established, upon the said last-mentioned tract or parcel of land, an University or College, for the purposes of education, and the advancement of learning in this Province, with a competent number of Professors and Teachers, to render such establishment effectual and beneficial for the purposes intended; and

277

if the said 'Royal Institution for the Advancement of Learning' should so erect and establish, or cause to be erected and established an University, then upon condition also that one of the Colleges to be comprised in the said University shall be named, and perpetually be known and distinguished, by the appellation of 'McGill College'; and if the said 'Royal Institution for the Advancement of Learning' should not so erect and establish, or cause to be erected and established, an University, but should erect and establish, or cause to be erected and established, a College only, then upon the further conditions that the said College shall be named, and perpetually be known and distinguished, by the appellation of 'McGill College'; and upon condition also, that until such University or College be erected and established, the said 'Royal Institution for the Advancement of Learning' do and shall permit and suffer my said wife, and in case of her death, the said Francis Desrivieres, to hold, possess and enjoy the said last-mentioned tract or parcel of land, dwelling-house, buildings, and premises, and to recover, have, and receive all and every the rents, issues, and profits thereof to and for her and his use and benefit: and upon this other and express condition, that if the said 'Royal Institution for the Advancement of Learning' should neglect to erect and establish, or cause to be erected and established, such University or College as aforesaid, in manner aforesaid within the said space of ten years, to be accounted from the time of my decease, then and in such case the said conveyance and assurance so made to the said 'Royal Institution for the Advancement of Learning' shall, from and after the expiration of the said space of ten years, become and be absolutely null and void, and all and every the estate, right, title, and interest of the said 'Royal Institution for the Advancement of Learning' of, in, and to the said last-mentioned tract or parcel of land and premises shall cease and be determined, and be as completely extinguished as if such conveyance and assurance had never been made or executed: All which conditions, restrictions, and limitations shall, in apt and sufficient language, be fully expressed in such conveyance and assurance. And upon trust that the said John Richardson, James Reid, John Strachan, and James Dunlop, or the survivors or survivor of them, or the heirs, executors, or curators of such survivors or survivor of them do and shall permit and suffer my said wife or, in case of her death, the said Francis Desrivieres, to hold, possess, and enjoy the said tract or parcel of land, dwelling-house, buildings, and premises, and recover, have, and receive the rents, issues, and profits thereof until the making and executing of the said conveyance and assurance so as aforesaid to be made to the said

'Royal Institution for the Advancement of Learning'; and if
the said 'Royal Institution for the Advancement of Learning'
should refuse to accept and receive the said conveyance and assurance of the said last-mentioned tract or parcel of land and
premises, upon the conditions, restrictions, and limitations herein
before expressed and directed, of and concerning the same, or
should, after the making and accepting of the said conveyance
and assurance neglect to erect and establish, or cause to be
erected and established, such University or College as aforesaid,
in manner aforesaid, within the said space of ten years, to be
accounted from the time of my decease, or if, from any legal
cause, matter, or thing, the said trust so as aforesaid to convey
and assure the said last-mentioned tract or parcel of land and
premises to the said 'Royal Institution for the Advancement of
Learning,' in the manner herein before directed, should be in-
capable of being accomplished or carried into effect, or otherwise
become, or be, or be deemed or construed to be invalid, illegal,
or inoperative, then and in either or any of those cases upon trust,
and that they the said John Richardson, James Reid, John
Strachan, and James Dunlop, or the survivors or survivor of
them or the heirs, executors, or curators of such survivors or
survivor do and shall, from and immediately after the expiration
of the said space of ten years, by a good and sufficient conveyance and assurance, convey and assure the said last-mentioned
tract or parcel of land, dwelling-house, buildings, and premises
to the said Francis Desrivieres (if then living), and to his
heirs and assigns forever, or if the said Francis Desrivieres
should be dead, then to the legal heirs then living, and to their
heirs and assigns forever.

"I give and bequeath, from and out of the rest and residue of
my estates, real and personal, movable and immovable, which shall
and may remain after the fulfilment and satisfaction of the
several legacies in this my Will contained, the sum of *ten thousand pounds,* current money of the said Province of Lower
Canada, to the said John Richardson, James Reid, John Strachan,
and James Dunlop, *their heirs, executors, or curators,* upon the
trust, and to and for the intents and purposes, and upon the
conditions following, that is to say, upon trust, that they the
said John Richardson, James Reid, John Strachan, and James
Dunlop, or the survivors or survivor of them or the heirs,
executors, and curators of such survivors, do and shall pay the
said sum of ten thousand pounds (with the interest to accrue
thereon from and after the expiration of three years from my
decease) to the said 'Royal Institution for the Advancement of
Learning,' when and so soon as the said 'Royal Institution for

the Advancement of Learning' shall have erected and established, or cause to be erected and established, an University or College upon the last-mentioned tract or parcel of land, herein before directed to be conveyed to the said 'Royal Institution for the Advancement of Learning,' in manner aforesaid, *to be* by the said 'Royal Institution for the Advancement of Learning' *paid and applied towards defraying the expense incurred in establishing the said University or College,* and towards maintaining the same after it shall have been erected and established, in such manner and form, and under such regulations as the said 'Royal Institution for the Advancement of Learning' shall in this behalf prescribe. Provided always, that such University or College be erected and established within the space of ten years, to be accounted from the time of my decease: and if such University or College should not be so erected and established within the said space of ten years, then upon trust that they the said John Richardson, James Reid, John Strachan, and James Dunlop, or the survivors or survivor of them, or the heirs, executors, or curators of such survivor, from and immediately after the said expiration of the said space of ten years do and shall pay the said sum of ten thousand pounds, with all and every the interest accrued thereon, to the said Francis Desrivieres, if then living, to and for his use and benefit, or if dead, then to his legal heirs then living, to and for their use and benefit."

APPENDIX B

The Charter of McGill College

Victoria, by the Grace of GOD, of the United Kingdom of Great
Britain and Ireland, Queen, Defender of the Faith.

To all whom these presents shall come,

Greeting:

WHEREAS his late Majesty George the Fourth was graciously
pleased, by Letters Patent bearing date at Westminster, on
the Thirty-first day of March, in the Second year of his Reign,
to establish at Burnside, near the City of Montreal in the Province of Lower Canada, an University, the first College of which,
by the said Charter, is called "McGill College," which Charter is
in the following words:

"George the Fourth, by the Grace of GOD, of the United
"Kingdom of Great Britain and Ireland, King, Defender
"of the Faith.

"To all to whom these presents shall come,

Greeting:

"WHEREAS the Honourable James McGill, late of the City of
"Montreal in the Province of Lower Canada, now deceased,
"by his last Will and Testament, bearing date at Montreal the
"Eighth day of January, in the year of Our Lord One Thousand
"eight hundred and eleven, did give and bequeath a certain tract
"of Land near the said City of Montreal, with the dwelling-house
"and other buildings thereon erected, to Trustees, in trust, to con-
"vey and assure the same to the Royal Institution for the Ad-
"vancement of Learning, established by virtue of an Act of the
"Provincial Parliament of Lower Canada, made and passed in
"the Forty-first year of the Reign of his late Majesty, intituled 'An
"Act for the Establishment of Free Schools and the Advancement
"of Learning in the said Province,' upon condition that the said
"Institution should, within ten years from the decease of the said
"James McGill, erect and establish or cause to be erected and
"established upon the said land, an University or College for
"the purposes of Education and the Advancement of Learning

"in the said Province, with a competent number of Professors
"and Teachers to render such Establishment effectual and bene-
"ficial for the purposes intended; and also, upon condition that
"one of the Colleges, to be comprised in the said University,
"should be called McGill College; And whereas, the said James
"McGill, Esquire, by his said last Will, did further give and be-
"queath to the said Trustees the sum of Ten Thousand pounds,
"in trust, to pay the same with interest to accrue thereon from
"and after the expiration of three years from his decease, to the
"said Royal Institution for the Advancement of Learning, to be
"applied as soon as the said Institution should have erected an
"University or College on the said land towards defraying the
"expenses thereby incurred, and towards maintaining the said
"University or College so erected and established. And whereas,
"we have been humbly petitioned by the said Royal Institution
"for the Advancement of Learning, that we should be pleased to
"grant Our Royal Charter for the more perfect erection and es-
"tablishment of the said College, and for incorporating the mem-
"bers thereof for the purposes aforesaid, and for such further
"endowment thereof as to us should seem meet, We, having
"taken the premises into Our Royal consideration, and being
"desirous that an University or College should be established for
"the Education of Youth in the principles of true religion and
"for their instruction in the different branches of science and
"literature, are willing to comply with the prayer of the said
"petition, and to afford every assistance towards carrying the
"intentions of the said James McGill into execution.
"Therefore, know ye that We of Our special grace, certain
"knowledge and mere motion, have willed, ordained and granted,
"and do by these presents for Us, Our Heirs and Successors, will,
"ordain and grant, that upon the said land and in the said build-
"ings thereon erected or to be erected, there shall be established,
"from this time one College at the least for the Education of
"youth and students in the Arts and Faculties, to continue for-
"ever, and that the first College to be erected thereon shall be
"called McGill College; and that Our trusty and well-beloved
"the Governor of Lower Canada, Lieutenant-Governor of Lower
"Canada, Lieutenant-Governor of Upper Canada, the Bishop of
"Quebec, the Chief Justice of Montreal, and the Chief Justice
"of Upper Canada, for the time being, shall be Governors of the
"said McGill College, and that the said McGill College shall con-
"sist of one Principal, to be elected in manner hereinafter men-
"tioned, and who shall be, during his continuance in the said
"office, a Governor of the said College; of four Professors, to be
"also elected in manner hereinafter mentioned; and of Fellows,

"Tutors, and Scholars, in such numbers, and at such salaries,
"and subject to such provisions, rules and regulations, as shall
"hereafter be appointed by the Statutes, Rules and Ordinances of
"the said College; and We do by these presents for Us, Our
"Heirs, and Successors, will, ordain and grant, that the Prin-
"cipal and Professors of the said College shall be, from time to
"time, elected by the said Governors or the major part of them,
"as shall be present at any meeting to be holden for such elec-
"tion; and in case of an equality of votes, the officer present at
"such meeting, whose office is first described in order in these
"presents, shall have a double and casting vote: provided always,
"that the persons by whom such elections shall be made shall
"notify the same respectfully to Us, Our Heirs or Successors,
"through one of Our or Their principal Secretaries of State, by
"the first opportunity, and in case that WE, Our Heirs or Suc-
"cessors, shall disapprove of any person so elected, and shall
"cause such disapprobation to be notified to him under the Royal
"signet and sign manual, or through one of the principal Secre-
"taries of State, the person so elected as aforesaid shall immedi-
"ately, upon such notification, cease to hold the office of Principal
"or Professor to which he shall have been elected as aforesaid,
"and the said Governors shall thereupon proceed to the election
"of another person to fill the office of such Principal or Pro-
"fessor respectively, and so, from time to time, as often as the
"case shall happen.

"And we do by these presents for Us, Our Heirs and Successors,
"will, ordain and grant, that the said Governors, Principal and
"Fellows, and their Successors, forever shall be one distinct and
"separate body politic and corporate in deed and in word, by
"the name and style of 'The Governors, Principal and Fellows
"of McGill College, at Montreal, in the said Province of Lower
"Canada,' and that by the same name they shall have perpetual
"succession, and a common seal, and that they and their suc-
"cessors shall, from time to time, have full power to break, alter,
"make new, or change such common seal at their will and pleas-
"ure, and as shall be found expedient, and that by the same name
"the said Governors, Principal and Fellows, and their successors,
"from time to time, and at all times hereafter, shall be a body
"politic and corporate, in deed and in law, and be able and capable
"to have, take, receive, purchase, acquire, hold, possess, enjoy
"and retain.

"And we do hereby for Us, Our Heirs and Successors, give and
"grant full authority and free license to them and their suc-
"cessors, by the name aforesaid, to have, take, receive, purchase,
"acquire, hold, possess, enjoy, and retain, to and for the use

"of the said College, notwithstanding any statutes or statute
"of mortmain, any manors, rectories, advowsons, messuages,
"lands, tenements, rents, hereditaments of what kind, nature, or
"quality soever, so as that the same do not exceed, in yearly
"value, the sum of £6000 above all charges; and, moreover, to
"take, purchase, acquire, have, hold, enjoy, receive, possess and
"retain, notwithstanding any such statutes or statute to the con-
"trary, all or any goods, chattels, charitable and other contribu-
"tions, gifts and benefactions whatsoever; and that the said
"Governors, Principal and Fellows, and their successors, by the
"same name, shall and may be able and capable in law to sue
"and be sued, implead and be impleaded, answer and be answered,
"in all or any Court or Courts of record, or places of judicature
"within Our United Kingdom of Great Britain and Ireland, and
"Our said Province of Lower Canada and other Our Dominions,
"and in all and singular actions, causes, pleas, suits, matters, and
"demands whatsoever, of what kind and nature or sort soever, in
"as large, ample, and beneficial a manner and form as any other
"body politic or corporate, or any other Our liege subjects being
"persons able and capable in law, may or can have, take, pur-
"chase, receive, hold, possess, enjoy, retain, sue, implead, or
"answer, in any manner whatsoever.
"And we do by these presents for Us, Our Heirs, and Successors,
"will, ordain, and grant that the Governors of the said College,
"or the major part of them, shall have power and authority to
"frame and make statutes, rules and ordinances, touching and
"concerning the good Government of the said College, the per-
"formance of Divine Service therein, the studies, lectures, exer-
"cises, and degrees in Arts and Faculties, and all matters regard-
"ing the same, the election, qualification, and residence of the
"Principal, Professors, Fellows, and Scholars; the salaries, sti-
"pend and provisions for the Principal, Professors, Fellows,
"Scholars, and Officers of the said College; and touching and
"concerning any other matter or thing which to them shall seem
"good, fit, useful, and agreeable to this Our Charter: provided
"that no such statutes, rules and ordinances shall have any force
"or effect until allowed and confirmed by Us, Our Heirs or Suc-
"cessors; and also, from time to time, to revoke, augment or
"alter the same as to them or the major part of them shall seem
"expedient, subject always to Our allowance and confirmation as
"aforesaid, provided that the said statutes, rules, and ordinances,
"or any of them, shall not be repugnant to the laws and statutes
"of this Our Realm, and of Our said Province of Lower Canada;
"and We do hereby for Us, Our Heirs, and Successors, charge
"and command that the statutes, rules and ordinances aforesaid,

"subject to the said provisions, shall be strictly and inviolably
"observed, kept, and performed, so long as they shall respectively
"remain in force and effect, under the penalties to be thereby or
"therein inflicted or contained. And we do by these presents
"for Us, Our Heirs and Successors, will, ordain and appoint,
"that the Members of the Royal Institution aforesaid, for the
"time being, shall be Visitors of the said College. And we do
"further will, ordain, and grant, that the said College shall be
"deemed and taken to be an University, and that the Students in
"the said College shall have liberty and faculty of taking the de-
"grees of Bachelor, Master and Doctor, in the several Arts and
"Faculties, at the appointed times, and shall have liberty within
"themselves, of performing Scholastic Exercises, for the con-
"ferring such degrees in such manner as shall be directed by
"the statutes, rules, and ordinances, of the aforesaid College; and
"we do, by these presents for Us, Our Heirs, and Successors,
"grant and declare that these Our Letters Patent, or the enrol-
"ments or exemplifications thereof, shall and may be good, firm,
"valid, sufficient, and effectual, in the law according to the intent
"and meaning of the same, and shall be taken, construed, and
"adjudged in the most favorable and beneficial sense for the best
"advantage of the said Governors, Principal, and Fellows, and
"Scholars of the said College of Montreal aforesaid, as well in
"all Our Courts of Record, as elsewhere, and by all and singular
"Judges, Justices, Officers, Ministers, and other subjects what-
"soever, of Us, Our Heirs and Successors, any misrecital, non-
"recital, omission, imperfection, defect, matter, cause, or thing
"whatsoever, to the contrary thereof, in anywise notwithstanding,
"without fine or fee, great or small, to be for the same in any
"manner rendered, done, or paid to Us in Our hanaper, or else-
"where, to Our use. In witness whereof we have caused these
"our letters to be made Patent. Witness Ourself at Westminster,
"the thirty-first day of March, in the second year of Our Reign.
"(1821.)
"By Writ of Privy Seal,
"(Signed)   BATHURST."

And whereas it is deemed expedient for the interests of the
said College, and for the augmentation of its funds, and for
the better and more easy management of its affairs and the
government of the said College, to make certain alterations in
the provisions of the said hereinbefore recited and existing Letters Patent, which said alterations are and have been assented
to by the said Royal Institution for the Advancement of Learning and by the said Corporation of the said College:

Now Know Ye, that We, of Our special Grace, certain Knowledge and mere motion, have willed, ordained and granted, and by these presents do, for Us, Our Heirs, and Successors, will, ordain and grant that henceforth from the date hereof, the members of the Royal Institution aforesaid for the time being shall be and remain Governors of the said College, and shall have and exercise all and every the powers, authority and jurisdiction given and granted unto the Governors nominated and appointed in and by the said Letters Patent, save only in so far as the provisions of the said Letters Patent in that behalf are or may be by these presents altered; and shall also have and exercise all and every the powers, authority and jurisdiction given and granted under and by virtue of these presents;

And We do further by these presents for Us, Our Heirs and Successors, will and ordain, that henceforth from the date hereof, the Governor of Lower Canada, the Lieutenant-Governor of Lower Canada, the Lieutenant-Governor of Upper Canada, the Bishop of Quebec, the Chief Justice of Montreal, the Chief Justice of Upper Canada, and the Principal of the said College, shall not, nor shall any or either of them, as such Governor of Lower Canada, Lieutenant-Governor of Lower Canada, Lieutenant-Governor of Upper Canada, Bishop of Quebec, Chief Justice of Montreal, Chief Justice of Upper Canada, and Principal of the said College, be Governor of the said College, or use or exercise any power, authority or jurisdiction in or over the same in any manner or way whatsoever.

And We do further, by these presents, for Us, Our Heirs and Successors, will, ordain and grant, that the said College shall consist of one Principal, of such and so many Professors in the various Arts and Faculties as from time to time may be judged necessary and expedient by the said Governors, and of Fellows, Tutors and Scholars, in such numbers and at such Salaries, and subject to such provisions, rules and regulations as shall be appointed by the Statutes, Rules and Ordinances of the said College; that save and except for the purposes hereinafter specially mentioned and excepted, three of the said Governors shall be a sufficient number to be present at any meeting for the transaction of the ordinary business of the said College; that the determination of all questions, matters and things submitted to the said Governors at their meetings shall be made by the votes of the majority of those present, including the vote of the Governor presiding at such meeting, who shall have a double or casting vote in the case of an equality of votes thereat; that the President or Principal for the time being of the said Royal Institution, in all cases when present, shall preside at the said meetings, and in his absence the member of the said Royal Institution first or senior in order of appointment of those present at the meeting, shall preside thereat; that the Principal and all the Professors of the said College shall from time to time be elected by the said Governors or the major part of them present at a meeting specially convened and holden for the purpose of such election, and shall and may hold their respective offices subject to the right and power of a motion by the said Governors for the time being, at a meeting specially convened and holden for the said purpose; provided always that no less than five of the said Governors shall be present at every such special meeting for the purpose of election or amotion, and that special notice in writing of the time, place and object of every special meeting, by the Secretary of the said College, addressed to each of the said Governors, shall have been delivered by the said Secretary into the Post Office of the said City of Montreal at least fifteen days before the time appointed for such meeting; that within forty-eight hours after every such election or amotion, notice thereof in writing, sealed with the College Seal, signed by the Secretary of the said College or in his absence by the Governor who shall have presided at the meeting whereat such election or amotion shall have been voted, and addressed to Our Visitor of the said College hereinafter mentioned, for the time being, shall be delivered into the Post Office of the said City of Montreal; that every such election or amotion shall be subject to the review of Our said Visitor, whose determination thereon being signified in writing to the said Governors within sixty days after such delivery as aforesaid at the said Post Office of the City of Montreal, of the said notice of such election or amotion, shall be final and conclusive, unless the same by any order or orders to be by Us, Our Heirs or Successors made in Our or Their Privy Council shall be altered, revoked or disallowed as hereinafter is provided; that during the said last-mentioned period of sixty days the said election or amotion, as the case may be, shall have no force or effect; and that failing such signification within the said last-mentioned period, such election or amotion shall be and be held and taken to be by him approved and confirmed;

And We do further by these presents for Us, Our Heirs and Successors, will and ordain, that henceforth from the date hereof such election shall not be required to be notified to Us, Our Heirs and Successors, in the manner provided and required in and by the said Letters Patent, or in any other manner or way whatsoever;

And We do further by these presents, for Us, Our Heirs and Successors, will, ordain and grant, that the said Governors, Principal and Fellows, and their Successors forever, shall be one body politic and corporate, by the name of "The Governors, Principal and Fellows of McGill College," and by the said name shall have perpetual succession, and a common seal, and shall by the same name sue and be sued, implead and be impleaded, and answer and be answered unto, in every Court of Us, Our Heirs and Successors, henceforth from the date hereof, and shall no longer be known by the name in the said Letters Patent mentioned, and shall retain all and every the property, franchises, rights and privileges granted under and by virtue of the said Letters Patent, and belonging to the said Corporation immediately before the date hereof, and shall be and remain liable to all claims and duties to which immediately before the date hereof they were subject, save only in so far as by these presents may be otherwise specially provided;

And We do further by these presents, for Us, Our Heirs and Successors, will, ordain and grant, to the said Governors, Principal and Fellows, and their Successors, by the name aforesaid, full authority and free license to have, take, purchase, and hold, to them and their Successors to and for the use of the said College, any goods, chattels or personal property whatsoever; and also that by the name aforesaid they shall be able and capable in law, notwithstanding any Statutes or Statute of mortmain, law, usage or custom whatsoever to the contrary, to have, take, purchase and hold to them and their Successors to and for the use of said College, any other Manors, Rectories, Advowsons, Messuages, Lands, tenements, rents and hereditaments of what kind, nature, or quality soever, over and above the manors, rectories, advowsons, messuages, lands, tenements, rents and hereditaments in the said Letter Patent mentioned of the yearly value of six thousand pounds above all charges as in the said Letters Patent is set forth, but not for the purpose or with the view of re-selling the same; provided always, that the whole shall not exceed the yearly value of Twelve thousand pounds above all charges, such annual value to be calculated and ascertained at the period of taking, purchasing or acquiring the same;

And We do further by these presents, for Us, Our Heirs and Successors, appoint as our Visitor in and over for the said College, Our Governor General of Our said Province of Canada, for the time being, or in his absence the Administrator of the Government of the same for the time being; who shall exercise, use and enjoy all and every the powers and authority of a Visitor, for and in the name and behalf of Us, Our Heirs and Successors, of the said College in all matters and things connected with the said College, as to him shall seem meet, according to the tenor and effect of these presents, and of the laws in force in Our Realm of England in relation to such powers and authority;

And We do further by these presents for Us, Our Heirs and Successors, revoke and annul the power and authority in and by the said Letters Patent given and granted to the members for the time being of the Royal Institution for the Advancement of Learning, to be Visitors of the said College; and do will and ordain that henceforth from the date of these presents the power and authority so given and granted to the said members of the said Royal Institution to be such Visitors, shall absolutely cease and determine, and shall not be exercised or used by them or any of them;

And We do further by these presents, for Us, Our Heirs and Successors, will, ordain and declare that the Statutes, Rules and Ordinances from time to time framed and made by the said Governors of the said College, touching the matters and things in the said Letters Patent and in these presents enumerated, or any thereof, or for the revoking, augmenting or altering of any Statutes, Rules or Ordinances theretofore framed and made, so always as the same be not repugnant to the Laws of Our Realm or of Our said Province of Canada, or to the objects and provisions of this Our Charter, shall have full force and effect, without the Allowance and Confirmation of Us, Our Heirs and Successors, as ordained in and by the said Letters Patent; provided always, that a certified Copy of all such Statutes, Rules and Ordinances, sealed with the College Seal and addressed to Our said Visitor of the said College for the time being, shall have been delivered into the Post Office of the said City of Montreal, and that the same shall not have been disallowed by Our said Visitor, and such disallowance signified in writing to the said Governors, within sixty days after such delivery of such Copy into the said Post Office;

And We do by these presents, for Us, Our Heirs and Successors, expressly save and reserve to Us, Our Heirs and Successors, the power of receiving, and by any order or orders to be by Us, or Them made in Our or Their Privy Council revising, confirming, altering, revoking or disallowing, all or any of the decisions, sentences or orders so as aforesaid from time to time by the said Visitor to be made and rendered in reference to any such Statutes, Rules and Ordinances, or the disallowing thereof, or in reference to any matter or thing whatsoever, as to which any power or authority is by these presents given and granted to him;

And We do by these presents, for Us, Our Heirs and Successors, will, ordain and grant, that nothing herein contained shall be held, construed or considered to have in any manner or way whatsoever revoked, cancelled, abrogated or altered the provisions, powers, authorities and grants in and by the said Letters Patent ordained and granted, or any thereof, save and except in the particulars hereinbefore specially and expressly set forth; but that all and every the said provisions, powers, authorities and grants in and by the said Letters Patent ordained and granted, shall subsist and continue in full force and effect, save and except in the particulars aforesaid, in the same manner as if these Our Letters Patent had never been made, ordained or granted; And We do further by these presents for Us, Our Heirs and Successors, grant and declare that these Our Letters Patent, or the enrolment or exemplification thereof, shall be in all things valid and effectual in the Law according to the true intent and meaning of the same, and shall be taken, construed and adjudged in the most favorable and beneficial sense for the best advantage of the said College, and of the said Governors, Principal, Fellows and Scholars thereof, as well in Our Courts of Record as elsewhere, and by all and singular Judges, Justices, Officers, Ministers and other subjects whatsoever of Us, Our Heirs and Successors, any misrecital, non-recital, omission, imperfection, defect, matter, cause or thing whatsoever to the contrary thereof in any wise notwithstanding.

In witness whereof We have caused these Our Letters to be made Patent.

Witness Ourself at Our Palace at Westminster, this sixth day of July, in the sixteenth year of Our Reign.   (1852.)

By Her Majesty's command,

(Signed)   EDMUNDS.

APPENDIX C

On November 20th, 1899, the day after Sir William Dawson's death, a Memorial Service, attended by Governors, Professors, and students, was held in Molson Hall. Principal Peterson in his address said:

"Since we met in our various classrooms last week, a great and good life has been brought to its appointed end. Sir William Dawson had considerably overpassed the span of life of which the Psalmist speaks: it was 'by reason of strength' that it was for him well-nigh fourscore years. Ever since he assumed the Principalship in November, 1855—that is, for a period of exactly forty-four years—he has been the most prominent figure connected with this University. The last years of his life—since 1893—have been spent, it is true, in retirement from active work, but he has been with us in spirit all this time. Many of us know how closely, and with what a fatherly interest, he has followed all our later history. And now his life has closed, in great physical weakness, but happily unaccompanied by distress or suffering:

> " 'Of no distemper, of no blast he died,
> But fell like autumn fruit that mellow'd long.'

"Busy, active and strenuous all his days, he must have chafed, I fancy, during recent years under a growing sense of uselessness—almost an impatience at being laid aside from work, which had been to him so long the very breath of life; yet none ever said with more simple, childlike resignation, 'Thy way, not mine!' For such a painless passing out of life, no vote of sorrow need be struck. There is no sting in a death like his: the grave is not his conqueror. Rather has death been swallowed up in victory—the victory of a full and complete life, marked by earnest endeavour, untiring industry, continuous devotion and self-sacrifice, together with an abiding and ever-present sense of dependence on the will of Heaven. His work was done, to quote the Puritan poet's noble line: 'As ever in his great taskmaster's eye'; and never for a moment did he waver in his feeling of personal responsibility to a personal God. Others will speak

291

to you of his record as a scientific man. I shall permit myself only to say that few can have an adequate idea of the power and forcefulness revealed in the mere fact that one who had so onerous a part to play as a college head should have been able to keep up scientific work at all. A weaker nature would have exhausted itself in the problems of administration.

"He, himself, has left it on record, in his paper entitled, 'Thirty-eight Years of McGill,' that these years were 'filled with anxieties and cares, and with continuous and almost unremitting labour.' There are on my library table at the present time three volumes, in which three college presidents may be said to have summed up the lifework it has been given them to do for the institutions with which they were severally connected—Caird of Glasgow, Eliot of Harvard, and Gilman of Johns Hopkins. The first was a massive intellect which, in the security of a long-established university system, delighted to deal, in a series of addresses to the Glasgow students, with such subjects as the unity and progressiveness of the sciences, the study of history, the study of art, and the place in human development of Erasmus and Galileo, Bacon, Hume and Bishop Butler. The two American Presidents have lived more in the concrete, and they have put on record their attitude to, and their methods of dealing with, the various problems they have had to face in the educational world in which their work has been done. Alongside their memorial volumes I like to place a still more unpretending collection of 'Educational Papers,' which Sir William Dawson circulated among his friends. They mark the various stages, full of struggle and stress at every point, of his college administration, and they form a record of what he was able to accomplish—apart from his work as a geologist—in the sphere of education, for the High School and the Normal School of this city, for the schools of the province, and above all for McGill itself, which he found in 1855 a mere college with eighty students, and which he raised to the level of a great university with over a thousand.

"Not even in his well-earned retirement could he permit himself to be idle. To me, one of the most touching sights in the first year of my arrival here, was the indomitable perseverance with which every day the well-known figure of the old Principal would make its way, bag in hand, across the campus to the museum he loved so well, there to work for a time among the valuable collections which the University owes to his zeal, industry and devotion. It was in 1841 that he published his first scientific paper, and the activity which began then was continued down to the Thursday in the week before his death, when some reference to the mining industry of this country suggested to him that once more with failing hand and wearied brain he should put pen to paper on the subject of the 'Gold of Ophir.' And now he has entered into his rest,—affectionately tended to the last by the gentle care of a devoted and heroic wife, and solaced by the presence of a distinguished son and loving daughter. The world had no power to hold him any more. His work was done and his spirit yearned to pass beyond all earthly bounds.

"He is gone and we shall see his living face no more. But teachers and students alike may have ever with them the inspiration of his noble life and the stimulus of his high example. What he was to those who were so long his colleagues I leave others on this occasion to set before us. My closing words to the students of McGill must be the expression of a confident hope that the record of Sir William's life and work will always be an abiding memory in this place. If you will bear it about with you in your hearts, not only will you be kept from lip service, slackness, half-heartedness in your daily duties,—and from the graver faults of youth at which his noble soul would have revolted,—from dishonesty, sensuality and impurity in every form,—but you will be able, each in his sphere, to realise more fully the ideal of goodness and truth, so that at the last you, too, may hear the voices whispering as they have now spoken to him,—'Well done, thou good and faithful servant; enter thou into the joy of thy Lord.'"

APPENDIX D

THE PETERSON MEMORIAL ADDRESS

On January 16th, 1921, a University Service in Memory of Sir William Peterson was held in the Church of St. Andrew and St. Paul, of which Sir William was a member and where he had worshipped during his twenty-four years in Canada. The following memorial address was given by the Rev. Principal D. J. Fraser (Arts '93), D.D., LL.D., of the Presbyterian College.

"Sir William Peterson had a fine reverence for sacred things and a keen appreciation of church worship. In the absence of a college chapel, which leaves McGill still lacking one note of catholicity, it is fitting that the Service to his memory, although a distinctively University Service, should be held in this Church where he worshipped with both the understanding and the spirit during the twenty-four years of his life amongst us. He had the Scot's proverbial taste for a good sermon, and he exacted that the pulpit should deal with Christianity as a rational religion and should make its appeal to the intelligence of the people. Knowing as he did that the Bible is the foundation not only of individual and national character but also of a comprehensive culture, and regretting that many children through home neglect had their only knowledge of it from the lessons heard in church, he pleaded that the Scriptures be reverently and clearly read. He was one of our highest authorities on hymnology and church music; he loved to join in singing the familiar psalms and paraphrases and hymns, and he appreciated as few in the congregation could the majestic anthems rendered by the choir. He never wantonly absented himself from the Sacrament of the Lord's Supper, the Presbyterian ritual of which, in close keeping with the form of the original Holy Meal, naturally appealed to him. Intellectual and mystical, historical and sacramental elements entered into his worship.

"I think his last diet of public worship, except the one at which he was stricken, was a Memorial Service in this Church to those who would not return from overseas, when I gave the sermon on a text chosen from those immortal verses of poetic beauty which have just been read by his successor (Revelation

294

22:4-5). Those, however, who laid down their lives for the cause of Empire and Humanity do not all sleep in Flanders and in France. Although in delicate physical health, he threw himself with abandon into the grim struggle from its very outset; he undertook the work of colleagues who had enlisted; he carried in his heart a tender solicitude for the lads from McGill who were exposed to peril; he acted almost as confidential adviser to the Government's Department of Militia; he advocated ceaselessly by voice and pen the cause so dear to his patriotic soul, until he inevitably broke under the strain; and today we memorialise as bonnie a fighter and as genuine a hero as any whose name is on our military Roll of Honour.

"Sir William Peterson was greatest as a scholar. It is hardly necessary that I refer to his brilliant career as a classical student at Edinburgh and Oxford, his priceless legacy to scholarship in the works of the Latin authors he edited and translated, his successful administration of University College, Dundee, at an extremely difficult time in its history, and his guidance of the affairs of McGill during its period of phenomenal growth from 1895 to 1919; for many of you who were his colleagues are better qualified than I to estimate the value of these activities. He preserved to the end the instincts and habits of the scholar. When he enjoyed a period of freedom from his administrative duties it was to the libraries of America and Europe that he gravitated in the scholar's quest for old documents that would yield the scholar's joy of new discovery; and on his last holiday visit to Scotland, deprived by the war of access to the libraries of the Continent, he happened upon an unpublished document of the seventeenth century by what he modestly called 'a lucky chance.' We know, however, that these happy finds come only to those who have the genius of the literary discoverer, and characteristic of the textual critic is his parting message to us in his delightful description of his new-found treasure given in a magazine article under the prophetic title—'A Last Will and Testament.'

"As an educationalist Sir William Peterson was a mediator between the champions of pure learning and the advocates of the practical sciences. To him the University had a two-fold function; first 'to make good citizens,' and second 'to hand on the torch of knowledge to successive generations of students.' He believed that in order of teaching pure learning should precede applied science, that classical subjects should precede professional; but in spite of his Oxford training he could never be accused of sacrificing the practical in the University to the disciplinary. He recognised that the development of the pure sciences was effected in history by the practical needs of life and that the marvels of modern scientific activity are based on abstract and theoretical learning. He found a place for the classical and the specialised, the humanistic and the utilitarian, and his ideal was that the University should give practical men a sound training in theory and also keep theory in touch with practice. It was a blessing to McGill and to education in Canada that we had as our guide a believer in the humanities at a time when our youthful enthusiasm for the practical was in danger of blinding us to the ideal of our educational ancestors that the function of the school is to develop men and women of character.

"Principal Peterson was widely known as an ardent champion of Imperialism, although here he failed to carry with him some of his warmest Canadian friends; but it is not so generally known that he did a great and needed work on this Continent in the interests of Anglo-Saxon unity. He frequently visited the United States and gave addresses to universities, learned societies, Canadian clubs and similar influential groups, and he always appealed for mutual good-will between the two children of the same British mother. In fact he earned a more generous recognition there than in Canada or in Great Britain. Harvard and Princeton, Yale and Johns Hopkins conferred their highest honour on the representative of our national University, and acknowledged that it was not a mere international compliment but a real recognition of a scholar who had made lasting contributions to the cause of higher learning and human progress. He was also elected Chairman of the Board of Trustees of the Carnegie Foundation for the Advancement of Teaching. Holding an almost unique place among the College Presidents on this Continent, his words reached influential audiences and carried great weight. His first visit to the United States was in 1896, during the first year of his incumbency at McGill for the purpose of addressing the Phi Beta Kappa Alumni of New York, and he chose for his theme 'The Relations of the English-speaking Peoples.' It was the time of the Venezuela incident when there was imminent danger of misunderstanding between Britain and America. His plea for friendship is of special interest to us today when there is a highly organised propaganda for stirring up strife between the two nations, a propaganda that is causing real anxiety to the spiritual descendants of Britain in Canada and New England. In these chaotic days we do well to heed and herald his message on that occasion. 'It is well-nigh inconceivable,' he said, 'that in this age of the world's progress the two representatives of Anglo-Saxon civilization will ever enter on a fratricidal struggle to decide which shall be the greater. . . . The best guarantees for the continuance of mutual good-will are surely to be found in that of which I know we are all equally proud—community of race, language, literature, religion and institutions, together with the glorious traditions of a common history. . . . A racial federation between Britain and America would probably prove a potent factor in hastening the era of general disarmament. . . . The authority, more fortunate even than President Monroe, will lay impossible, and then it will be seen that every man who by rash action or hasty word makes the preservation of peace difficult has committed a crime not only against his own country but against civilization itself.' That last sentence obviously referred to President Cleveland. I was a student at Harvard at the time and every Professor whose classes I attended took the same attitude. By such appeals Principal Peterson helped to strengthen the body of American opinion that exists today against the intolerable thought of strife between the two peoples who have lived for more than a century in peace and harmony and mutual affection, and his weighty words are a warning to Canadians who share his imperialistic ideals against irresponsible criticisms of our friends and neighbours to the South. His Imperialism, while it gave him the vision of a commonwealth of nations within the British Possessions, did not blind him to the larger vision of the unity of English-speaking peoples, and to the still nobler vision of universal brotherhood of which his fellow-countryman sang under conditions of unrest very similar to our own :—

> " 'Then let us pray that come it may,
> As come it will for a' that,
> That man to man the warld o'er,
> Shall brithers be for a' that.'

"While Dr. Peterson was primarily a scholar and administrator, he was also a public-spirited citizen who mingled freely with his fellows in varied walks of life and who identified himself with many movements in the interests of human welfare. His last public address was to a group of our Greek fellow-citizens with whose propaganda against Turkish rule over their brethren in Asia Minor he rightly or wrongly sympathised. His chief public interest, however, was in education, and he not only served diligently on the Council of Protestant Instruction for the Province of Quebec but he gladly gave the encouragement of his presence and counsel to the teachers in primary and secondary schools throughout Canada at their annual gatherings; and one of his favourite pleas on these occasions was for the rightful place of English Literature—and especially Poetry—in the school curriculum. He magnified the office of the teacher and deplored the

apathy of the public towards those entrusted with the training
of the future manhood and womanhood of the nation. 'No expenditure,' he cried, 'is considered too great to be grudged on
war and armaments by land and by sea, on construction works
such as railways, bridges, harbours and naval stations, but the
needs of the common school rouse little, if any, interest or enthusiasm. And yet it is there that the national character is being
moulded.' He never ceased to protest against the narrow idea
that education consists merely in the acquiring of knowledge and
is to be measured by success in examinations; and he constantly
held up to the teachers of youth the need of caring for such
things as 'good manners, courtesy, consideration for others, respect for seniors, friendly politeness towards all.' He was also
an enthusiastic supporter of the teaching of music in the public
schools. He saw what had been accomplished by training in this
department in Scotland and Germany, for example, among peoples not naturally musical, and he feared that through our
neglect we might become a songless race. Himself finding in
music one of his exquisite delights, he endeavoured to bring to
the rural districts its elevating and enriching influence.

"Although not a social reformer in the popular sense of that
term, he was deeply interested in efforts for the betterment of the
community; and especially in the last years of his active life the
social situation in Montreal weighed heavily on his heart and con-
science. He beheld the city from his uptown coign of vantage
and the vision troubled him. The social evils of this great commercial centre challenged him to do something for the alleviation
of distress, the improvement of housing conditions, the preven-
tion of such slums as are a blot on the fair city which gave him
birth, the reduction of the infant mortality which is a scandal to
our population and the bringing of the simple joys and pleasures
of life to the greatest possible number. He saw so many worthy
separate agencies trying to grapple with the social problem without unity of purpose and co-ordination of effort, he saw the
churches so relatively powerless to effect any appreciable cure
because of their sectarian divisions, that he dreamed a dream
that McGill University might do in this respect what the existing
agencies and churches were helpless to effect, that it might become
not only the inspirer of a great passion for social redemption
and not merely a school for the scientific training of social
workers, but also a unifying centre of our manifold social efforts
where existing agencies might be strengthened and stimulated and
co-ordinated. This is really the thought that lay behind his
organizing the Department of Social Service in the University.
Whatever we may think of his method of ministering to the

crying social needs of our time and place, we cannot doubt the sincerity of his purpose and the intensity of his desire. It was also his solicitude for the students coming up from the country and smaller towns to this populous centre, exposed to the moral perils of a great city, that kept him strongly appealing for dormitories under University supervision and control, an appeal to which we turned a strangely deaf ear, but to which, we are thankful to say, he lived long enough to see a fairly generous response.

"One hesitates to refer to the personal qualities that endeared him to his intimate friends. I always detected in his life a certain undefined loneliness. The scholar's shyness and the isolation of his exalted position hardly account for it. A humanistic scholar in a University where the practical departments were making greatest progress, engrossed in his intellectual interests in the solitude of his upper chamber while the busy commercial world went heedless by, always leisurely in the midst of a most active life, a man of religious reticence who was misunderstood because he did not make a noisy profession of his faith, an old country-man in a new land that he never could quite call 'home,' a controversialist skilled only in the use of the rapier and compelled at times to enter the lists with those who wielded the bludgeon, a subtle humourist who must 'carry on' with the prosaic and matter-of-fact, a lover of his own fireside who must of necessity be socially advertised with the vulgar, his spirit dwelt apart from the busy world in which he served.

"Loyalty was the supreme virtue in his ethical code, and disloyalty was to him the unpardonable sin. No man could have done for McGill what he did and not make academic enemies. He found a group of professional schools, each more or less autonomous, and he transformed it into a University. His ideal of the unity of learning made it necessary that he should run counter to the traditions of the various schools in seeking to co-ordinate all departments of study, and he exposed himself to criticism, just as President Eliot of Harvard did in his similar work for his University; but I never heard him speak a disloyal word of any of his colleagues. No man could have advocated Imperialism as he did without making political enemies, and many a vigorous attack was made on him by young Canadians; but I do not recall any spoken word or any printed sentence of his that dragged his advocacy of Imperialism into the realm of party politics or personal controversy. I know how true and generous he was to one of his friends who always found in him a congenial fellow-worker in the things of the spirit. I also know how large a place he kept in his heart for the students,—rejoicing in their success, proud of their manly conduct, heart-sad over the tragedy of guilt and shame that befell any one of them. He had a warm heart, although he did not wear it on his sleeve for daws to peck at. To me as I go about the College yard he is a spiritual presence, summoning me to do my best, to be accurate, fearless, loyal to the truth as I know the truth, and loyal to those for whom I hold the truth in stewardship; and such a spiritual comrade he will be while memory lasts. My experience is that of many of you who were fond of him and of whom he was fond, and our tribute to his memory, while quite unworthy, has at least, what he would most desire, the merit of sincerity.

"Students of McGill, our former Principal is gone and we shall see his living face no more. But the stimulus of his high example remains with us. It is fitting in conclusion that I repeat to you the inspiring and earnest words with which he ended his address to the students at the Memorial Service to his illustrious predecessor, Sir William Dawson, twenty-one years ago :—'My closing words to the students of McGill,' he said, 'must be the expression of a confident hope that the record of Sir William's life and work will be an abiding memory in this place. If you will bear it about with you in your hearts, not only will you be kept from lip-service, slackness, half-heartedness in your daily duties, and from the graver faults of youth at which his noble soul would have revolted, from dishonesty, sensuality and impurity in any form, but you will be able, each in his sphere, to realise more fully the ideal of goodness and truth, so that at the last you, too, may hear the voices whispering, as they have now spoken to him, "Well done, thou good and faithful servant, enter thou into the joy of thy Lord." ' "